BSA

Boarding
Schools'
Association

GOOD PRACTICE
in
BOARDING
SCHOOLS

Edited by Tim Holgate
Director of Training
Boarding Schools' Association

DEDICATION

This book is dedicated to the hundreds
of hard-working boarding staff throughout
the country who give unstintingly of their
time and energy to care for the young people
in our schools.

A catalogue record for this book is available from the British Library

ISBN 0-9538435-1-3

CONTENTS

CONTRIBUTORS

Marigold Bentley – Works on peacemaking for Quaker Peace and Service.

Dr John Coleman – Director of the Trust for the Study of Adolescence.

Peter Dix – Headmaster of Port Regis.

Gill Dixon – Housemistress of senior girls at Oakham School.

Brian FitzGerald – Reporting Inspector for the Independent Schools' Inspectorate, formerly Her Majesty's Inspector with responsibility for boarding.

Philip Hardaker – Vice-Principal of Sherborne International College.

Dr Roger Harrington – Medical Officer to Stowe School, a general practitioner in Buckingham, President of the Medical Officers of Schools' Association.

Tim Holgate – Director of Training for the Boarding Schools' Association, formerly a housemaster at Marlborough College and Head of Warminster School.

Helen Holland – Counsellor and trainer, Director of Helen Holland and Associates.

Candida Hunt – Counsellor and trainer, Assistant Director of 'Family Links'.

Emma McKendrick – Headmistress of Downe House School.

Angus McPhail – Warden of Radley College, formerly Head of Strathallan School.

Sue Mickleburgh – Training Officer for the Eating Disorders Association.

Dr Roger Morgan – Chief Inspector for Oxfordshire Social Services and author of *National Boarding Standards.*

Clive Thorpe – Director of Studies (International) and a housemaster at Framlingham College.

Adrian Underwood – National Director of the Boarding Schools' Association, formerly a housemaster at Kingham Hill School and Head of Moira House School.

ACKNOWLEDGEMENTS

I wish to thank those who have contributed to this book: their willingness and enthusiasm to share their experience and expertise have been much appreciated. I am similarly grateful to the many heads and members of staff of boarding schools up and down the country who have shared their own experience and current practice, and who have been so supportive of our professional development initiatives, many of which have benefited from the generous support and sponsorship of the Department for Education and Employment. My thanks are due also to the Officers and Executive of the Boarding Schools' Association for their support, and to Professor Ron Best for kindly writing the Foreword.

There are three other people I wish to thank by name. Shirley Lee of the Faculty of Education at University of Surrey Roehampton has been most helpful and supportive throughout this project. Adrian Underwood, National Director of the Boarding Schools' Association, has been tireless in his enthusiasm and has provided valuable and much-appreciated encouragement. Finally, I wish to express my gratitude to my wife, Anne, for her invaluable help and support.

Tim Holgate

FOREWORD

Professor Ron Best
Dean of the Faculty of Education, University of Surrey Roehampton

Amongst the important figures of post-1788 Australian history, four come immediately to mind. They are the explorers Blaxland, Evans, Lawson and Wentworth. In my school days they were known to all as the discoverers of the mountain ranges and river systems which meandered across the map of New South Wales, then found on the walls of every primary school in the state.

They also gave their names to the houses of the secondary school I attended in Parramatta in the mid-1950s. And for good reasons. They had shown courage, fortitude and a taste for adventure which would serve as an excellent role model for the post-war generation, and they were a constant reminder of some historical facts which even the least able child would presumably remember.

But they had some practical advantages, too. There were four of them, a nice round number when it came to inter-house sports and other competitions, and the initials – B, E, L and W – punctuated the alphabet quite neatly for allocating pupils to houses according to surname. That there were no actual 'houses' whatever to be seen in this boys' state comprehensive day school was not at all odd. All secondary schools had houses and I thought no more about it.

It was not until the late seventies, when researching pastoral care in UK comprehensive schools, that I came to realise that the house (or 'vertical') pastoral system was but one of many vestiges of the predominantly private boarding institutions which accounted for so many of the schools in this country in the 18th and 19th centuries. That these schools were also most often of religious or charitable foundation was but another contrast with the typical county schools which were the focus of our research.

There were two very important similarities between a good day school and a good boarding school: both accepted the concept of the role of the teacher as *in loco parentis*, and both were concerned for the development and well-being of the child as a whole person. These are central to a concept of education which goes beyond the preoccupation with subject knowledge and measurable competencies which seems to have dominated government policy and curriculum prescription in the last twenty years. Teachers are there to care for the child as a whole person and not (as one commentator put it many years ago) just as "an empty bucket to be filled with knowledge". From this perspective, the potential of what we know as pastoral care and personal-social education is enormous.

While there has been a good deal of research and publication about the care and support of children in the day school sector, and a great many in-service staff development opportunities provided on such topics as bullying, counselling, peer support and pastoral management, the needs of children in the boarding sector have been relatively neglected. This seems to me to be a great shame. Arguably, it is in the distinctive context of the boarding experience that the teacher *in loco parentis* should come most visibly to the fore. Moreover, the problems which beset all children – and, perhaps, especially those in adolescence – achieve a heightened prominence in a setting where youngsters are thrown together for twenty-four hours a day, with neither frequent contact with parents and siblings (and not all our boarders have either), nor a daily opportunity to leave the demands of schooling behind them if only between 4 p.m. and 9 a.m. the following day.

For these reasons alone I am proud that the Faculty of Education at University of Surrey Roehampton has come to be involved in the provision of training for boarding school staff, and I value the collaboration we have with the Boarding Schools' Association in helping to raise the standards of boarding practice. This is but a part of a much larger picture of development in the boarding sector, evidenced also in the re-launch of an Independent Schools' Inspectorate and in the establishment of National Boarding Standards against which the quality of provision may be evaluated. These initiatives, together with the growing opportunities for initial training and continuing professional development, augur well for the future.

In this context, a book which has as its focus the challenges and changes in boarding education at the beginning of a new century could not be more timely, and I congratulate all those who have played a part in bringing it to publication. I am sure it will serve as essential reading for anyone who is involved in boarding provision, but I hope it will attract a much wider readership, not least amongst colleagues involved in day schools and in the training of teachers for all parts of the education system. For this is a sector from which we all have much to learn.

ABBREVIATIONS

BEA	Boarding Education Alliance
BSA	Boarding Schools' Association
DfEE	Department for Education and Employment
EDA	Eating Disorders Association
EFL	English as a Foreign Language
GCSE	General Certificate of Secondary Education
HMI	Her Majesty's Inspector
ISC	Independent Schools' Council
ISI	Independent Schools' Inspectorate
ISIS	Independent Schools' Information Service
LEA	Local Education Authority
MOSA	Medical Officers of Schools' Association
NBS	National Boarding Standards
NHS	National Health Service
OFSTED	Office for Standards in Education
PSE	Personal and Social Education
UCAS	Universities and Colleges Admissions Service

INTRODUCTION BY THE EDITOR

"The world is passing through troubled times.
The young people of today think of nothing but themselves.
They have no reverence for parents or old age;
they are impatient of all restraint;
they talk as if they knew everything;
and what passes for wisdom with us, is foolishness to them.
As for the girls, they are immodest and unwomanly in speech, behaviour and dress."

Peter the Monk, 1274

It would be tempting to think that little has changed since the days of Peter the Monk! However, the task of looking after young people living and working away from home is now a challenging and, at times, stressful and complex affair. Gone are the days when the adult's word was absolute and the boarding school had little communication with parents or accountability to society and the law. Boarding staff have to resolve and deal with a multitude of problems and issues, and need to be respected as professionals in their own right.

This book has been written to fill a current gap in the literature. Firstly, it offers boarding staff a source of ideas and reference, to assist in their day-to-day work. Secondly, it provides background reading to support professional development, both that carried out within schools as well as the various training courses and conferences run by the Boarding Schools' Association. It aims, thirdly, to focus on issues of good practice, and many of these will be relevant to those managing the care of young people living away from home and those inspecting such provision.

The variety of styles and views expressed in this book reflect the authors' diversity and breadth of experience. Some of the chapters have an intentionally formal tone, underlining the important statutory obligations and responsibilities that we share in safeguarding and promoting the welfare of pupils. Others are written by boarding practitioners, who share their thoughts and experiences in the boarding house and the wider school setting. There are, nevertheless, a number of common themes and threads running through the book, and cross-referencing between chapters is provided where appropriate.

The early chapters set the scene with an optimistic view of modern boarding, looking at the needs of the young people in our care and how welfare provision in the boarding school can meet such needs, as children and young people grow and develop. The legal framework that supports boarding welfare is clearly outlined. After painting a picture of the adolescent dilemma, the book looks at the key skills involved with helping and communicating with pupils. Issues concerning confidentiality are explored further in a separate chapter. Tensions do occur, of course, in such close communities and we consider ways of countering bullying and other forms of difficult behaviour, as well as resolving conflict. The safety of the boarding environment and of the activity that takes place within it leads on to the organisation and communication structures which help the house to run smoothly, and to the need for clear policies and procedures. The role of senior pupils is addressed, as are the needs of the very youngest boarders and those from overseas. We examine the nature of eating disorders and their link with low self-esteem, and consider the management of a range of other pastoral issues. The final chapter draws together many of the underlying themes, and focuses on the need to assess welfare provision with a view to planning for future changes and improvements. The postscript offers some thoughts for those about to embark on the task of running their own house.

The final sections aim to support staff development and stimulate further reading and research. A number of case studies develop issues raised in the chapters and will allow staff to discuss and debate their response to different scenarios. A list of reference material is provided for those wishing to delve into areas in greater detail. A summary of much of the current welfare legislation relevant to boarding schools is included in an appendix.

The National Boarding Standards, developed by all school associations and those involved in boarding education, are reproduced here in full. The Standards have now been adopted unanimously by the constituent bodies on the National Boarding Standards Committee, and were submitted to central government in June 2000. Further details of the background to this significant initiative are included in Appendix 2.

Throughout the book, references to staff and students have, wherever possible, avoided the uncomfortable use of his/her and she/he. It must be understood that, unless otherwise made clear, reference to a student or member of staff of one gender also implies the other. It should also be pointed out that the views and opinions expressed in the chapters are those of the authors, and do not necessarily represent those of the Boarding Schools' Association.

It is my hope that this book will stimulate thought and interest, and contribute to the welfare and care of young people in boarding schools and elsewhere.

CHAPTER

1

Boarding Today and Tomorrow

Adrian Underwood

"The dread of beatings
Dread of Being Late
And greatest dread of all, the dread of games"

John Betjeman, 1921

"I like living with my friends. The independence
allows me to feel more confident and I find being at
home more rewarding."

Boarding pupil, 2000

My first real encounter with boarding was in 1971 when I plunged in at the deep end on being appointed to a house of 45 boys. As I look back on the 29 intervening years of my life in boarding schools, I am conscious that we have all lived through a part revolutionary and part evolutionary phase in boarding. That phase and its successor will be explored in this chapter.

In the last 20 years there have been two major changes. Firstly, the monolithic pattern of boarding has changed into one of variety and choice. Secondly, boarding has moved from the opaque to the transparent.

For many years there was only one pattern. Schools were single-sex, all-boarding, mainly full of pupils from within the UK and only offered a 'full boarding' option with the occasional break in the term. That pattern has now changed and the boarding 'offer' is now diverse and caters for the needs and aspirations of 21st century families.

That is not to say that the 'full boarding' option has disappeared. It certainly has not and is strongly supported by families both in the UK and from abroad. There are a good number of schools which have decided to continue to offer full boarding with all the qualities of integration, community and 'available time' which stem from such a commitment. Equally, there are schools which have developed new forms of boarding, namely weekly, 'flexi' and occasional. These have their own challenges and opportunities, and have developed as a direct result of a number of social factors.

Firstly, in the family of today, more often than not both parents are in the workplace[1]. Thus, the concept of weekly boarding appeals, where children can be fully involved in the life of the school during the week, when their parents have little quality family time at their disposal. At the weekends, the family can relate positively and recreate and re-charge together as a family for the week ahead. Equally, many families who choose the boarding option are urban based and know the real frustrations of trying to offer a range of extra-curricular activities to their children when these are so affected by transport arrangements in our over-crowded cities. All these frustrations melt away in the boarding environment, where the extra-curricular facilities on one site are of a very high quality and always available. Double income families are here to stay and the transport problems in our cities give no sign of disappearing. Thus, the boarding option will continue to fulfil the needs of many families.

Boarding schools have also recognised the value of 'flexi' and occasional boarding. Both styles of boarding fulfil other needs. Many a parent's evening is affected by having to collect children from school late at night after an event: occasional boarding offers a solution to this. Flexi-boarding is an equally attractive concept to many families where various circumstances mean that the availability of boarding on a 'flexi' basis offers a safe, secure and positive environment on selected nights during any given week.

Boarding schools worth their name have a commitment to the inherent values of boarding and, thus, the offers of 'flexi' or occasional boarding are underpinned with the belief that the short-term boarding experience will be valuable in itself, and may well lead to boarding being chosen as the preferred form of education.

A further area of development in the boarding market has been the provision of sixth form houses. The competition at 16–18 in this country is intense and sixth formers have a wide choice on offer to them. Whilst some senior schools have retained the 13–18 (or 11–18) vertical house structure, many have built specialist sixth form houses. There is no doubt in my mind that, having enjoyed a good boarding education to 16, the sixth form years provide the icing on the cake. Equally, many boarding pupils wish to live in a separate, more adult environment at this time.

There is also clear evidence from the annual ISIS Census that many post-GCSE day students opt for a boarding education in the sixth form. A sixth form house offers a complete pre-university experience. It offers development of study habits, especially self-motivation, time management, career discussion, university applications, management of self in terms of domestic chores and cooking.

The process of choice is also an area which has seen revolutionary change in recent years. Occasionally, in spite of the work of the Boarding Education Alliance and schools' own promotional work, articles antagonistic to boarding still appear in the media. When reading them, one can only feel that the authors are lost in their own time-warp, as none of them refers to today's boarding experience. It has to be admitted that, in the era to which most of these articles refer, boarding for some pupils was not an uplifting experience. The articles always refer to children being 'sent away' to school. The reality, as proved by the Boarding Education Alliance Pupil Survey (December 1999) is that 80 per cent of the choices made to board today are made by the pupil alone or the pupil in consultation with the family – a far cry from being 'sent away'.

But this new process of choice brings with it its own challenges. If pupils are recognising the benefits of a boarding education, it is essential that schools continue to maintain their quality and strive to offer the best possible boarding environment in this new century.

'Transparency' lies at the heart of the recognition of boarding as a quality education today. For many years, boarding schools were closed environments where only children of a certain class were educated and from which only myths emanated. Today we live in an accountable age, and rightly so.

Thus, boarding schools are, perhaps, the most inspected in the education sector. One group of 'inspectors' is the parents, both potential and current. The 'new' parents are not themselves children of boarders. Indeed, studies show that the majority of parents paying boarding fees today were not boarders themselves. These potential parents who visit our schools are well aware of two significant elements. Firstly, they have drawn up their budgets and know that to educate a child as a boarder from 11 to 18 will cost them at least £150,000 per child, and from 7 to 18 over £200,000. They are also aware of the 'quality control' element in any business today, and will expect the same monitoring of quality in a boarding school.

Today's boarding parents will also expect to play a part in the life of their child's education, which contrasts distinctly with the concept of 'sending their children away' and being unaware of the life of the school. This applies, to a lesser extent, to overseas families but even so in an age of air travel, overseas families visit more regularly. The 'quality control', therefore, is not just by word of mouth of the pupil but by regular experience of the school environment in person.

The growth in the international dimension of boarding has been dramatic. The ISIS Census for 2000 shows a 9·8 per cent increase over 1999 of overseas pupils entering UK ISC schools. Whilst there has been a significant reduction in the take up of boarding places by members of the armed forces, diplomatic families and families on overseas business postings, the number of foreign nationals and expatriate pupils in our schools is now 9,167 out of 69,525[2].

With this growth has been the need to recognise even more the specific responsibilities we have for pupils from overseas. In 1985 I took myself to the Far East for a three-week tour of boarders' families. The scales fell from my eyes. I quickly realised that we were blinkered by the parochial attitudes of our English seaside town and, as a staff, did not really appreciate the particular needs of our pupils from overseas. On my return, I instituted a programme of awareness with a simple basis: did we all assume, because we had day pupils, that our 'voice' implied that all pupils could go home every night and enjoy parental support? If not, then how did we differentiate our attitude in our classes and activities for the benefit of our boarders, particularly those whose parents were over 6,000 miles away? (See Chapter 14.)

So much has changed since 1985 but, even so, the BSA heads were challenged at their annual conference in 2000 by Elizabeth Nixon in her presentation "The *in loco parentis* role – who is responsible?". Elizabeth, a former Chairman of the Diplomatic Spouses' Association, has spent her life abroad with the Diplomatic Service and has much experience of children at boarding school in the UK. The text of her address is reproduced in ***Boarding School***[3], No. 16 (January 2001) and makes valuable reading to anyone responsible for any boarders from overseas.

As Elizabeth acknowledged, technology has greatly improved communication with overseas parents. This technology has to be used, however, not just by pupils to e-mail their parents regularly, but by all those responsible for the welfare of boarders, to ensure that overseas parents are as well informed as parents twenty miles across the county.

The Internet has revolutionised communication between boarders and their families, and between house staff and boarders' parents. All schools I visited this year have Internet access for their pupils, most having access in each house, and some in each bedroom. Indeed, as schools plan new boarding houses, one of the essential elements in these plans is the integral Internet system for each house.

Those responsible for pastoral care in all its aspects, including medical, can now communicate with overseas parents more regularly and discuss joint home/school strategies for dealing with a particular situation with regard to a boarder in their care. A letter by airmail is no longer an acceptable form of communication in any time of stress or crisis.

Added to the parental expectation of boarding schools are the expectations of government and society. Boarding schools experience a stream of interested parties in the form of potential parents and pupils, politicians, journalists and inspectors (Social Services, ISI and OFSTED).

With a few reservations, this new order has been welcomed, indeed embraced, by the boarding world. Journalists who wish to write about boarding as it really is today are given the opportunities they wish, to visit schools and talk freely with both pupils and staff. Some suspicions remain, but not of the order of 1991 when I left a journalist alone in my study with 10 pupils for an hour or so. I was asked if I knew what I was doing, and could only reply that if we were not confident in the abilities of our boarders to speak openly and positively about their boarding experience, then what did we think we were offering them?

Inspection of the boarding environment has always been with us, but more under the spotlight since the Children Act (1989). Some early experiences of some Social Service inspections were not easy, but trust and partnership has developed on both sides.

In the decade which has passed since the first welfare inspections, many in boarding and in the inspectorates have become aware that a national framework for inspection was needed. Thus, in 1998, the National Boarding Standards Committee was formed. The composition of this committee and the standards themselves can be found in Appendix 2. The unanimity and positive partnership between the different bodies represented on this committee meant that, after two years of drafting, re-drafting, trialling both inspection methodology and reporting procedures, a set of 53 standards for boarding were offered to the Government in June 2000 for consideration.

During the life of this committee, the Care Standards Act came into being and, from 1st April 2002, there will be a National Care Standards Commission responsible for all residential provision in England. As the boarding sector had anticipated such a development, it is fervently hoped that the Standards developed by the national committee are adopted by Government and form the basis for inspection of boarding under the new act. There are continuing discussions about the inspection regime, and it is another positive sign for the sector that these discussions are actively involving those within boarding with a wealth of boarding experience.

'Duty of care' is a phrase which has been synonymous with the boarding world since it started. But over the years, and particularly in the last decade, it has taken on more powerful significance. Today's housemistresses and housemasters, house tutors and matrons are faced with a greater range of boarding legislation than ever before and also a commitment to ensuring that care goes beyond 'looking after' or 'protecting', and aim to ensure the most positive, wide-ranging and happy educational experience for each boarder in their charge.

Development in boarding today is all about 'investment in quality' and, first and foremost, that investment is in the quality of staffing. It has been recognised in recent years that, good as it was, 'learning as you went along' is no substitute for a structured programme of professional development for all involved. Our schools today are committed to professional development in all aspects of boarding education in the best interests of their pupils. Thus, the Boarding Schools' Association has seen an upsurge in applications for its courses leading to university validated Certificates of Professional

Practice in Boarding Education. In addition, boarding staff are constantly using opportunities for in-service education in pastoral care, counselling and other aspects of boarding life.

The BSA programme of professional development is supported and sponsored by the Department for Education and Employment. The DfEE's support extends to publications, and recently the BSA/DfEE have published ***Running a School Boarding House: A Legal Guide for Housemasters and Housemistresses***[4]. This type of publication and the book of which this is a chapter are indicative of the investment in quality staff to care for the boarders of today.

Investment in quality also very much applies to the boarding environment. A recent ISIS survey showed that millions of pounds are currently being invested in new boarding houses. Today's houses mirror family homes and as one parent told me "my son's bedroom at school is much better than he has at home". Thus, the idea that Spartan surroundings are good for the soul is another boarding myth.

Investment in new boarding houses and refurbishment of older ones consider the needs of boarders at different ages and stages of their lives (see Chapter 2). The size and shape of studies and bedrooms are significant to matters of social interaction and also privacy. Communication tools for each boarder must be high on the list of priorities as well as the ability to personalise individual space and enjoy a range of social areas. Boarding houses have always been places of positive activity, but equal consideration has to be given to the provision of areas where a boarder may 'chill out' at times when a complement to positive activity is required.

And what of the future? Clarissa Farr and Stephen Winkley, in their presentation at the annual BSA Heads' Conference 2000 in Torquay, confirmed that there were 740,000 UK families who could afford boarding, as against just over 74,000 boarders currently in ISC and state boarding schools. Thus, part of the challenge is to make the boarding option attractive to these families and, at least, make them aware of the qualities of boarding, and how a modern boarding education may benefit their children and the wider family life.

Clarissa and Stephen gave some very clear pointers in their presentation as to how marketing can be positively used in this regard[5]. For too long the boarding sector has shied away from promoting its qualities. Now, with the success of the *Boarding*

Education Alliance and the support from over 270 schools for its successor *B21 (Boarding in the 21st Century)*, there is an awareness that boarding, as an industry worth £1 billion per annum, should be promoting itself as positively as any other comparable industry. Moreover, with the 21st century boarding 'offer', there is so much transparent quality to promote.

My view is that the number of schools offering boarding may well decrease in the future. However, those schools who have made and continue to make significant investment in their boarding will attract a strong clientele who recognise the particular qualities and value for money which boarding offers to both pupils and their families.

References and Notes

1. *Millennial Families* – a response from the Boarding Education Alliance.

2. ISIS Annual Census 2000.

3. Published by the Boarding Schools' Association.

4. Available from the Boarding Schools' Association.

5. Boarding School, No. 16, January 2001.

CHAPTER

2

Meeting the Needs of Young People

Tim Holgate and Brian FitzGerald

In an era when the standard of care given to boarding pupils is increasingly examined under the microscope, it is important that boarding house staff are aware of the needs of young people as they grow and develop throughout their time in the school. In doing so, they can have a clear framework and sense of purpose for meeting these needs, and providing levels of pastoral care and welfare that meet today's high standards and levels of accountability. The organisation of the boarding house, the deployment of staff, the development of the physical environment of the house, together with the systems, structures and procedures (both school-wide and house-based) all need to be implemented with clear objectives and outcomes in mind.

> *"Pupils need to be aware of what is expected of them and how the arrangements for their care are intended to work. Staff need to understand the school's principles and procedures for the care of pupils, so that they can respond to a child with confidence. This in turn will help the child to feel secure.*[6] *"*

Boarding staff will find it helpful to clarify and agree on the principles that underpin life in the boarding house. These can set out the philosophy or mission of the house (or school), by which welfare and the development of pupils may be promoted, and their needs met.

The opening statement[7] of the section on Standards in the Children Act Guidance and Regulations makes it clear that *"there should be a statement of the principles on which the life of the [boarding] school is based"*.

Some schools like to outline the rights of pupils, parents and resident staff, and these can be incorporated into a statement of principles. It would be expected that boarding staff at all levels, as well as pupils, would collectively agree and support these general principles from which clear aims and practice for boarding in a particular house or the whole school can be developed. The boarding aims should, obviously, be related to the whole school aims or mission statement and linked, as appropriate, to the school development plan. Figure 2.1 outlines a possible statement of principles.

Before translating these principles into clear aims and objectives for boarding, and establishing the welfare structure and day-to-day management of pastoral care systems in the house, it may be helpful to consider and clarify the needs of the pupils in a particular boarding house, to help their development throughout their time in the school. Good pastoral care does not happen by accident or osmosis, nor can it easily be inherited or borrowed from successful practice in a different house: it needs to be created and shaped in response to the pupils' changing needs. Clearly, if the needs of the pupils change, as may well happen with different intakes and new initiatives developed in the school, then so should the aims and provision of boarding welfare.

The house should contribute to its pupils' development in a number of areas. A. H. Maslow (1954) has defined human needs on five levels:

❖ **physical needs** (hunger, thirst, sleep)

❖ **sense of security and safety** (protection against danger or deprivation)

❖ **sense of belonging** (and of being loved; desire to belong to a group)

❖ **self-esteem and self-respect** (need for recognition and appreciation)

❖ **self-realisation** (self-fulfilment; self-development; creativity)

Figure 2.1 – Example of a Statement of Principles

The following are the ten principles upon which boarding in this school is based.

❖ The development of the whole person and the communication of values are vital.

❖ Being an open and trusting school, boarding is based upon mutual respect for all its members.

❖ Each boarder has the right to be able to work, play and relax free from abuse, intimidation, harassment, teasing and bullying.

❖ There is equality of opportunity and respect for all boarders, regardless of ethnicity, culture, gender or disability.

❖ Each boarder and each member of staff is to be treated as an individual, and with respect by other pupils and by staff.

❖ Although living together, staff and boarders acknowledge the right of each other to privacy.

❖ Each boarder has the right to extend his or her intellectual growth in an atmosphere of positive encouragement and in conditions that are conducive to learning.

❖ All boarders should be able to develop physically, spiritually, intellectually, morally and socially.

❖ Despite the distance separating boarders from their families, links with parents are seen as an indispensable part of the support and development of boarders.

Boarding houses obviously meet the first two levels of need, in their basic provision of accommodation and the pupils' physical environment, but then so do most other settings of residential care. Boarding, therefore, needs to create the right atmosphere, climate and conditions to meet the final three levels, which can be so much more easily met when there is a strong, supportive and tolerant community, and where the talents and aspirations of all its members are valued. We would all recognise the importance of the complementary role of the child's family, although many staff will acknowledge the additional demands of caring for those for whom this family support may not be strong.

Clearly, then, the boarding house has a crucial role to play in meeting the needs of all its pupils. Most importantly, there is the statutory requirement to safeguard and promote children's welfare by ensuring protection against suffering significant harm or neglect.

This represents a real challenge for boarding staff who will, from experience, recognise that so-called normal development patterns of children and young people vary so widely, both chronologically in terms, for example, of early and late puberty, and the sequence in which they occur. They will recognise that the different aspects of typical development will occur at different ages and stages in any given child, and that abnormalities in development may not be easy to spot (Bee[8], 1997).

For example, by the time a child starts boarding at preparatory school, say at age eight, his ability to reason and deduce is in its early stages of development, and the physical changes of puberty are usually some way off, but his social and moral development may be reasonably well advanced. By senior school age, many children are well into the traumas of adolescence, and social and emotional development often takes a new turn, with many of the frustrating symptoms of adolescence. The ability to reason and make moral choices is clearly more advanced, and arguments about the rights and wrongs of decisions and the actions of others are often hotly debated.

The boarding house and school thus need to provide opportunities for the development and growth of the pupils in their care in the following areas:

- ❖ social

- ❖ moral

- ❖ spiritual

- ❖ emotional

- ❖ physical

- ❖ intellectual and cultural

The opportunities provided may need to be related as appropriate to the school's curriculum provision and general pastoral care. In creating systems of care related to the needs of pupils, allowance will be made for individual differences between boys and girls, among pupils of the same age, and with pupils of different ages.

> *"[Staff] need to be aware of boarders who may not be part of an established peer group, and who may suffer isolation. Such isolation may be the first step towards bullying, and is more likely to affect newcomers, or children who are recognisably different in some way from the rest.*[9]*"*

The challenge for boarding staff often lies in resolving the conflict that can arise between the needs of an individual (say, one who needs a good deal more sleep than average) and the needs of the community (who may all be accommodated in shared dormitories). This will frequently become acute when dealing with pupils whose behaviour is a cause for concern. Should an offence which would normally warrant a well-understood and accepted response be dealt with in the same way if a pupil, for example, has just suffered a major disappointment or even bereavement? The whole question of the fairness and consistency of sanctions and punishments must be rationalised in terms of the pupils concerned. The dilemma is, again, to balance the needs of the individual, in terms of treating each case on its merits, with the needs of the community, in terms of consistency and fairness.

The seemingly unpredictable timetable for physical growth and development is one of which boarding staff will be particularly conscious. Even within the range of typical development, differences in the age of puberty can be alarming and difficult to handle for many young people, and this will often straddle the preparatory / senior school transition.

A particularly early or late puberty can have significant psychological and emotional effects on a child living at home, let alone one having to cope with the experience of communal living with peers. Birch[10] (1997) maintains that boys who are early maturers often find that their greater strength and size gives them an advantage over their peers, particularly in sport and in earlier self-confidence in relationships. Studies have shown that the reverse is often true with late-developing boys. However, it is sometimes easy to assume that the advanced physical development of a boy brings with it early emotional or moral development as well, and it is often these big boys who are scolded for not "acting their age". One needs to remind oneself that, within the six foot 13-year-old frame, a little boy is just as likely to be lurking inside. Equally so, a boy or girl who is less well developed physically than his or her peers, may suffer considerable embarrassment and trauma, with teasing and bullying, particularly in respect to physical activities and in showers or bedrooms.

Research has suggested that girls who are early developers may be more self-critical about their body image and, being taller than their peers (and also many boys of similar age), may be at a disadvantage. Some studies suggest that it can lead to poorer performance in school. Later in adolescence, it is suggested, such girls have better coping skills (Simmons[11] *et al.*, 1983).

Planning for the development of young people will probably involve many of the following, depending on the age range and circumstances of the house:

- developing spiritual and moral awareness; promoting clear expectations of positive behaviour, and a sense of right and wrong;

- cultural development, involving an appreciation of one's own culture, as well as those of other ethnic groups and nationalities;

- making decisions, perhaps through house or school councils, taking initiative, learning from mistakes;

- developing responsibility for themselves, others, and the environment; and understanding the benefits and demands of increasing independence;

- development of leadership opportunities;

- developing a sense of service, and of making a positive contribution to the house, school and wider communities;

- preparation for the next stage (senior school, college, career or Gap year);

- developing and examining relationships, the effect of exclusion or loneliness;

- developing positive attitudes towards others of, for example, different gender, ethnicity, culture, religion, disability, sexual orientation;

- learning to lead a healthy life style, the importance of exercise, diet and sleep, the effects of substance abuse;

- discussing sexual development and sexuality;

- learning to respect privacy.

Many schools (and indeed boarding houses) will outline the aims underpinning the community life in the boarding house and these, again, will help to guide and cement the day-to-day welfare and pastoral provision.

> *"[Schools] . . . should include a clear set of aims for the provision of boarding. There should also be clear guidelines and procedures for boarding that are not just statements of details of organisation.*[12] *"*

Figure 2.2 shows an example of boarding aims.

The outcome of these should be to create, provide and maintain a high level of pastoral welfare for pupils within which those of all ages can flourish, develop and fulfil their potential. Translating these aims into practice can also help to push through needed changes and reforms, and help to identify how to use and deploy available resources more effectively (see Chapter 17). Some of the systems that will be in place are considered by Best[13] *et al.* (1995) on three levels.

- **Reactive pastoral care** provides the response and support for personal problems, in terms of guidance, counselling and support. Hamblin[14] (1978) has called this "emotional first aid".

- **Preventive pastoral care** results from anticipating pupils' needs and critical incidents, and will provide coping strategies (*e.g.* for difficulties with relationships, handling bullying).

- **Developmental pastoral care** contributes to the personal and social lives of pupils, and enhances the quality of their lives. Although often covered in a formal PSE setting, boarding staff have unparalleled opportunities to contribute in a more informal and less structured way, for example, by building pupils' self-esteem or assertiveness, giving them opportunities to develop independence and initiative.

Figure 2.2 – Example of Boarding Aims

In boarding, we aim to:

❖ develop the whole person, a desire for truth and a respect for others;

❖ produce an open and trusting ethos in which each boarder feels able to approach any other member of the community (staff or pupil), confident in the knowledge that he or she will be treated and respected as an individual;

❖ create an atmosphere of tolerance, openness and trust in which teasing, harassment and bullying would find great difficulty in developing;

❖ provide the conditions for boarders to develop their intellectual talents through well structured homework conditions, access to staff and other pupils, participation in activities and in an atmosphere which values effort;

❖ provide a range of activities, hobbies and opportunities related to age and maturity that will assist in the personal, social and cultural development of each boarder;

❖ safeguard and promote the welfare of each boarder, by providing an environment that is, as far as possible, free from physical hazards and dangers of any sort;

❖ provide accommodation that is comfortable and suited to the needs of boarders, according to age and maturity, and which provides adequate levels of privacy;

❖ develop boarders' responsibility for self, for others and for the environment;

❖ develop boarders' qualities of leadership and ability to work as part of a team;

❖ encourage boarders to contribute to the needs and welfare of others in the house and school, as well as those in the wider community;

❖ provide suitable conditions for boarders to feel able to turn to members of staff to share the good things in their lives, as well as seeking advice, counselling and support during times of difficulty.

Meeting pupils' needs and enhancing their development will thus have a major role in influencing welfare provision and the day-to-day management and organisation of the boarding house. Boarding staff will, obviously, consider the aspects in the following sections[15].

ORGANISATIONAL/MANAGERIAL PROVISION

Arrangements for academic work

The house should ensure good conditions for private study and structured homework. Pupils may need to have access to staff or other pupils for academic help. Younger pupils, who may not have work-space available in their bedrooms, need to have somewhere to continue their homework after the end of the formal preparation period if, for example, they have been late in starting after a sporting fixture. Space also needs to be available for older pupils who may be working on public examination projects. This requirement needs to be taken into account in the way in which older boarders' rooms are arranged. The working conditions and environment should be conducive to good concentration and, for younger pupils, a degree of effective supervision may be needed.

Sleeping arrangements

These, again, should be related to the different ages of the pupils, the location of the sleeping areas being linked to the different bed-times of younger and older pupils. The deployment of staff and senior pupils within the house will, no doubt, be looked at to achieve satisfactory levels of supervision and care. Within the limitations of the building and available rooms, many houses will recognise the benefits of pupils having different (and perhaps more private) accommodation as they progress up the school. In senior schools, the balance between communal living in dormitories and the greater privacy of bedsits will need to be addressed. The proximity of bathrooms and WCs to the different sleeping areas should also be considered. Roger Morgan[16] (1993), in his survey of the views of over 2000 boarders in Oxfordshire, established that the lack of privacy was considered by both preparatory and senior pupils as the worst aspect of sleeping in a boarding school.

Activities/hobbies

These are always a good way to give boarders further opportunities to pursue and develop interests in their own time, particularly if the school's extensive facilities are available, as appropriate, in their free time during the day and in the evenings and at weekends. Both cultural and physical opportunities need to be available and competitions, both between houses and within the house, can help to bring the house community together. Free and structured time for younger pupils needs to be balanced appropriately. Houses will also look at off-site visits and expeditions for supplementing what is organised in school (but see Chapter 9 for organisation of off-site expeditions).

Standards of accommodation

Standards of accommodation are nowadays much higher in boarding schools than in the days of yore. Facilities in the house will, at some stage, need to be upgraded as part of a planned rolling programme of refurbishment, and any housemaster or housemistress needs to know where this fits into school development and financial planning. Adequate provision of communal areas, suited to the age range of pupils in the house, should cater for their need to read or work quietly as well as watch television or let off steam in an appropriate way. Noise levels and privacy aspects will need to be addressed when reorganising the use of existing space, to provide the sort of comfort levels expected by twenty-first century pupils and their parents. One should also keep an eye on the comparability of accommodation standards between houses, and particularly between boys' and girls' houses in a coeducational school. Morgan[17] (1993) identifies aspects of boarding accommodation that constitute the pupils' 'best buy'.

Opportunities for tutoring

The boarding school is likely to have a comprehensive structure for guidance and tutorial support for all its pupils, and each house will need to look as well at its own provision. How effective are procedures to monitor pastoral as well as academic progress and development? Is there a range of appropriate adults for boarders to turn to if they have a problem? Is it possible to provide both male and female staff support in the house? The boarding house has an excellent opportunity to provide informal counselling and support as well as a more formal and structured system. The house tutor team can often be deployed to allow each to look after a particular year group.

DEVELOPING POSITIVE ATTITUDES; ETHOS AND CULTURE

Communication of values

This is not easy for a new housemistress or housemaster to achieve before she or he has a clear feel for the house and its pupils. It has to be based on mutual respect and trust, and clear and unambiguous communication that the welfare of each individual boarder is paramount. All house staff need to make it clear just what they stand for, an easier task perhaps if they have been involved together with the formulation of boarding principles and aims. It can help if staff ensure that there are plenty of opportunities for them to talk to the house, either together in assemblies or meetings with individual year groups.

Development of leadership

Whatever the type of school or the age range of its boarders, it is important to develop a sense of responsibility among pupils, particularly the top year group who, whether they are part of a formal prefect system or not, will inevitably have to display leadership and show initiative (see Chapter 12).

Eliminating anti-social behaviour

A key task for all house staff must be to create and sustain an atmosphere and climate hostile to anti-social behaviour. All boarders need to recognise that bullying, theft and vandalism can do more to erode a sense of community and respect for each other than almost anything else. Pupils should be in absolutely no doubt that they all have a corporate responsibility to promote this attitude.

> *"[Discipline] should be based on good personal and professional relationships.*
>
> *[It] is of paramount importance for the growth, welfare and development of pupils, particularly so in boarding schools, where pupils have to co-exist and grow up with peers who exhibit varieties of behaviour.*[18] *"*

Equality of opportunity

Although most schools (and houses) will probably have a very short statement promoting equal opportunities and rights, the boarding house is the place where positive attitudes towards others can be fostered. This is especially important with pupils having widely differing needs and backgrounds, particularly those who have to cope with some disadvantage. Staff should be vigilant to ensure that pupils, for example, with learning difficulties, from different cultures or religious backgrounds, or those who may have anxieties about their sexuality, are not marginalised, isolated, or suffer from low self-esteem.

Promotion of a healthy lifestyle

Boarding staff should take every opportunity around the house, particularly in their informal dealings with pupils, to promote an awareness of appropriate diet, exercise and adequate sleep. Although house staff will sometimes have to adopt a disciplinary role when incidents involving smoking, alcohol and illegal drugs are concerned, they should also use the opportunity wherever possible to talk about the social and health implications of these.

COPING WITH DIFFICULTIES

Many of the pupils at one time or another, some more frequently than others, find communal life in a boarding community stressful and difficult to cope with. This is where the strength of the community comes to the fore, and all in the boarding house (particularly the house staff) need to be alert and sensitive to individual needs of pupils coping with difficulties. Staff need to be able to find the time to help pupils who find boarding uncomfortable and who lack the skills to cope with communal living, and the independence and initiative that it may demand of them. Specifically, this will involve:

❖ supporting pupils who find the lack of privacy hard to come to terms with;

❖ developing strategies to combat boredom and lack of motivation;

❖ handling sympathetically those who find the separation from home particularly difficult, together with any resulting homesickness that may result (cited in ***School Life***[19] as one of the worst things pupils found about boarding, although some would point out that current flexible and open policies for communication with parents and access to home may have helped to address this);

- finding the time to help those who suffer from loneliness and difficulty in making friends;

- helping pupils plan and prepare for a future which may cause anxiety, whether it be the move to senior school, or higher education;

- helping pupils to cope with the burden of high expectations, possibly unreasonable academic pressure inadvertently caused by ambitious parents, or the conflict experienced by the multi-talented child pulled in many different directions at once.

Not only the senior house staff, tutors and matrons are likely to be involved in helping pupils cope with particular difficulties; other staff involved in the running of the house may be used as *confidantes*. This suggests the need for *all* house staff to be trained in the accepted codes of response to boarders, and in such matters as child protection and the school's anti-bullying guidance. (See Chapters 3 and 11.)

Boarding staff are at the focal point of a child's life at school, as the following diagram reminds us.

Figure 2.3

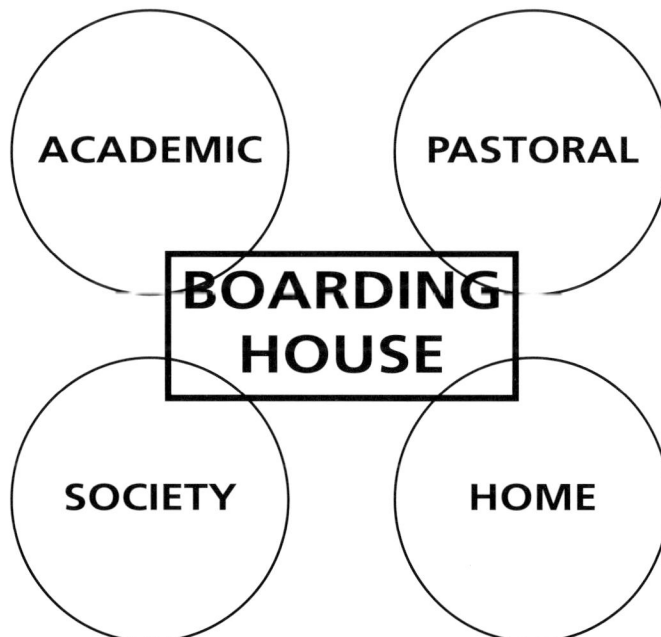

This provides, simultaneously, a supreme challenge and a high reward for staff. Boarding house life, and the people who live and work there, provide the means and the opportunity by which young people can be helped to balance the academic pressures and demands, ever-increasing in an era of league tables and uncertain university selection; the student's pastoral and communal life, with the demands of friends, foes, peer pressure and establishing relationships; the influence of society, the media and contemporary culture; and the expectations and standards of home and family.

The house staff are the key people who help young people cope with so many of the challenges and pressures that are part of growing up in the 21st century. One only has to consider the following to be reminded of some of the issues they feel they have to cope with and worry about.

self-esteem	*friendships*
bullying	*boys / girls*
sex and sexuality	*appearance / body shape*
conformity / individuality	*peer pressure / opinions of others*
clothes / fashion	*parents*
academic pressures	*employment prospects*

It is one of the miracles of life, and the great success of boarding, that so many young people emerge, not only unscathed, but enhanced from the experience! For them, Maslow's five levels of human need have been more than met.

References and Notes

6. Department of Health, **The Children Act 1989: Guidance and Regulations (Volume 5 – Independent Schools)**, The Stationery Office – para 3.1.4.

7. *Ibid.*, para 3.1.1.

8. Bee, Helen (1997), 8th ed., **The Developing Child**, Longmans.

9. Department of Health (1995), *The Children Act 1989: The Welfare of Children in Boarding Schools (Practice Guide)*, The Stationery Office – para 6.46.

10. Birch, Ann (1997), *Developmental Psychology*, Macmillan.

11. Simmons, R. G., Blyth, D. A., McKinney, R. L. (1983) in *Girls at Puberty*, Penguin.

12. Department of Health (1995), *The Children Act 1989: The Welfare of Children in Boarding Schools (Practice Guide)*, The Stationery Office – para 6.4.

13. Best R, *et al.* (1995), *Pastoral Care and Personal-Social Education – Entitlement and Practice*, Cassell.

14. Hamblin, D. H. (1978), *The Teacher and Pastoral Care*, Blackwell.

15. Department for Education and Employment, *Boarding Accommodation – A Design Guide* (Building Bulletin 84), The Stationery Office, 1996. This will provide further references for accommodation aspects.

16. Morgan, Roger (1993), *School Life – Pupils' Views on Boarding*, London, HMSO.

17. *Ibid.*

18. Department of Health, *The Children Act 1989: Guidance and Regulations (Volume 5 – Independent Schools)*, The Stationery Office – para 3.9.2.

19. Morgan, Roger (1993), *School Life – Pupils' Views on Boarding*, *op cit.*

CHAPTER

3

Boarding Welfare and the Law

Roger Morgan

Few of us, thankfully, spend our days considering the wording of the law in relation to our day-to-day work with pupils – little would otherwise be done. However, a knowledge of what the law requires us to do – and not to do – in relation to the welfare of pupils is both important and helpful, particularly when tricky questions arise over a decision which is out of the ordinary and may carry risks for a pupil or ourselves, or when things begin to go wrong.

The welfare duty of boarding staff towards the pupils in their care comes mainly from the Children Act 1989, and there are other parts of that Act, not specifically to do with boarding schools, that also directly affect boarding practice in particular circumstances. This chapter is intended to provide a basic general knowledge of how the Children Act applies to everyday boarding practice – both on the proverbial 'wet Monday evening' in the boarding house, and also when issues develop beyond the school's established precedents and policies and require decision-making based on the key principles in the legislation about our duties towards pupils. My intention is to sketch the relevant legal context to daily welfare practice in boarding, rather than to concentrate on specific cases. It is also important to stress that the law is not static – and the Children Act in particular is subject to major changes affecting boarding welfare, happening over the period 2000 to 2002. This chapter therefore includes reference to those changes, and their impact on practice after that period, compared with the past.

Some caveats must always be made at the start of any chapter offering interpretations of the law. This chapter is not a definitive statement of the law, and cannot be relied upon as such; nor can it constitute advice for any particular case. The former requires direct reference to the law itself, together with relevant current government guidance and up-to-date legal precedent from the courts, while the latter requires obtaining legal advice on the specific circumstances of concern. The fact that the Children Act is changing in relation to the pre-2000 position makes it even more important that up-to-date guidance and case law is consulted before taking major decisions based on interpretation of the law. Because laws have a habit of being amended over time, it is also important if ever referring directly to them to check that the version being read is the latest one, incorporating any amendments that may have been made. (See Appendix 1.)

This chapter is mainly concerned with the welfare provisions of the Children Act 1989, this being the law relating to the welfare of boarders, and of the Care Standards Act 2000, being the law bringing amendments to the Children Act welfare responsibilities, and in particular to the way they are inspected and monitored. There are of course other specialist aspects of legislation, not dealt with here, which affect aspects of boarding practice, as they do other kinds of work – for example, employment legislation in relation to staff, health and safety at work legislation, fire, planning, building control, vehicle, and food safety legislation. Boarding practice, as all other aspects of our working lives, is also affected by the Human Rights Act, which came into force on 2nd October 2000 and, as precedents and case law develop, there is likely to be a 'Human Rights' dimension to both our interpretation of all laws (the Children Act included) and to many individual cases.

We are all likely to have to differentiate between the pupils' plea "that's against my human rights" when objecting to legitimate actions or restrictions, and what may be a genuine breach of such rights. It is reasonable for boarding staff to assume that they are not breaching human rights if they are acting in accordance with both the letter and the spirit of the National Boarding Standards once these are implemented – although human rights case law may of course lead to amendments in the standards, as indeed in legislation itself, in the future. In making decisions on matters not covered in standards, it is important to recognise that in relation to certain issues – such as privacy, child protection and the nature of punishments – there is now a higher premium placed upon staff to act reasonably because of the incorporation of human rights legislation into UK law.

The law can also be supplemented from time to time by government Regulations; these too have the force of law (they are generally termed 'secondary legislation', Acts of Parliament themselves being the 'primary legislation'). Regulations can be made by Ministers wherever an Act of Parliament gives them the power to issue such Regulations to extend, interpret or amend the law in a specific area. The clue that Regulations might be around is any wording in an Act of Parliament on the lines of ". . . by such Regulations as the Secretary of State may determine", or ". . . the Minister may specify in Regulations . . .". Some Acts also give the government the power to issue guidance, standards or directions to someone on what they should do. This is not itself law, so that you do not break the law by not following such guidance, standards or directions – but whether or not it was followed would certainly be used as the basis for decisions if something were to go wrong or in any court case.

The Children Act

Over the years since it was passed, it has become common for people to blame the Children Act for interfering with the application of common sense to looking after children – particularly troublesome ones. We have all heard the statement that the Children Act stops us from intervening in various ways to discipline children or prevent them from behaving unacceptably, that its pro-child provisions can enable the challenging child to cause unchallenged mayhem, and that the Children Act stops us from previously innocent actions such as putting a comforting arm around the shoulder of a child who has just heard that a favourite pet has died at home.

In fact, the Children Act itself says very little that is specific about what should and should not be done in boarding, beyond the general, obvious and acceptable duty to look after children properly. It does none of the things listed above. The Act does however establish that boarding schools must by law look after their boarders' welfare – hardly a new concept. How that is to be done is not in fact set out in the legislation, but in documents such as government guidance documents and the National Boarding Standards, effective from April 2002, which fill in the detail of day-to-day required boarding provision and practice.

The key section of the Children Act 1989 that impacts directly on boarding practice is Section 87. This section contains two key elements (plus a host of procedural details) – firstly, the statement of the legal welfare duty the Act places upon boarding schools in looking after their boarders, and secondly the legal requirement for external inspection or monitoring of how boarding schools carry out that welfare duty.

The welfare duty

The core statutory duty placed on boarding schools by Section 87 of the Children Act is to "**safeguard and promote the child's welfare**". This is the primary legal duty that boarding brings for the school, and it is the basis of all the requirements of the National Boarding Standards. The following briefing points are offered to help define and interpret this duty, its scope, and the changes affecting it from 2002.

❖ The inclusion of the term "**safeguard**" in the school's legal duty clearly means that the school and its staff should do whatever they reasonably can to protect boarding pupils from harm such as accident or physical injury, physical or sexual abuse (from outsiders, adults at school, and other pupils), bullying, emotional harm, anything that interferes with their normal social, emotional or physical development, harmful discrimination, and any form of neglect. It requires the school to provide its boarders with adequate and appropriate facilities for their needs, such as suitable boarding premises, staff supervision, support and protection, catering and security. It is important (and professionally reassuring) that the legal duty is to take positive steps to safeguard boarders – it does not impossibly require that boarders never ever suffer harm despite reasonable safeguards to avoid it. The key is that, if harm occurs, it should not be through the failure of the school and its staff to provide adequate safeguards.

❖ The Children Act elsewhere (in Section 31) contains the concept of "**significant harm**" to describe the harm that pupils should be safeguarded against. The inclusion of the term "significant" clearly excludes minor everyday issues such as a minor grazed knee on the games field, and focuses our duty on safeguarding boarders from what might be termed "occurrences with consequences" – that is, anything which has major or long-lasting negative consequences for the pupil, particularly if what caused it was unnecessary, was something that one might reasonably have expected to be avoided, or which happened through taking an excessive risk.

❖ The Act legally defines **harm** as meaning ill-treatment or the impairment of health or development. It further defines **health** as meaning both physical and mental health, **development** as meaning physical, intellectual, emotional, social or behavioural development, and **ill-treatment** as including sexual abuse and "forms of ill-treatment which are not physical". In deciding whether harm to a child's health or development is in fact "**significant**", the Act requires a comparison with what could reasonably be expected of a similar child. It is important to know that these definitions require schools to safeguard boarders against situations and occurrences with harmful emotional or social consequences, as well as physical ones, and that boarding provision needs to be sufficiently supportive of boarders' educational well-being to avoid harm to their intellectual development. The Children Act duty is not solely a matter of avoiding child abuse.

❖ The Act does not in fact use the term 'boarder', nor does it refer anywhere to a 'boarding school'. The welfare duty (to safeguard and promote welfare) applies to **any child the school accommodates**, while that child is accommodated by the school. This means that the school has to safeguard and promote the welfare of any child either accommodated (essentially meaning overnight as well as by day) on the school premises, or in any other accommodation arrangements made by the school away from the school's premises. This includes pupils staying with staff, with school-arranged (rather than parent-arranged) guardians, in school-arranged lodgings – during holidays as well as term time – and on overnight trips abroad (including hotels, field study centres, exchange visits, adventure or leadership courses and cadet camps). Because the duty focuses on accommodation of children, it also applies to children who are not necessarily boarders – obviously to weekly or flexi-boarders while accommodated at or by the school, but also to day pupils staying overnight, and to visiting pupils the school may accommodate from elsewhere – such as a visiting team. The duty also applies to children other than its own pupils who may be accommodated by the school without their parents or other carers of their own, such as children attending holiday courses run by the school (rather than by another entirely separate organisation to which the school simply lets its buildings). The duty to safeguard and promote the welfare of any accommodated child extends throughout the day while they are being accommodated, as well as in 'boarding time' and overnight. Perhaps ironically, the Children Act welfare duty does not apply to day pupils who are not accommodated overnight by the school.

- ❖ The welfare duty relates to any **child**. This means any pupil or other child or young person aged under 18. The school does not therefore have a legal welfare duty under the Children Act towards any pupil aged 18 or over, as that person is legally an adult (although the school can of course expect an adult pupil nevertheless to comply with the welfare arrangements in place for younger pupils, as a reasonable condition of continuing to board at the school). The welfare duty of a boarding school applies equally to children of all ages under 18. Despite common belief, it does not differentiate between pupils aged under or over 16, although of course the means of safeguarding and promoting the welfare of boarders can and should reflect the age of the boarders concerned.

- ❖ The term "child" in Section 87 of the Children Act is in the singular, not the plural. Thus the school has a specific welfare duty towards **each individual boarder** (or other child accommodated), not only to the boarding population as a whole. This becomes significant when there is an individual boarder who does not 'fit in', has a particular individual need or problem, is perhaps not really placed at the right school, or is part of a minority group within the school. The welfare duty applies specifically to each of these individuals and, once a child is accepted for accommodation by the school, his or her welfare has to be safeguarded and promoted as is individually necessary.

- ❖ Because the Act applies to children accommodated by the school, it does not apply to the **children of staff** who are directly accommodated by and with their own parents – even if on school premises – because there is then a direct parental responsibility for their own children's welfare instead. However, it does apply to children of staff if they are being looked after as boarders with other boarding pupils, rather than directly by their own parents.

- ❖ The welfare duty is imposed on **the person (or body) running the school** – but is also delegated through the head and members of staff with responsibilities for boarders and boarding. The Children Act imposes the formal duty on the proprietor of the school, on any other person responsible for conducting the school, and (from 2002) on the governing body of a state boarding school. In practice therefore, the primary welfare duty is formally imposed on a school's governing body, trustees or an owner-head; the school's staff, who have delegated duties from the proprietor, head, governors or other "relevant person", have always to act in accordance with the duty to safeguard and promote the welfare of all accommodated pupils. It is helpful for staff to have individual job descriptions which clarify what aspects of boarding are their responsibility and thus where they have particular responsibility delegated to them to take action to ensure that the welfare duty is being met. This also means that staff (such as school nurses, chaplains and counsellors, who traditionally have a degree of independence within the school, and staff such as domestic, catering and maintenance staff who are not specifically employed to work with pupils) still have a duty to take action to safeguard and promote the welfare of any boarder, including informing the appropriate people, if they receive information – for example an allegation or suspicion of abuse – that any pupil's welfare is at risk. A boarder cannot legitimately be left at risk of significant harm through a staff member's wish to avoid breaching the confidence of that pupil or another pupil or person.

❖ Last, but certainly not least, the inclusion of the word "**promote**" in the school's statutory welfare duty means that the school has a statutory duty, not just to keep its boarders safe, but also to provide them with a pro-active welfare, as well as educational, service. The pastoral side of boarding is therefore not simply an adjunct to accommodation, but a primary statutory duty of every boarding school towards every individual boarder. The Children Act itself does not define the nature or day-to-day content of this pro-active welfare function, but what is required 'on a wet Monday evening' to satisfy this duty is set out in the National Boarding Standards issued by the government from 2001 under the Care Standards Act 2000 (prior to that, it is contained in the various welfare standards documents of local social services authorities, and in the wider government guidance which was issued on the Children Act in 1991).

The Care Standards Act 2000 has amended aspects of the Children Act 1989 from April 2002. One of these changes is that, from that date, the statutory welfare duty, which before that date only applies to independent boarding schools, is extended to apply fully to all types of boarding school – including Local Education Authority maintained boarding schools and non-maintained special schools. As a result, from 2002 all these categories of boarding school come under the same set of National Boarding

Standards and the same welfare inspection system, replacing the variety of existing local standards and inspection systems. Before that date, LEA boarding schools have not been legally required to have separate welfare inspections, and non-maintained special schools have been subject to far more varied and flexible monitoring of their own welfare duty by local social services authorities under a different section of the Children Act. The only boarding schools to have a different set of welfare requirements and a different form of inspection from 2002 are those required to register as children's homes (how this happens and what it means is described below). It is also worth noting that, from 2002, the same statutory welfare duty and inspection system applies for the first time to Further Education Colleges accommodating students under 18.

National Boarding Standards (see Appendix 2)

What matters to staff with day-to-day responsibility for the care of boarders is what they should do, and not do, provide and prevent, in order to meet their welfare duty under the Children Act. From April 2002, the detailed requirements are those set out in National Boarding Standards issued by the government, which were developed and piloted with schools and their associations as well as existing boarding welfare inspectors and government departments. This standards document contains specific minimum standards, with detailed criteria for each, that apply from 2002 to all boarding schools (there are separate sets of national standards for special schools, schools that have to register as children's homes, and for Further Education colleges). They are designed so that, if followed, the school will in most cases be adequately safeguarding and promoting its boarders' welfare – that is, fulfilling the statutory welfare duty. They are also designed to be appropriate to all types of boarding school without requiring standardisation or curtailing the proper individuality of each school, and to focus on positive pastoral and welfare outcomes (or risks) for boarders, rather than upon systems and structures for their own sake.

Having stated that the National Standards will ensure adequate fulfilment of the welfare duty in most cases, it must be acknowledged that there are times when meeting the standards will not be enough, and schools must take action not envisaged in the standards in order to ensure that boarders' welfare is safeguarded and promoted. There may also be particular circumstances where it will be necessary to do more than meeting the relevant standard in order adequately to safeguard and promote welfare –

remembering that the standards are in law *minimum* standards and thus not the maximum that could be done. Examples might be where it is necessary to provide special support and make arrangements to counter difficulties arising when the home countries of two groups of boarders living together at school are engaged in military conflict, or where additional security measures are necessary in a school experiencing intruders.

Before April 2002, the definition of expected welfare practice in boarding has been as set out in government guidance documents (not law, but statutory guidance to be followed by inspecting social services authorities) – particularly in Volume 5 of the Guidance and Regulations series issued by the Department of Health on the Children Act, and a subsequent amendment and further guidance circular to inspecting authorities (Department of Health Circular LAC (95) 1). Individual local social services authorities have since 1991 developed and issued their own local standards guidance for schools and used these in their Children Act welfare inspections. A main objective of the replacement of these local standards by a single set of national standards from 2002 has been to produce consistency of welfare requirements upon schools across the country.

The National Boarding Standards are not themselves law, but are issued under a new clause of Section 87 of the Children Act which empowers the Secretary of State to publish national minimum standards for safeguarding and promoting the welfare of boarders. The legal impact of these standards (from 2002) comes from the fact that the law states that the national standards shall be taken into account in any decision by a welfare inspectorate about whether a school has failed to safeguard and promote the welfare of any child it accommodates, and also in any other legal proceedings (under any other legislation) in which it is alleged that the school has failed to safeguard and promote the welfare of any child it accommodates.

Unlike some other national minimum standards issued by the government for other settings, those for schools are not accompanied by Regulations with the force of law in themselves – the one exception to this is that, for schools registered as children's homes, there is a set of Children's Homes Regulations with the effect of law that must therefore be fully complied with. In summary, boarding schools which are not children's homes should comply with the National Boarding Standards because these define how to meet their legal welfare duty, and to avoid being found to have failed to safeguard and promote a child's welfare, while boarding schools which are children's homes must also keep to the letter of the Children's Homes Regulations.

Children's Home registration

There is a single, simple and clear criterion which triggers the need for a school to be registered as a children's home. This is whether it accommodates (*i.e.* overnight as well as by day) pupils for more than a total of 295 days in any 12-month period. Before April 2002, a school needs to register as a children's home if it accommodates four or more children for over 295 days a year; from April 2002, under the terms of section 1 of the Care Standards Act 2000, the requirement to register is triggered by accommodating only one child for over 295 days in a year. Prior to 2002, only independent schools (not LEA or non-maintained special schools) have to register if they exceed the 295-day limit; from April 2002, all types of school need to register if they meet this criterion.

A school must register beforehand as a children's home if it *intends* to provide residential accommodation for the relevant number of children – that is, if this is a planned service. If the school does not intend to provide such a service but finds itself accommodating a pupil for over the critical 295 days in an emergency (perhaps because a boarder's travel home arrangements have failed for a long vacation), registration is not triggered by this happening for one year only, but is required if the same thing happens two years running.

There are two important features to know about what counts towards the 295-day criterion. Firstly, it relates to actual individual children – the school does not have to total the accommodation of different children. Secondly, the law specifically includes arrangements for accommodation made by the school, as well as accommodation actually on school premises, towards the 295 days; overnight stays with school-arranged educational guardians, on residential field trips, or spending holidays lodging with staff, have to be counted towards the total. In practice, a school should identify their 'longest accommodated pupil' – counting both nights spent on school premises and elsewhere arranged by the school – and if one or more pupils total over 295, then decide whether to apply for children's home registration to continue or develop this extended accommodation service, or to rearrange things to keep below the 295-day limit next year.

Some schools will wish to register as children's homes as well as schools, because they wish to provide more accommodation than most schools during the year. This will particularly apply from 2002 to many residential special schools. Registration as a children's home does not mean that the school in any way ceases to function as a school and becomes something else – it is effectively a licence to operate, and a duty to provide, an enhanced level of care service to pupils because they live for such a high proportion of the year at school rather than at home or elsewhere. Registration as a children's home has five main consequences for a school.

* It becomes subject to the standards for children's homes instead of the National Boarding Standards or their predecessors (the 2002 national minimum standards for children's homes have however been written to be properly applicable to schools).

* It becomes subject to the statutory Children's Homes Regulations and therefore to a more legally binding set of welfare requirements.

* It receives more frequent welfare inspections.

* Because it is registered with the inspecting authority (which other schools are not), that authority can take enforcement action directly against the school if that should become necessary on welfare grounds.

* The registering authority can impose specific conditions of registration that the school must comply with.

Before April 2002, independent schools needing to register as children's homes should apply to their local social services department. After April 2002, application should be made to the National Care Standards Commission, as the new national registration authority.

Educational guardians

Although the term 'guardian' is often used in the school world to refer to someone who acts on a parent's behalf, particularly for overseas pupils, and who may accommodate a pupil at exeats and during holidays, this use of the term does not appear at all in the Children Act. An educational guardian is not the same thing as a 'legal guardian' (as might be appointed by court), does not have the same legal powers in relation to the child, and in fact has no formal legal status at all under the Children Act. An educational guardian (even if appointed through an agency) can only be someone providing informal support or accommodation on behalf of either the parent or the school. If the educational guardian is appointed or provided by the school, then the school remains responsible for the pupil's safety and welfare, under its Children Act welfare duty, all the time the pupil is with the guardian. If the child's parent has appointed the guardian, then the parent, rather than the school, carries responsibility for the child's welfare while with that guardian.

It is therefore vital that the school and the parents are both clear which of them is responsible for the appointment of an educational guardian, and therefore for the welfare of the boarder while with that guardian. It is risky for this to be a grey area, or to discover that the parent and the school have made different assumptions about this. If it is unclear, perhaps because the parent is accepting the school's suggestion of a possible guardian, the school would be well advised to take legal advice on the wording of documents between parent and school to make it clear who holds the welfare responsibility for the child. There is absolutely no reason why a school should not appoint educational guardians for pupils, as a perfectly legitimate school-provided service – but it needs to be clear that the school should check, supervise and take responsibility for its guardians in the same way as it does for its boarding staff, and also that time accommodated with school-appointed educational guardians counts towards any pupil reaching the 295-day criterion for possible children's home registration for the school.

In loco parentis

We frequently speak of boarding staff standing *in loco parentis* to the pupils in their care. However, school staff cannot by law fully substitute for a child's parents, and it is important to analyse how school staff stand in relation to a child's parents.

Section 3 of the Children Act 1989 defines parental responsibility as "*all the rights, duties, powers, responsibilities and authority which by law a parent of a child has in relation to the child and his property*". It is essential that the school knows, and has recorded, who has such parental responsibility – it is not always obvious, because the term "persons with parental responsibility" can include others than a child's natural parents (for example, being given parental responsibility by a court order or by being appointed as a child's legal guardian under the terms of a parent's will if there is no other surviving parent). Each person with parental responsibility for a child can act alone, without reference to other parent(s) or person(s) with parental responsibility – thus any person with parental responsibility for a boarder can take relevant decisions for the pupil, even if not the parent in usual contact with that pupil – although it would not be unreasonable for a school to check the situation with the parent with whom they are usually in contact.

Neither a school nor its staff acquire parental responsibility for a boarding pupil because the parents have passed the day-to-day care of that child to the school. The Children Act (in Section 2) is very clear that parents cannot in fact pass their parental responsibility to anyone else, including a school: "*a person who has parental responsibility for a child may not surrender or transfer any part of that responsibility to another*". What a "*person with parental responsibility*" can do is to arrange for some or all of their parental responsibility to be met by one or more persons **acting on the parent's behalf**. In other words, when a parent places the child in school as a boarder, they cannot give full parental responsibilities to the school staff, but they are asking school staff to provide day-to-day care of the child on their behalf.

All the school's care and decision-making for a boarder is effectively delegated from that child's parent (or someone with parental responsibility for the child). This has two important consequences for schools. Firstly, it is important to be clear what care and decision-making the parent has in fact delegated to the school – the school cannot assume that whatever it wishes to do will be covered by the parental delegation implied by placing the child at school. If a parent is delegating aspects of their child's care to the school, there may be aspects that they do not intend to delegate, or they may attach 'strings' to their delegation (*e.g.* over medical treatment). This is why it is wise to secure prior specific parentally-signed permission for unusual activities and decisions, such as medical treatment (including first aid and giving of analgesia by school staff), visits abroad, or participation in unusual and potentially high risk activities. Secondly, because the parent has delegated day-to-day care tasks to the school, it is salutary to remember that the parent can equally well rescind any part of their delegation to the school at any time.

While school staff are looking after a boarder, they do have clear rights to act reasonably in the child's interests, in addition to their overall welfare duty to safeguard and promote the child's welfare. Section 3 of the Children Act clearly states that someone who does not themselves have parental responsibility for a child, but (as do boarding staff) has care of the child, "*may (subject to the provisions of this Act) do what is reasonable in all the circumstances of the case for the purpose of safeguarding and promoting the child's welfare*".

In making a decision affecting a boarder, such as in emergency, it follows that what staff should do is firstly to make sure that they take all the circumstances into account (including all their information and knowledge about that pupil and the present situation), secondly that they can show that they acted reasonably, and thirdly that what they decided to do was in order to safeguard or promote the welfare of the child(ren) concerned. This is a vital sentence from the law for boarding staff to bear in mind for guidance when they find themselves with their backs to the wall, on their own and responsible, in an emergency.

To help decision-making, and to prepare for possible subsequent explanations or defence, staff would in making difficult, contentious, evenly balanced but high risk, or emergency decisions, be well advised to follow the 'three Rs of decision-making' – have and write down their **Reasons** for the decision or action, check that what they are deciding or doing is clearly **Reasonable** in the circumstances in which they find themselves and on the information they have or can reasonably get, and keeping a **Record** of what they decide and why. (As a tip, the best record is always the one made at the time and kept unaltered, however rough and whatever more formal and sophisticated reports or records may be made.)

As a general guideline, staff can be expected to act in looking after their boarders as a good parent would if they were in the school situation rather than at home. As staff are acting on delegated authority from the child's parent, with their own legal duty to safeguard and promote welfare, it may be a relief that the fact that a child may claim "my parents let me" does not necessarily mean that their parents would expect the school staff to "let them"! School staff taking all the circumstances into account with their own welfare duty in mind can clearly decide that something a child may do at home is not permitted at school.

Court Orders

Since boarding staff are expected to act reasonably, but subject to the provisions of the Children Act, they need an awareness of other provisions of that Act that are not directly written for schools. Principally amongst these is knowledge of the various court orders that may affect the care of a child under Section 8 of the Children Act. It is wise for the school to ask at initial registration, and subsequently to re-check, whether any court orders affecting care of the child are in force – this may be important information if there are disputes between parents, or someone other than the usual parent arrives at school to see the child or take them out of school.

These 'Section 8 orders' include: a **Contact Order**, which allows visits, stays and contact for the child with the person named in the order; a **Prohibited Steps Order**, which effectively places out of bounds something a parent could otherwise do, and requires the specific permission of the court for the specified step to be taken; a **Residence Order**, which defines a person the child must live with (and incidentally makes it illegal to take the child out of the United Kingdom without the written permission of everyone with parental responsibility for the child, or of the court – important to know about when arranging a school trip abroad); and a **Specific Issue Order**, which gives a court direction on an aspect of the care of the child which might otherwise be decided by a parent. Boarding staff therefore need in their records a clear statement of, firstly, who has parental responsibility for each of their boarders and, secondly, any of these or other court orders directly affecting care of the child. Staff should of course comply with the terms of any such court order.

Child protection

Although not the whole of a school's welfare duty, child protection is a central element in discharging the duty to safeguard children's welfare. The National Boarding Standards set out clear requirements which schools should follow very closely in relation to three vital elements of child protection: the safe recruitment of staff, response to allegations and suspicions of abuse inside or outside the school, safe practices in day-to-day supervision of pupils and countering bullying. Schools should always follow these standards and criteria closely – and I would suggest that boarding staff reading this paragraph should, for their own and their pupils' protection, now check their school's own practice against those standards and criteria.

It is particularly important to check the operation of systems such as staff recruitment procedures, which are often left to operate 'on autopilot' most of the time but which may land the school in major trouble if they fail. It is a devastating truth that even though we have higher profile fire precautions and drills, pupils are probably more at risk of harm from abuse than they are from fire and that, in common with most services for children, most schools are from time to time targeted by individuals as a means of gaining access to children to abuse.

There are common failures to watch out for in staff recruitment procedures:

❖ some categories of adults to whom the school gives access to pupils may be likely to escape routine police and other recruitment checks, such as ancillary, domestic, driving and visiting activity staff;

❖ many schools operate more than one recruitment system (*e.g.* a separate one for non-teaching staff) which may not both be of equal rigour;

❖ government checking systems may themselves fail to check non-teaching staff unless the school clearly indicates on the request form (*e.g.* by attaching a note) that these are to have substantial unsupervised access to children in a boarding school;

❖ such procedures may fail to identify and chase up breaks in the process (*e.g.* a new member of staff who fails to return a provided police check consent form, or a check not received back for some reason from the government checking system);

❖ some staff awaiting satisfactory clearance may need very close supervision on site if they arrive at school before their clearances have arrived.

It is important that boarding staff, and particularly those in charge of houses, know exactly which of their staff and any other adults in contact with boarders have been satisfactorily checked for unsupervised access to children, and that they arrange a reasonable level of 'chaperoning' for staff or outside visitors or instructors not recruitment-checked who have contact with pupils. Again, having read this far, you may wish now to satisfy yourself that you do know which adults in your own boarding setting have been recruitment-checked, which need chaperoning, and what would be a reasonable way and level of chaperoning for these in your setting.

There are some child protection issues that the National Boarding Standards cannot reasonably lay down in immutable black and white print for all schools, but which are nevertheless important to fulfilling the welfare duty in the boarding house. Two of these are what is acceptable in terms of physical contact with children (which will vary according to age, gender, children's needs, whether the child is distressed, and the type of school), and what should be the school or house practice in relation to one-to-one time spent alone with a child.

One approach to such issues, given that universal absolute stances are not feasible, is that every boarding staff group should discuss these, in relation to what will and will not properly safeguard and promote pupils in their particular circumstances, as well as reduce risks to themselves of allegations being made, and establish clear norms for their setting. This has the virtue of ownership by all staff involved, of fitting the setting, and of agreeing norms for sensitive areas of boarding life which clearly place limits around and identify any individual beginning to drift outside the agreed safe practice. The Children Act does not say that no staff may be alone with a pupil, nor that no staff may touch a pupil – but obviously such actions must be reasonable, appropriate and in line with the welfare duty towards that pupil. Individual staff needing to act reasonably at all times are helped by knowing where and when they may themselves be vulnerable, or be seen as putting anyone else in a vulnerable position, and what are the established and openly discussed norms of their own staff group.

If staff receive an allegation of abuse of a pupil, or themselves suspect this, they should follow the actions required under the National Boarding Standards (included in Appendix 2). Section 47 of the Children Act gives the local social services authority for the area in which the school is situated the statutory duty to make 'enquiries' (often termed child protection investigations) whenever they have reasonable cause to suspect that a child is suffering, or is likely to suffer, significant harm (as defined in the Act). Because this duty is given to the social services authority rather than to schools, it is important that if any member of staff (including ancillary staff as well as teaching and boarding staff) receives an allegation of, or themselves suspects, abuse, this is referred promptly to the local social services authority to investigate, and that the school does not itself try to carry out an internal investigation (unless this is agreed with the social services authority child protection staff). Where the allegation or suspicion concerns events at the boarders' home elsewhere in this country, rather than at school or locally to the school, the matter should be referred to the local social services authority for that area. Again, the National Boarding Standards set out the requirements for school child protection policies on responding to allegations and suspicions of possible abuse. It should be noted that the transfer of welfare inspections from social services authorities to the National Care Standards Commission in 2002 does not change the child protection investigation functions of local social services authorities, and therefore allegations or suspicions of abuse should continue to be referred to those authorities.

Welfare inspections

Alongside the welfare duty placed by the Children Act upon boarding schools, is a duty upon an external inspectorate to carry out regular inspections to check that schools are adequately fulfilling their welfare duty and to take action if they are found not to be fulfilling that duty adequately. Since October 1991 and until April 2002, local social services departments are responsible for this inspection duty; from April 2002, the new National Care Standards Commission is responsible. In Wales, the National Assembly rather than the National Care Standards Commission will then have the responsibility for welfare inspection. There is provision in the Children Act for an inspecting body other than social services authorities or the National Care Standards Commission (or National Assembly in Wales) to apply to become accredited by the Secretary of State to carry out welfare inspections of boarding schools and Further Education colleges under the Children Act, but at the time of writing no other body has been accredited under this provision.

The inspection of boarding welfare is separate from, and additional to, inspection of the school's educational provision, and is carried out to assess firstly whether the school is currently adequately safeguarding and promoting boarders' welfare in accordance with the relevant standards (from 2002, the National Boarding Standards), and secondly whether there has been any failure to fulfil this welfare duty in relation to one or more children.

The inspectorate has wider monitoring powers than solely carrying out inspection visits, although these are for most schools the main contact staff will have with the inspectorate. Social services authorities (until April 2002) and then the National Care Standards Commission (after April 2002) can "*take such steps as are reasonably practicable to enable them to determine whether the child's welfare is adequately safeguarded and promoted while he is accommodated by the school*" (Section 87 of the Children Act). In addition to inspection visits, this can include requesting information from the school (for example, staffing information or notifications of major incidents), carrying out investigations of any complaints made about the school to the inspectorate, and seeking information from other organisations, such as the local fire service and the local social services department child protection investigation staff in relation to any possible child protection enquiries that may have involved them.

Properly authorised inspectors (carrying both an identity card and a document specifically authorising them to carry out inspections – school staff may refuse entry to anyone claiming to be an inspector without such documents) have the right of access (for the purposes of inspection) to premises, boarding pupils and any records the school is required to keep in relation to its welfare duty, including any computer-held records, pupil files, staff personnel files (*e.g.* to check records of staff recruitment checks) and the school's pupil health (as opposed to NHS) records. From 2002, inspectors of the National Care Standards Commission are required to carry out their inspections according to a nationally laid down methodology.

It should be noted that the power of entry for inspectors does not require prior notice, and that 'unannounced' visits can therefore be made by an authorised inspector. Two changes to the legal power of entry to boarding school premises by inspectors take effect in 2002. Firstly, the pre-2002 limitation that inspectors can only enter premises at "any reasonable time" is amended to empower them to enter "at any time" (thus strengthening the right of inspectors to visit whenever they consider it necessary) and, secondly, the pre-2002 power of entry to school premises currently accommodating children is extended to give inspectors the power of entry to premises which are going to be the school's premises in the future. The power of entry relates to the school as a whole, and is not limited to boarding houses.

The law requires the details of the premises, children and records to which inspectors can have access to be defined by the Secretary of State in Regulations (with the force of law once made). At the time of writing, the relevant detailed Regulations can be found in the back of Volume 5 of the Department of Health's 1991 Guidance and Regulations series under the Children Act. Such Regulations can be updated or replaced at any time, and it would be advisable to check that any set of such Regulations consulted is current. It is an offence for anyone to "intentionally obstruct" an inspector from exercising their powers under Section 87 of the Children Act (for example, preventing or refusing legitimate access to premises, children or records, or failing to assist them in accessing computer held records if asked). Schools will however be reassured to know that complaints procedures will be available to them to use if they consider that the actions or demands of an inspecting authority, or of its individual inspectors, are unreasonable, or themselves interfere with the welfare of children.

Each inspection leads to an inspection report, which before 2002 does not have to be published, but from 2002 is likely to be a publicly available document. This report may include both recommendations to the school for changes or improvements to welfare arrangements to avoid falling below an acceptable standard of practice and keep in line with the requirements of the published standards, as well as more general welfare advice which constitutes suggestions rather than requirements from the inspector. The school should clearly implement recommendations made to bring, or keep, the school's boarding provision in line with the required standards.

Apart from those schools registered as children's homes, the boarding welfare inspectorate cannot itself take direct enforcement action against the school for failing to safeguard and promote the welfare of its boarders. What the inspectorate can however do if it considers that there has been a failure in safeguarding and promoting welfare is to send a formal notification of that failure to the Secretary of State in the case of an independent school or a non-maintained special school, or to the local education authority in the case of a maintained LEA boarding school. A notification to the Secretary of State can lead to enforcement action against the school, initially requiring remedial action and ultimately, in serious cases, resulting in closure of the school or its boarding provision. There is provision for appeal in each case. It is worth noting that the inspectorate has a clear duty to make a statutory notification of failure to safeguard and promote welfare if it considers that such a failure has occurred – it does not have discretion to decide not to make the notification, for any mitigating or other reason, once it considers that the failure has occurred.

Conclusion

It is not expected that many boarding staff will often need to refer to the terms of the law; the day-to-day working document for reference about the welfare duty will be the boarding standards. It is hoped that this chapter will serve as a signpost to the legal provisions of the Children Act should the reader need to consider an issue or their actions in relation to the welfare duty in the light of the relevant legal principles.

In order to check one's own welfare practice in legal terms, I do however suggest that the reader should now consider the following six key questions.

1. Do I personally have a working knowledge of the National Boarding Standards?

2. Is our everyday boarding practice in line with those standards?

3. Do I know which aspects of boarding welfare are my particular responsibility?

4. Where the school has been inspected under the Children Act, do I know and has the school implemented any recommendations made in the last boarding welfare inspection report?

5. Has my own staff group discussed and agreed how to deal with issues such as physical contact and time alone with pupils, and am I content that our practice does safeguard and promote welfare as well as avoid staff being unnecessarily vulnerable?

6. What aspect of our boarding provision might be seen as least likely to safeguard and promote boarders' welfare, and is there anything it would be reasonable to do about it?

CHAPTER

4

The Nature of Adolescence

John Coleman

What is adolescence?

While this is an important question to ask, the answer is not a simple one. In the first place, no one is entirely sure when the stage begins. For some, it may be at 13, the first 'teen' year, while for others it may be at the start of secondary school. For those who prefer a physical marker, the beginning of puberty is the obvious moment. Yet puberty itself is very complex, with different elements – the growth spurt, wet dreams and so on – occurring at different times. The picture is further confused by the fact that, during the 20th century, puberty has occurred approximately one month earlier every decade. Today, many boys and girls in the top class of any primary school will have started puberty – are these 10- or 11-year-old children adolescent?

The situation is even more confused at the upper end of the age range. If legal definitions are to be relied upon, you are adult in some respects at 16, in other respects at 17, and yet others at 18. Continued education and training after 16 for almost all young people in our society leads to prolonged dependence on the family. Adulthood is postponed and more and more young men and women remain at home until their early 20s. At what point can we truly say that a teenager becomes an adult?

Understanding adolescence

There is general agreement that adolescence is best understood as a transition from childhood to adulthood. Transitions have special characteristics. They involve change, and they require adjustment to new circumstances. Because of uncertainty about what lies ahead, those involved in transitions may experience considerable anxiety about the future. They may also feel a sense of loss for what has been left behind.

The adolescent transition results from the operation of a number of pressures. Some of these, in particular the biological and emotional pressures, are internal; while other pressures, which stem from peers, parents, teachers, and society at large, are external to the young person. Sometimes these external pressures carry the individual towards maturity at a faster rate than he or she would prefer. For example, friends or the peer group may encourage young people towards early sexual behaviour. On other occasions, parents or other adults may act as a brake, holding the adolescent back from the freedom and independence which he or she believes to be a legitimate right. It is the interplay of these forces which contributes more than anything to the success or failure of the transition from childhood to maturity.

While very many young people cope with the transition reasonably well, there are of course a minority who run into difficulties. It is the problem behaviour of this group that is so prominent in the public eye. Adolescent suicide and self-harm, drug and alcohol abuse, delinquency, teenage pregnancy – all these pose pressing problems not only for parents, teachers and other professionals but for society at large. In Britain, work in all these areas has made possible a greater understanding of the factors which cause problem behaviour.

First, it is clear that the family plays a key role in affecting the adjustment of the young person. A parent who provides support at the right time, who values the young person and endorses his or her aspirations, and who is able to set appropriate boundaries, will reduce the likelihood of problem behaviour. On the other hand, research also shows that erratic or inconsistent discipline, a lack of parental concern, and poor monitoring and supervision, are all strongly associated with the development of difficult behaviour among teenagers.

Second, some attention needs to be paid to the context or setting in which the individual grows up. It seems clear, for example, that for a child to be looked after by a local authority, with all the rejection and the disruption of family ties involved in such a placement, can be extremely damaging. Other children may experience family poverty, they may live in circumstances of deprivation on an inner city estate or in an isolated rural area, or they may have parents engaged in chronic conflict and violence towards each other. To grow up in such circumstances is likely to have long-term disruptive effects on young people.

Grown-up or not?

In seeking to understand adolescence, a concern for many writers has been the impact upon young people of not having a clearly defined status in society. It may well be that this is an issue not unrelated to the problem behaviours we have been discussing. Not knowing whether you are grown-up or not has a number of implications. First, it is intensely frustrating for adolescents. The feeling of not knowing where you stand, of not knowing exactly how you are going to be treated – as a child or as an adult – can be very difficult to cope with. If society does not have a framework and clear benchmarks to tell you when you have reached adulthood, how can the individual young person work it out for himself or herself? The second implication is that adults feel confused about adolescence, but adults generally have to play a game in which the rules are being made up as they go along. In this game the institutional framework, such as the law, school rules, and so on, are of little help. Third, the uncertainty of status often serves to place young people in positions where they have very little power, and where damaging stereotypes can flourish easily.

Sexuality may be taken as one example of this, for here stereotypes of 'promiscuity' and 'permissiveness' interfere in the way adults perceive young people, and reduce the chances that boys and girls will receive the support the education, and the medical care that they need. Sexuality is a particularly good illustration of this problem in the United Kingdom because of what has come to be known as the Gillick case. Briefly, it was as a result of this case that the House of Lords issued a judgement in 1985, indicating that a young person under 16 does have the right to confidential medical treatment and contraceptive advice, but only under certain conditions (see Chapter 6). Unfortunately, such conditions (e.g. that, unless the girl receives confidential advice or treatment, her health is likely to suffer) are open to varying interpretations. A number of subsequent 'clarifications' have been issued by the Department of Health but, from the adolescent's point of view, the situation remains far from clear.

While we cannot be certain exactly how the Gillick case has affected adolescent sexual behaviour, what little research there is seems to indicate that young people have experienced increased uncertainty about their rights in relation to medical treatment. Such uncertainty has repercussions far beyond the issue of contraception. Here is something that really matters to adolescents, and yet it must appear to them that the adult world is unable to assist them or to give them clear guidance in a sensible way. Such a message cannot be the right one to be sending to those growing to maturity in the 21st century.

Of course this problem is reflected in many areas, apart from sexuality. The dramatic change during the 1980s and 1990s in the way young people make the transition from school to work is an indication also of the difficulty of assuming an adult status. Whereas, in earlier decades, well over half of all adolescents in Britain left school to go to work, today virtually no one does so. The setting up of a wide range of training schemes for the 16- to 19-year age-group may possibly have reduced youth unemployment, but it has also had the effect of creating an occupational twilight zone where young people are neither pupils nor working – a poor preparation for adulthood.

Conclusion

Young people face a harsher world today than they did thirty years ago. Poorer job prospects, more limited housing, increased rates of family breakdown, and fewer resources in education are just some of the social changes which have occurred and which will have had a direct effect on adolescents. Uncertainty continues to be a major issue for all youngsters as they move through the teenage years. As we look beyond the year 2000, it seems important to recognise some of the most obvious needs of young people, and encourage adults to be better informed about this stage of development.

The fact is that, in large part, adults find this stage a puzzling and confusing one. Many talk of 'dreading the teenage years', hardly a basis for good relationships between the generations. The situation is not made any easier by the absence of good quality information about adolescence. While much attention is given to babyhood and early childhood, those who want to learn about the adolescent stage of development have to hunt far and wide for the right book or set of training materials. Professionals in the youth field could undoubtedly do more to provide better training and assistance to enable adults to understand this stage more clearly. Ignorance breeds anxiety, but it also leads to poor parenting and relationship skills. Young people need adults to be better informed about adolescence because it is only in that way that their parents, as well as teachers and others, can give them the most effective support.

CHAPTER
5

Counselling and Communication Skills

Helen Holland and Candida Hunt

Introduction

The essentials of effective communication, and how these attitudes and skills can be used to help young people in difficulties, are the principal topics of this chapter.

Most of the qualities and skills needed to communicate well in the way that is labelled 'counselling' are ingredients in all healthy, supportive relationships. The most important of these is a real respect for the other person – not necessarily of his or her behaviour, but of the person as a whole.

The principal difference in a counselling relationship is that only one person brings difficulties, and the other person is there to offer help and support. This does not mean that the 'counsellor' has all the solutions, and simply doles them out to the 'client': the task is to help the client's efforts to find his or her own solutions. When people are first cast in a counselling role they often feel anxious that they will not be able to come up with all the right answers. Be reassured – we don't have to. If, as counsellors, we provide all the answers to other people's questions, we become omnipotent and they become helpless. One of the key elements of a helping relationship is to enable the other person to solve his own problems more effectively – by acknowledging his feelings, by thinking clearly both about how he feels and how he behaves, and thus empowering him to take charge of and for himself. Any of us, when we are troubled, can be helped by another person using this approach with us.

Many people think that the essence of good communication is to talk well; in fact, it is to listen well. Active listening communicates to the other person a genuine interest in what she is saying, a genuine desire to understand her point of view. This is true of all supportive relationships. The chapter will explore some of the ingredients for active and supportive listening.

Our emotional health

If we are to attempt to model helpful attitudes to young people, we need first to think about our own attitudes, behaviour and relationship skills. In order to offer help to others, we need first to turn to ourselves. In his book ***Emotional Intelligence***[20], Daniel Goleman encourages us to consider five key areas of emotional and social development.

1. Knowing our emotions: developing awareness of the wide range of feelings we experience.

2. Managing our emotions: handling our own difficult feelings in a way that promotes our emotional well-being.

3. Motivating ourselves: marshalling our emotions to help us act on our own behalf.

4. Recognising and accepting emotions in others: the development of empathy.

5. Handling relationships: building on self-awareness and empathy, the art of relationships is based on skill in managing our response to emotions in others while also managing and effectively expressing our own.

Developing these qualities will help us in all our relationships, personal and professional. They enable us to develop effective communication skills in our dealings with pupils in all school contexts, not just at the moment that a young person needs help. If we demonstrate 'emotional literacy' in everyday encounters with pupils, they will much more readily turn to us for help when they are in trouble. Modelling and spreading these skills and attitudes to the whole community can have widespread benefits.

"Boys fortified by emotional awareness and empathy are less likely to inflict hurt on others and more resilient under the pressure of cruelty that comes their way[21]."

Helping young people meet their needs

If young people are asked what they most want from adults, they often reply "To be listened to". (Adults also want to be heard and appreciated, of course.) A common complaint of young people of all ages is that adults talk to (at) them, but do not listen to their point of view. We will consider listening and responding skills later in this chapter. First, let us focus on the recognition and understanding that encourage our acceptance of an individual; this is essential for genuine listening to take place.

A principal need of young people is to believe in themselves. The adults in their lives can either foster self-belief, self-acceptance and a high self-esteem, or hinder these qualities. Criticism, belittling, humiliation, sarcasm, blame – all these are a hindrance. Praise and encouragement, acceptance and support – these help to build up high self-esteem.

Children with poor behaviour almost invariably suffer from low self-esteem; those who are generous to others, realistic about their own strengths and weaknesses, and are generally purposeful and relaxed, are likely to have higher self-esteem. When considering a child in difficulties, it is particularly worthwhile to pause and ask ourselves in what way his self-esteem may be under threat. We can think of self-esteem as having five elements:

❖ a sense of belonging
    "Do I fit in here?"

❖ a sense of identity
    "Who am I?"

❖ a sense of security
    "Am I safe?"

❖ a sense of competence
    "Can I do it?"

❖ a sense of purpose
  "Where do I want to go?"

A child may be struggling in one or more of these areas. For example, a pupil of different ethnic origin from others in her class may not be sure whether she belongs in the group; if she is teased or singled out because of the colour of her skin, she may not feel safe. If English is not her first language, she may also be anxious about whether she is competent enough to achieve the tasks she is set. Another youngster may be struggling because his parents are divorcing; he too is likely to be wondering where he belongs, and his sense of his own identity will need adjustment. This demonstrates that, while individual circumstances may differ, the categories of self-esteem can still apply.

Each of us has a hierarchy of needs, which begins with physical survival, moves through emotional, social, and intellectual to spiritual needs. For example, children who are tired or hungry will find it difficult to concentrate in the classroom. Those who are distressed about events at home may withdraw socially.

This framework helps us reflect on where children may be blocked from moving forward. We all want recognition, acceptance and to feel that we are significant. Children attempt to get these needs satisfied by seeking attention. All children need attention. If this need is not met as a result of their receiving positive attention, they will still seek it: negative or hostile attention is better than being completely ignored – unrecognised, insignificant. Traditionally, children have often found it easier to gain negative attention than positive attention: if two or three children are playing together happily, or a child alone is busily and harmlessly occupied, we tend to "leave well alone" and ignore them; yet as soon as there is conflict, or the child's activity becomes annoying or messy, we turn our attention to them – often critically. If this is the only attention they get, children will begin to behave in undesirable ways more and more often. If we pay them attention when they are co-operating, they will co-operate more. Remember:

Negative attention encourages negative behaviour
Positive attention encourages positive behaviour

When young people behave inappropriately they may have unmet needs, and their actions are often ill thought out attempts to redress the balance. It is particularly important when working with and supporting young people to distinguish in our own minds between the way they behave and who they are – to see beyond inconvenient, antisocial or unacceptable behaviour to the person. Of course, not all distressed people behave in ways that have a negative impact on others, but it is important to be aware of our reactions and to avoid judging the whole person because of one aspect of his behaviour. In the heat of the moment, it can be a real challenge to us as adults to recognise that poor behaviour is usually the inappropriately expressed outward sign of inner distress.

Children misbehaving are nearly always endeavouring to find significance. They may do this through seeking attention, trying to prove their power, or even by seeking revenge.

To counter these behaviours, we must help the young to make positive and constructive use of their desire to be significant. There are also children who go unnoticed because their behaviour is not troublesome (though they may be labelled lazy or unfocused). However difficult it seems, encouragement is an essential element in helping all these children.

The attention-seeker whose behaviour an adult finds irritating can be asked to contribute helpful tasks. It is important wherever possible to ignore the misdemeanours and focus on the actions that are acceptable and desirable. So Jimmy, instead of being told to stop fiddling with the safety-pins, is asked to help fold sheets. Remember that the behaviour we focus on is the one that will be repeated.

The young person endeavouring to prove his or her power can do so actively or passively. The adult's reaction is to feel angry or to force obedience. The results can be very unpleasant.

Guy was an Australian Gap student, inclined to throw his weight around, but also willing to learn from his mistakes. An altercation took place in the school dining-room one lunch-time when he accused Tom, a pugnacious fifth-former, of not having cleared the table adequately. Chairs were thrust angrily aside and voices raised as the two young men sought to master each other. A housemaster, coming into the room, wisely pretended not to notice what was happening, and called for Guy to accompany him on some task. Once outside, he suggested Guy should handle such a situation less confrontationally in future. The Australian did more than that. He made a point of apologising to Tom for his loss of temper, and asked what Tom suggested as the best way of obtaining co-operation from himself and his peers. The result? A remarkably good relationship between the Gap student and the fifth-formers. They respected both his willingness to apologise and his genuine attempt to disengage from the power struggle.

Dealing with young people who are determined to seek revenge can be very disheartening. We can feel ashamed of our own desire to lash back in retaliation. Our outrage at unkind, even vicious, behaviour serves only to intensify it and, even if we recognise what is happening, it can be very difficult to respond effectively because the child is unlikely to cease his actions, indeed will push even harder to hurt us. The adult's role is to offer chances for co-operation and to teach the child to handle honest feedback; it takes time and trouble to build the rapport that will enable this to happen.

It is necessary to offer young people clear boundaries and clear guidance about their helpful and unhelpful behaviour, and to challenge without criticising or shaming them. This is not always an easy thing to do, particularly when we ourselves are upset or angry. Here are two different ways a matron might respond to deal with her exasperation at a constantly untidy dormitory.

Blaming "You" message:

> *"You are the worst dormitory in the house! You are all so untidy and thoughtless, you make me really angry. You should be ashamed of yourselves – and if you don't pull yourselves together you'll be in real trouble."*

Clear "I" statement:

> *"I feel frustrated and angry when I see an untidy dormitory. People's belongings get lost or damaged, and the cleaners can't do their job properly when rooms are in a mess. I expect all of you to look after your things and help to keep the room tidy; I will be back at 6 o'clock to see that you have sorted it out."*

In the first of these examples, the children may feel resentful and angry, or laugh away their discomfort by mimicking Matron's 'nagging' voice. In the second example, they are much more likely to co-operate and tidy up: Matron stated honestly how she felt about the situation, generalised her description of the problem by avoiding the use of the word "you", and gave clear guidance about what was to be done.

Throughout childhood, young people need adults who can provide the right combination of acceptance, empathy, structure, challenge and expectations. In adolescence, the situation is complicated by the desire for approval from their peers, the urge to take risks and experiment, and the sense of despair that can strike even the most successful student. With sound self-esteem and the ability to think through situations, adolescents are much better equipped to deal with this period of their lives.

Rapport: the key to counselling skills

The key to this whole chapter is a recognition of the importance of emotional literacy. Research summarised by Daniel Goleman in **Emotional Intelligence** demonstrates that it is of far greater consequence than being clever (the kind of intelligence traditionally valued and tested in IQ tests) or acquiring technical expertise. As he says, "*We can be effective only when the two systems – our emotional brain and our thinking brain – work together*". Attitudes and skills modelled and practised by the adults in a school community, rehearsed in PSE classes, reflected on in assembly and chapel, enable young people to develop a sensitivity towards themselves and others that will stand them in good stead all their days. Conversely, lack of these competencies may seriously hamper their academic and working careers and their personal relationships.

The American psychiatrist Carl Rogers has identified the essential ingredients for any helping relationship[22]. His "core conditions" are unconditional positive regard, congruence and empathy. He was himself surprised, after considerable research and reflection, at the simplicity of the conditions needed for helpful changes to take place. The conditions may be simple in principle, but their practice is demanding.

Total acceptance (Rogers' unconditional positive regard) of another person's view of the world **as it seems to them** offers a real challenge – generally we like to impose our own view of an event or attitude described by someone else. By congruence, Rogers means that the counsellor is "freely and deeply himself" – being genuine rather than wearing a mask or presenting a façade. Empathy, the third core condition, is the ability sensitively to be aware of what someone else may be feeling, to 'read' the other person's emotions. Again, we often superimpose how we ourselves might feel in a given situation rather than staying open to the emotional experience of someone else.

An accepting attitude towards another – for example, of a child's desire to have fun – does not mean that we have to tolerate inappropriate behaviour, such as having fun at unsuitable moments. Rather, we must teach the child to discern what is and is not appropriate at any particular time, while making clear that we understand and accept the child's desire for fun – accepting his feelings without condoning his behaviour.

Empathy enables us to avoid humiliating and misinterpreting other people in our everyday dealings with them. It is also the most effective way of signalling our wish truly to understand another person, in any relationship – and particularly at a time when our principal aim is to offer help.

Congruence – sincerity or genuineness – allows us to be straight with each other. Children are adept at sensing a mismatch between deed and word, between word and thought; they dislike hypocrisy. When we are honest with them about how we are feeling, without blaming them or making them responsible for our feelings, we are modelling an emotionally literate attitude. If we honestly own our personal feelings about undesirable behaviour and are clear about what behaviour we expect, they are more likely to take responsibility for themselves. If we blame and criticise them (and it is difficult to be critical of behaviour without sounding critical of the person – confusing the sinner with the sin), they are likely to feel resentful, angry, guilty or upset, and to focus their attention on these reactions rather than on thinking about how they might choose to change their behaviour.

Rapport is established – or the opportunity for it missed – at any or every encounter around the school. A nod, a smile, a greeting, a word of thanks, all make connections between people. They can also serve as our introduction to a few words of conversation. Just telling the young what you have noticed about them can be helpful.

- ❖ "Thanks for holding the door open, Peter. I noticed you doing very well on the cricket pitch yesterday. How many runs did you make in the end?"

- ❖ "Hello, Jenny. I'm glad to see you, as I've been wanting to tell you how much I like the painting of yours in the hall – the one of the windmill."

- ❖ "It's not always easy being a prefect, is it, Adrian? I thought the way you handled that dispute in the quad yesterday was very tactful."

On other occasions a pupil can be invited to help with a task or chatted with as a match is watched. Questions that show real interest and invite genuine answers need not touch on personal topics, but the interaction can prepare the ground for future encounters. The pupils identify this or that member of staff as someone who is easy to talk to, someone who seems truly interested in their opinion, and store the memory for future reference. These positive interactions also help to raise pupils' self-esteem.

Time to talk: listening and supporting

When the need or opportunity to talk more seriously arises, listening and counselling skills really come into their own. People often say "But there isn't enough time!" Our response is that quality matters more than quantity. Well-established rapport means that trust has already been gained, and we can offer an opening that will sometimes be taken up quite quickly. If not, and depending on the situation, we can simply offer a quiet reminder along the lines of "Look, if you want to talk I'm here", and perhaps try again another time, or mention our concern and the pupil's reluctance to a colleague whose approach might be more successful.

Openings should be tentative, and show respect for the young person's ability to manage his or her own needs. Having said that, it is also important to be genuine and reflect the relationship you have already established with that particular pupil. Thus you might be a forthright personality and issue a cheery invitation to chat, but you should also try to match the child's character and approach a quieter one more quietly.

Finding a private space is essential, and it needs to be in a place and at a time that will be free from interruptions. In all our interactions, and particularly when we want to be helpful to others, it is important to consider our manner. Body language says even more than tone of voice in communication; in inviting someone to talk openly with us, we need to maintain an open, comfortable posture, positioning ourselves at the same level as the pupil and at an appropriate distance. We also need to place ourselves so that eye contact is possible but not forced. Remember that different cultures have different attitudes to eye contact, and individual interpretations of acceptable body language.

Once the talking has begun, the listener indicates by nods, 'mmhms' or 'uh-huhs' that she is paying close attention. Echoing the last few words or repeating a phrase shows that we are really attuned. There is no need to speak in order to fill a silence if the other person stops talking. Waiting indicates trust in the other's ability to find the right words. If she seems really stuck, she can be encouraged with a phrase such as:

- ❖ "It's not easy, perhaps, to find the right words. . . ."

- ❖ "I can see this is difficult to talk about. . . ."

- ❖ "You seem to be thinking hard. Could you say a bit more about . . . ?"

The core of active listening is reflecting or paraphrasing what the speaker has just described, with the intention not simply of repeating what has been said, parrot-fashion, but rather with the sincere wish to clarify and to check our understanding. The temptation is often to respond immediately with our own thoughts; when we resist that and truly seek to confirm what we have just been told, the speaker feels not merely heard and accepted but also encouraged to continue.

To work well, paraphrasing must be a genuine attempt to show that the listener is checking she has got the story right. On the one hand, it is very simple. Wait for the full stop, ask yourself what you have just heard and then rephrase it as accurately as you can.

In effect, you are asking:

- ❖ *"This is what I think you said. Have I got it right?"*

You are implying:

- ❖ *"It's important to me that I really understand your point of view."*

If you have genuinely misunderstood, you will be corrected. If you have got it right you will know, by the expression on the speaker's face, the response:

"Yes, and what's more. . . ."

A paraphrase can reflect both words and feelings, and this is where our skill at empathising is so important. We recognise the anger or the disappointment underlying a statement, and gently mention it. Or we pick up the contradiction between the flatly told tale and the resentment we sense is burning beneath. Tentatively, we offer our interpretation of the other's story and its attendant emotions, and our reward is a further sharing of confidences.

The framework for active listening (see Gerard Egan, ***The Skilled Helper***[23]) is to:

- identify, explore, clarify the problem;
- seek to understand the problem and identify possible alternatives;
- work to develop action strategies.

We hear the story, exploring its ramifications with a view to understanding it ourselves and, more importantly, to enabling the speaker to gain insight and develop self-awareness. Then, and only then, can goals be identified and action taken.

To help the understanding, to develop the story and deepen the insight, we sometimes need to ask questions. Again, we must tread delicately. Questions should be for the benefit of the speaker rather than the listener, enabling him to consider more thoroughly the situation presented. The danger, especially when adults question children, is that we take control and follow our own line of thinking. So we must ask through statements or 'open' rather than 'closed' questions, and offer ones that invite further thought and suggest new perspectives. Examples of statements and open questions might include:

- "Perhaps you could tell me about. . . ."
- "What else might you like to say about that?"
- "How do you think your Mum felt then?"

Closed questions are those that can be answered just by saying "Yes" or "No"; they tend to feel interrogatory, and to close down rather than open up exploration of a difficult topic. At all costs avoid asking the question "Why?", which at the very least puts the other person on the spot, and usually implies judgement, even blame.

When the time to finish approaches, indicate that the interview is about to draw to a close. Summarise what you have heard, offer the opportunity for a follow-up session, clarify any other help that is needed, and end in a way that will enable the young person to move back into the everyday world. For example:

- "Take a few deep breaths before you go back to lessons."

The summing up is a reminder of the ground covered, and again shows that you have truly been listening. Clarifying can also be useful when someone is presenting a multi-faceted problem. You can counteract a feeling of helplessness by saying:

- ❖ "You've told me this and this and this. Which bit would you like to tackle first?"

Or you step momentarily into your role of tutor or housemistress, and deal with practicalities:

- ❖ "Let's see. You can talk to Mr Brown about the missing coursework, and I'll mention the games kit to Matron. Is that all right with you?"

and then revert to the role of listener:

- ❖ "Jamie, do you want to say more about . . . ?"

Such conversations need not be extended and lengthy. A skilled listener can evoke a very swift response in terms of the actual story, and also do much to restore a young person's confidence. Accurate reflection and skilled questioning help the pupil to develop self-awareness and a sense of responsibility.

When the problem has been thoroughly aired, we need to resist jumping in with our own solutions, to avoid thinking: right, I have explored the issues sensitively, I now understand the problem or the behaviour – here's the answer. Our offering of advice at this stage can undermine all the good work we have done in listening so carefully. Instead we must encourage the speaker to come up with his own options to choose from, his own goals. We can help to ensure that these goals are attainable and that they are broken down into small achievable steps, and we can point out, if necessary prohibit, options that are dangerous or illegal; but our aim must continue to be to empower the young person and encourage his sense of responsibility. Our role is to offer information or practical back-up if it is requested, and then to keep contact so that evaluation is possible at a later date. This may be an entire reworking of the options or merely a raised eyebrow as you pass in the corridor. "Everything okay now?" And in some cases, particularly when an intimate matter has been discussed, a child may never want to refer to it again. We must respect that silence.

When the child is stuck for answers or seems to have few resources to draw on, then we might offer suggestions or suggest strategies, but it is really important that he chooses from among them and adapts them to his own style and situation. The less confident can be encouraged by examples of how others overcame difficulties, or perhaps taught visualisation techniques.

Kate was a very musical girl who was becoming increasingly diffident about playing the piano in public. She shared her fears with her housemistress, who recognised that part of the problem was Kate's desire to please her highly ambitious parents. They talked through the choices that lay ahead of her and the decisions to be made about university or music college, and Kate was able to see the importance of following her own heart in the matter. As for the coming performance on Prize Day: "I just know I'm going to make a hash of it. I'll walk on to that platform and shan't be able to remember a note". Her housemistress suggested that, instead of focusing her attention on what might go wrong, Kate should picture herself taking some deep breaths beforehand, walking on and smiling at the audience, taking time to adjust her stool and look at the music, playing beautifully and feeling the nervous tension ebbing away. She could even imagine herself playing a wrong note and calmly keeping going, knowing that hardly anyone in the audience would have noticed. By replacing the old frightening image with this more realistic picture, Kate calmed and reassured herself – and, of course, gave a splendid performance.

Metaphors also serve to make sense of difficult situations and ways of overcoming them. "Imagine you are in a boat without oars. What do you need to do?" or "It's like when you miss a try at rugby. . . ."

Other conversations, not targeted on particular problems, can offer the opportunity to develop self-esteem and self-discipline. On these occasions, perhaps in a tutorial or PSE lesson or in a house group, it is useful to ask questions and to provoke discussion. Questions can challenge the young to reflect on themselves and their behaviour, to think about, challenge and develop their attitudes and values.

- ❖ What do you want from life? school? friends? family?

- ❖ What do you want to achieve? to accomplish? – today? this term? this year?

- ❖ Is what you are doing helping you in this?

- ❖ What could you do otherwise?

- ❖ What are your plans? Where do you go from here?

- ❖ How are you going to work things out?

Our task is to help young people see themselves as pro-active, able to take the initiative, to monitor their own behaviour – and to make good choices about their lives.

Supporting young people through loss and change

Just talking through a problem often eases it and helps the other person find new solutions. However, some troubles cannot be resolved. When distress must be borne, our task is to help the young person come through a time of loss, bereavement or change. We need to recognise the different stages that may be passed through, and be able to accept all the difficult feelings that may arise. As adults involved in the day-to-day care of young people enduring profound troubles, we need to exercise discretion and discernment. When is it appropriate to have a quiet chat and encourage all the feelings of anger and despair to pour out? When should one divert, engage or leave alone? It can be useful to ask the child herself what is most helpful. Make sure there is opportunity for privacy as well as time for companionship. And do not underestimate the importance of ritual. It is worth, for example, recording the anniversary of a death and other important dates such as the deceased person's birthday, and approaching the child quietly on the eve of such a day:

- ❖ "Would you like to come and light a candle in the chapel tomorrow?"

   or

- ❖ "Today's a special day, isn't it? Are you going to ring your Dad?"

It can be as difficult for a child to cope with divorce as with death. The young need to know that no blame attaches to them, and that their feelings of pain, anger and dismay are natural and acceptable – and will not disappear overnight. Boarding schools can be a haven for children whose families are for one reason or another not providing a secure environment. Calm everyday routines, supportive adults, opportunities to express oneself through sport or study or music – all these can sustain and heal.

Dual role

How can a member of staff play the dual role of both Person in Authority and Sympathetic Listener? This seems to cause more concern among adults than among young people, who are well able to accept the duality if the adult concerned can also do so. Adults need to be clear about boundaries, and manage both roles with discretion and respect. Rather than the roles being in conflict, there are considerable benefits in making use of counselling skills and attitudes outside the particular supportive conversation where we are seeking to befriend a child. A disciplinary role is underpinned and given greater authority by the pupil's recognition of and respect for someone who clearly respects and wishes to understand him.

> *Andrew, aged 12, was a pleasant and cheerful member of the school. Tall and sturdy, he was not particularly academic, was occasionally disruptive but worked adequately and did well on the sports field. Then life at home became miserable as his parents' marriage began to fall apart. Andrew grew sulky and belligerent, causing real trouble in the classroom and attacking some of the smaller boys in the house. One day an incident took place right outside the head's office window. Andrew was called in, to stand before his desk and be duly admonished. He stood sullenly silent and departed in a huff. Later that afternoon, he was called to his tutor's room. "Listen, Andrew. Both you and I know that what happened this morning was quite unacceptable. Bullying is always wrong." Silence. In a quieter, warmer tone of voice the tutor added, "Actually, I realise that right now things are difficult for you at home. It can't be easy to have that on your mind." Further silence. More slowly and tentatively, the tutor followed this up with "I guess you must be feeling pretty angry and confused, kind of churned up inside. Sometimes in such situations it helps to talk." Andrew scowled, fidgeted, and then slowly began to speak. He and the tutor spent ten minutes or so exploring how it felt to have one's world so shaken. The tutor concluded, "We'll have to stop in a couple of minutes when the prep bell goes, but I want you to know that this hurt and these difficult feelings will go on for quite a while. Rather than punching someone or disrupting a lesson, come and tell me about it. If not me, then someone else. Talking does help, I promise." Andrew was no longer unkind or troublesome in the weeks beyond.*

A word of caution

In our eagerness to help a child in difficulties, we may sometimes be tempted to do too much. We have already looked at the need to foster self-belief and a sense of competence in those we are trying to help, so as to avoid encouraging the idea that only we can sort out their problems. Additionally, there are two other possibilities of which we need to be aware. The first is to try to be too clever, and to push for more exploration and disclosure than feels comfortable to the child. It is important to be respectful of the child's ability to know what is manageable for him, and not to try to force the pace. The second difficulty is to recognise when you are feeling uneasy about or overwhelmed by the problems a child faces and, when you are out of your depth in either knowledge or experience, to talk about it with the youngster and agree together what further help might be beneficial.

A final word – of encouragement

The idea of trying to help a child in trouble can sometimes seem daunting. We wonder whether we are up to it, whether we will make matters worse or perhaps open a can of worms that we won't know how to deal with – our anxiety can take many forms. In fact, the best help is often the simplest: an empathic attitude and the ability to be a kindly listener, coupled with a genuine acceptance of the other person and a real belief in his or her ability to grow and change. Offer this to the children in your care, and you will help them to flourish.

References and Notes

20. Goleman, D. (1996), *Emotional Intelligence*, London, Bloomsbury.

21. Kindlon, Dan and Thompson, Michael (1999), *Raising Cain: Protecting the Emotional Life of Boys*, London, Michael Joseph.

22. Rogers, Carl (1990), *The Carl Rogers Reader*, Constable.

23. Egan, Gerard (1990), *The Skilled Helper*, Pacific Grove, Brooks/Cole.

CHAPTER
6

Confidentiality
Roger Harrington

Confidentiality in schools is often a difficult matter, particularly in schools' medicine and, in my executive role with the Medical Officers of Schools Association (MOSA), I have regularly received queries about this from school doctors, nurses, heads and bursars. Often the problem is centred on the apparent conflict between the heads and bursars, who expect to know more about the pupils than the doctors and nurses are prepared to divulge, and the doctors and nurses themselves who are uncertain about how much information they can and should divulge.

Let us begin with a few definitions:

Con	– *"with"*
Fidere	– *"to trust, believe or confide in"*
Confidence	– *"confiding of secrets"*
In confidence	– *"a condition of secrecy"*
In one's confidence	– *"allowed to know his secrets"*
Confidential	– *"imparted in confidence"*
	– *"to be kept secret"*
	– *entrusted with secrets".*

In all these there is the implication of trust and secrecy.

The following is a letter sent by a parent to a school bursar and it demonstrates the parent's erroneous belief about his right to receive medical information about his son.

"I write in response to your letter concerning the extras that are outstanding. I require you to satisfy me of the following:

1. *A full breakdown of the late payment charge;*

2. *What are Matrons' runs? (I assume I am not sponsoring someone for the marathon.) Please justify.*

I understand my son had a consultation with a consultant surgeon and his fee is £60, which I am quite happy to pay. However, I do believe I am entitled to a written report on the consultation, and I would ask you to ensure I get one.

I am enclosing a cheque for £440·63 in good faith and an expectation of satisfactory explanations of the points I have raised.

Yours sincerely"

If I had been approached by the bursar requesting that a report be forwarded to the father, as a school doctor I would have handled this by asking the boy to see me. On the assumption that the boy was deemed competent (see below), I would then have sought his written permission to tell his father what had gone on when he had seen the specialist. I would then write letters to the father and bursar explaining the situation and emphasising the confidential nature of the information in question. In fact this was a split family and, although the boy's mother knew what had been going on, father had not been kept in the picture. As he paid the school fees, he thought he had an automatic right to know about his son's medical condition – hence his rather forceful letter!

There is so much more information available these days, and how many times do we find ourselves saying – "keep it under your hat", "between you, me and the gatepost", "within these four walls", "don't let this go any further, but . . ."?

There have been monumental legislative changes in the past decade or so which have affected schools, those who work in them and the children. The Education Acts of 1988 and 1993, the Children Act 1989 and the Parents' Charter have made schools more accountable, established league tables, increased parental influence and made us review the way we deliver pastoral care.

As professionals, teachers, nurses and doctors, and given the roles we play in boarding schools, we are in a unique position to receive information about the pupils, and we have to devise systems to handle all that comes our way. Information circulates in all directions. We hear about a pupil's friends, family, academic progress, illnesses, mis-demeanours, sexual encounters, etc. Most of this is not controversial, contentious or requiring secrecy – but some is, and this is where we all make value judgements about whether we keep it to ourselves or tell someone else. We use a number of factors – amongst other things, the nature of the information itself, how we received it, its content, our assessment of it – to make that judgement. But also there has to be a framework in the school for handling information, a framework which creates the right environment to protect the pupil.

Let me now discuss the information which, in my judgement, is potentially sensitive and should be subject to confidentiality, how it should be handled, medical confiden-tiality and the constraints that I am under as a doctor, general practitioner and school medical officer and, finally, discuss some of the most sensitive issues of all, such as contraception, pregnancy, abortion and so-called 'under-age sex'.

I have already mentioned information regarding friends, family, illnesses, etc. More specifically, what events in the course of a pupil's school life are going to have the most impact?

- bereavement – close friend, parent, grandparent, family pet

- parental separation/divorce

- serious physical/mental illness

- suicide or attempted suicide

- substance abuse including alcohol, tobacco and illegal substances (*e.g.* cannabis, ecstasy, heroin or cocaine)

- eating disorders – anorexia nervosa and bulimia

- physical abuse – sexual abuse, actual rape or bullying

- sexual problems – contraception, pregnancy and abortion

- ❖ academic problems

- ❖ disciplinary matters

The information about any of these may come from any source, and the school must be prepared to handle it. For example, bereavement or parental separation would probably be notified to the house by the family, and the house would pass on the information accordingly to the head and administrative staff if necessary. However, I have seen a young man present with vague aches and pains which were due to unhappiness about the break up of his parents' marriage, about which he was told nothing. Disciplinary and academic problems are going to be reported by the staff involved and may then go to the head, housemaster or housemistress, and parents as appropriate.

The other situations listed are perhaps more sensitive ones and, from my point of view, have a medical involvement in part or whole. Eating disorders might be reported by the house staff but, on occasions, I have even seen the pupil's peers report that 'Bloggs' is eating very little or appears to be losing weight. The school doctor would then institute help as appropriate, which might include referral to a specialist, counselling at school or even a spell at home with obvious parental knowledge.

With alcohol or substance abuse, I think it is reasonable that every head would want to know what was going on. If drugs are being passed around the school, it is mandatory that the head and his staff know, if only for the protection of the wider school community. In this specific situation, divulging information may be part of helping the child, and not just a means by which disciplinary procedures are invoked, and the child is perhaps expelled. (See Chapter 15.)

Child abuse, sexual abuse or rape are clearly very serious matters as, almost certainly, there will be police and social services involvement, and the school's policies with regard to child protection issues will be invoked.

The overriding fact governing my behaviour with regards to information is that I have a duty of confidentiality to my patient. This, with only a very few exceptions, transcends every other consideration. In the school situation, this obligation to my patient is greater than that which I owe to the school which employs me, or to the parents of the pupils, and it is vital that schools, governing bodies and parents recognise this. Medical confidentiality does not distinguish between the various conditions and circumstances I have listed. I owe the same duty to a pupil attending with a cold as I do to one attending to discuss drug abuse or a termination of pregnancy. And nor is there any distinction between the subject of the consultation, the treatment given or even the fact that the consultation has taken place – in other words, I am not at liberty to disclose any fact about the consultation to any third party without the patient's consent. To disclose that 'Bloggs' attended to discuss contraception carries the same ethical weight as to disclose that 'Bloggs' attended at all.

Why, you might ask, does it have to be as rigid as this? Because, in medical matters, the doctor/patient relationship is sacrosanct – and for any doctor to be able to do his best for his patient, and for him to be able to have access to all the relevant information he needs for this, the patient must be secure in the knowledge that, if he imparts any information to the doctor, it will go absolutely no further without his or her consent. And, in general, this is the situation in schools.

Obviously, I am aware that the head is acting as an agent for the parents, is *in loco parentis*, and that if he does not have certain information he will be unable to act efficiently and expeditiously. Equally, I am aware that, in reality, for the school itself to function the school doctor must try to steer a middle course, balancing the demands of the school, and the level of information required by the head, against the duty he owes his patient. One situation where obviously there has to be compromise is where the school (and then the parents) has to know when a pupil is admitted acutely to hospital, if only to explain the sudden absence! In fact, this information should only be imparted with the pupil's consent but what happens in reality, in say this acute situation of hospital admission, is that the school doctor makes the decision, the sanatorium sister rings the house staff and the sister or house staff then inform the parents. Confidentiality has probably been breached, but I cannot see that it can happen in any other way.

At Stowe, I hope I have covered this problem in the following way. The parents of all new pupils are sent a so-called medical query paper which asks for details of current health, past medical history, current treatment, drug and other allergies, etc. It also sets out the school's medical policy and the parents sign and return it, hopefully before the child enters the school. I have included a paragraph about confidentiality as follows:

> *"In accordance with the school doctor's and nurse's professional obligations, medical information about pupils, regardless of their age, will remain confidential. However, in providing medical care for a pupil, it is recognised*

that on occasions the doctor or nurse may liaise with parents or guardians, the head teacher or other academic staff and house staff, and that information, ideally with the pupil's prior consent, will be passed on as appropriate. With all medical matters, the doctor and nurse will respect a pupil's confidence except on the very rare occasion when, having failed to persuade a pupil or his or her authorised representative to give consent to divulgence, the doctor or nurse consider it in the pupil's better interests, or necessary for the protection of the wider school community, to breach confidence and pass information to a relevant person or body."

It may be necessary to amend this paragraph according to the ages of the pupils and the type of school (*e.g.* preparatory or senior, day or boarding, coeducational or single sex and state or independent).

Matters concerning the professional conduct and discipline of registered medical practitioners and registered nurses are overseen by the General Medical Council (GMC) and the United Kingdom Central Council (UKCC) respectively. Any doctors or nurses who breach confidentiality could find themselves the subject of a disciplinary hearing by their respective professional body. A consequence of being found guilty is erasure from the register with an almost certain loss of livelihood for that doctor or nurse.

The GMC has recently revised its advice to doctors in a document ***Confidentiality: Protecting and Providing Information*** (September 2000). Section 1 deals with patients' right to confidentiality and states:

"Patients have a right to expect that information about them will be held in confidence by their doctors. Confidentiality is central to trust between doctors and patients. Without assurances about confidentiality, patients may be reluctant to give doctors the information they need in order to provide good care. If you are asked to provide information about patients, you should:

- *seek patients' consent to disclosure of information wherever possible, whether or not you judge that patients can be identified from the disclosure;*

- *anonymise data where unidentifiable data will serve the purpose;*

- *keep disclosures to the minimum necessary.*

You must always be prepared to justify your decisions in accordance with this guidance."

This new guidance places increased responsibilities on doctors to keep patients informed about, and get agreement to, the disclosure of information. It sets out the framework for respecting patients' rights while ensuring that information needed to maintain and improve health care is passed to those who need it. The additional duties to obtain consent and to anonymise data tie in with developments in law, including the Data Protection Act 1998.

Nurses' obligations are similar, and the UKCC's 'Guidelines for Professional Practice' state:

> *"To trust another person with private and personal information about yourself is a significant matter. If the person to whom that information is given is a nurse, midwife or health visitor, the patient or client has a right to believe that this information, given in confidence, will only be used for the purposes for which it is given and will not be released to others without their permission. The death of a patient or client does not give you the right to break confidentiality."*

There are situations where confidential information may be disclosed to a third party, and some of these are:

❖ when the patient, or a person properly authorised to act on behalf of the patient, gives informed consent;

❖ when the information is passed between members of a health care team caring for that patient;

> [In schools, the team might consist of the school doctor and his or her partners, nurses, physiotherapists, chiropodists, psychologists and counsellors. Additionally, some individuals outside the health care professions might be involved in looking after pupils, such as house matrons and other lay staff providing pastoral care. It is the doctor's responsibility to ensure that appropriate consent is obtained to divulge information, that pupils and parents understand a doctor's and nurse's professional constraints and how, why and

when information might be disclosed to a team member, and finally that all the team members understand and observe confidentiality.]

❖ when a medical emergency means that a patient's consent cannot be obtained (*e.g.* serious accident or unconsciousness);

❖ when it is considered that disclosure without the patient's prior consent is in their medical interests;

[The doctor may judge that, because of immaturity, illness or mental incapacity, the patient is unable to give valid consent. The patient must be informed before disclosure, and it should be recognised that the judgement of whether a patient is capable of giving or witholding consent to treatment or disclosure must be based on his or her ability to understand the situation, and not solely on age. This is an important factor in schools because of the wide range of ages encountered.]

❖ when it is believed that the patient is a victim of neglect or physical or sexual abuse;

[In schools, doctors and nurses must be aware of the statutory obligations they have with regard to child protection issues.]

❖ when the information is required or requested for medical teaching, research or audit;

❖ when it is judged that disclosure is in the public's interests and failure to disclose may expose a patient or others to risk of death or serious harm;

❖ when satisfying a specific statutory requirement (*e.g.* notification of a communicable disease);

❖ when ordered by a judge or the presiding officer of a court, or if summoned to assist a coroner, procurator fiscal or other similar officer in connection with an inquest or comparable judicial investigation.

Whatever the circumstances, a doctor must always be prepared to justify his actions if he decides ultimately to disclose confidential information.

Confidentiality and sexual matters is the one area in schools where problems can and do arise. On the one hand, there is the line taken by the school, the head and the governing body, and almost certainly this will be that intimate sexual relationships between pupils are forbidden, that they are against the school rules. This will be upheld for many different reasons:

* the personal beliefs of those making the rules;

* the desire to be seen to be giving what is perceived as a moral lead in the current climate;

* the wish to put forward a particular image for that school – that sexual intimacy is discouraged;

* it is what the parents want and the reason why they send their child to that school in the first place.

On the other hand, there is the inescapable fact that, increasingly, teenagers are sexually active and, in the school situation, doctors have to try to balance the requirements and demands of the school against those of the pupils.

The following are the policy guidelines which MOSA has put forward with regard to contraception.

1. *Every school doctor should be prepared to offer contraceptive advice and, if appropriate, provide contraception subsequently, including emergency contraception, to any boy or girl of any age.*

2. *Contraception should only be provided after full and adequate counselling and discussion, with the pupil realising fully the implications of his or her actions.*

3. *Pupils should be encouraged to discuss contraceptive matters with their parents or those acting in loco parentis.*

4. *The school doctor owes a duty of confidentiality to the boy or girl and must not break that confidentiality, except in the most extreme circumstances.*

5. *If the school doctor decides it is necessary to break that confidentiality, he must discuss this with the boy or girl, and then be fully prepared to justify his actions.*

6. It is the duty of the school doctor to inform the school of his policy with regard to the provision of contraception.

7. The school doctor must be aware of the potential for conflict between his position and that of the school authorities and parents.

It has to be made clear that confidentiality will be maintained, as surveys would suggest that this is the crux of the problem: young people are fearful of consulting their doctor because they feel that their parents will be told or, in schools, the head will be informed. Equally, I believe that the school doctor must inform the school of his position with regard to contraceptive provision and then be aware of the potential for conflict, all the time having the best interest of the pupils uppermost and encouraging them to talk to their parents, guardians or whoever is *in loco parentis.*

The duty of confidentiality which is owed to a person under 16 is as great as that owed to any other. Regardless of whether or not the requested treatment is given, confidentiality of the consultation should still be respected, unless there are convincing reasons to the contrary.

A person is a minor until 18 years of age but the Family Law Reform Act 1969 Section 8 allows persons under 18 years of age to consent to medical treatment. In fact, any competent young person, regardless of age, can independently seek medical advice and give valid consent to medical treatment. Competency is understood in terms of the patient's ability to understand the choices and their consequences, including the nature, purpose and possible risk of any treatment, or conversely the consequences of refusing treatment. Parental consent to the treatment is not necessary.

This current legal position was established in 1985 after the much publicised court case, *Gillick versus the West Norfolk and Wisbech Area Health Authority and the Department of Health and Social Security.* Mrs Gillick, who had five daughters, sought an assurance from the local health authority that they would not give advice and treatment concerning contraception to her daughters whilst they were under the age of 16 without her prior knowledge and consent. She failed to receive such an assurance and the case eventually reached the House of Lords. The conclusion of the Appeal Court was that a girl under 16 did not, by virtue of her age, lack legal capacity for consent to contraceptive advice and treatment by a doctor. The doctor has a discretion to give contraceptive advice or treatment to a girl under 16, without the parents' knowledge and consent, provided that the girl has reached an age where she has a sufficient understanding and intelligence to enable her to understand fully what is being proposed. And the phrase 'Gillick competent' has entered the lawyers' jargon book.

One of the Appeal Court judges, Lord Frazer of Tulleybelton, put forward five points which a doctor should particularly consider when consulted by people under 16 for contraceptive advice.

1. The doctor should establish whether the patient understands the potential risks and benefits of the treatment and advice given.

2. The value of parental support must be discussed. Doctors must encourage young people to inform parents of the consultation and explore the reasons if the patient is unwilling to do so. It is important for persons under 16 seeking contraceptive advice to be aware that, although the doctor is legally obliged to discuss the value of parental support, the doctor will respect their confidentiality.

3. The doctor should take into account whether the patient is likely to have sexual intercourse without contraception.

4. The doctor should assess whether the patient's physical or mental health or both are likely to suffer if the patient does not receive contraceptive advice or supplies.

5. The doctor must consider whether the patient's best interests would require the provision of contraceptive advice or methods or both, without parental consent.

So where does all this leave us in schools? There is much information available at present which, in the school setting, comes from different sources. Some is more sensitive than others and there must be a framework in place to handle all types of information, from that which may be freely available to that which demands total confidentiality. The school doctor is in both a privileged and a difficult position. He is contracted by the school to provide a range of services while, at the same time, if he is a general practitioner, he will probably be contracted to his local Health Authority to provide general medical services for the pupils who are registered with him as patients. For various ethical and contractual reasons, his obligation to the pupils is greater and, with very few exceptions, he owes them a duty of confidentiality at all times. He must be mindful of the needs of his patients but also of the school's rules and requirements. It is totally reasonable to expect that the parents or guardians will be informed of all cases of illness and accident, but it has to be recognised that there will be some more sensitive health matters which the pupils will not wish their parents or the school to know about – and the doctor must respect this while, at the same time, attempting to persuade the pupil that it will be better to discuss the matter with their parents or whoever is acting *in loco parentis.* It is more than likely that such matters are going to be concerned with contraception, other sexual matters, alcohol and drug misuse. If the doctor considers that it is in the pupil's best interests for him to disclose information to the school or parents, then he must tell the pupil accordingly and be prepared to justify fully his actions at a later date if necessary.

The outcome of the Gillick case was that doctors could not provide contraception for the under-16s *carte blanche,* but only after careful consideration, and I think in the end Mrs Gillick helped both doctors and their young patients by opening the debate and clarifying the issues.

With termination of pregnancy, the same strictures and guidelines must apply and, again, the pupil must be persuaded to inform her parents. However, her wishes must be respected if she refuses. Although the parental right to know about the health of their children might seem, on the surface, overwhelming, we have seen that, for various reasons, it is not; and similarly with respect to any rights of the school to know. Also, I have not mentioned child protection issues but there are differences because of the statutory requirement to divulge information (see Chapter 3).

I believe that there is a way ahead – a middle course. If all of us who are responsible for the health and welfare of the pupils communicate, we can work hand in hand to do the best for them and, if we can remain focused on their best interests, I think that, in the majority of cases, we shall not go far wrong.

CHAPTER

7

Reducing Bullying in Boarding Schools

Brian FitzGerald

Bullying is a serious matter and schools need to treat it as such. It is probably endemic in schools, as it is in society at large. The incidence of bullying is more common than many schools realise or are prepared to admit. This is changing, but much goes un-recorded and frequently the victim and even his or her parents have been made to feel the guilty party.

What is bullying?

In any survey or investigation, a school needs to have a clear definition understood by all. It is a conscious abuse of power an individual or a group has over other individuals or groups. In bullying there is a conscious desire to hurt, threaten or frighten. There may be persistent teasing or name-calling, queue-barging, malicious gossip, fagging, racial or sexual harassment, extortion, emotional abuse, damaging or stealing the property of the victim, physical or sexual abuse. It may also involve coercing the victim into acts that he or she does not wish to do. In **Bullying at School**[24], Professor Dan Olweus defines bullying in the following way:

"A student is being bullied or victimised when he or she is exposed, repeatedly and over time, to negative actions on the part of one or more other students."

In ***Bullying: don't suffer in silence***[25], the anonymous author refers to most bullying incidents having three things in common:

❖ it is deliberately hurtful behaviour;

❖ it is repeated over a period of time;

❖ it is difficult for those being bullied to defend themselves.

Bullying may well start with the exclusion of a child from a friendship or peer group or the non-acceptance of a newcomer. Such isolation, or 'indirect' bullying, of individuals within a peer group is a particularly insidious form of bullying. Although it may not be a precursor of more overt, 'direct', physical forms, it can be a very hurtful and damaging experience. It is important that staff consciously note peer group relationships and how they change from time to time.

Staff and parents need to work closely together to recognise the first signs of isolation. This may be the first stage in more overt bullying, and is more likely to affect newcomers or children who are, for some reason, recognisably different from the others. Ethnic or cultural discrimination and abuse may occur in such circumstances. Dealing with children who are isolated, whatever their background, needs to be very sensitive and tactful, especially as some children may naturally prefer to be on their own.

More extreme cases of direct bullying may or may not develop from isolation, and it is possible for isolation to be quite separate from direct bullying. Isolation and other forms of bullying are very serious matters: they are likely to produce withdrawal or more active deterioration of behaviour, deterioration in academic achievement and, in extreme and tragic cases, lead to attempted or actual suicide.

The extent of bullying

A national survey of Norwegian school children indicated that 7 per cent were bullies and 9 per cent were victims, and that some 17 per cent of the victims were both victims and bullies[26]. In a survey for an in-service course for a mixed boarding school in England, it was found that as many as 30 per cent of boarders in the boys' houses had been the victim of bullying between September (the beginning of the year) and April. It averaged about 20 per cent for all houses. Twenty per cent admitted having taken part in bullying someone else, and the response to having seen bullying take place was about 50 per cent.

The results of this confidential survey came as a surprise to the teachers in the school. It was a caring and pleasant institution. It was significant, however, that no programme of training was provided for senior pupils for the pastoral responsibilities and duties they had to carry out. It was also significant that considerable variation occurred in the incidence in reported bullying among the houses. This probably reflected the wide range and inconsistency of practice brought about by a lack of overall boarding policies, procedures and guidance (see Chapter 11).

In a survey of 2,600 boarding pupils in Oxfordshire[27], Roger Morgan found that bullying was severe, frequent or persistent enough to be reported as the 'worst thing' about boarding by 7 per cent of preparatory school pupils and 4 per cent of secondary pupils. These figures appear low, but it must be remembered that they represent only those who saw bullying as the worst aspect of their lives at school.

Whether the incidence of bullying in boarding is greater or less than in day schools is not clear. Among individual schools, as with houses, there appears to be considerable variation. The experience of the Oxfordshire Social Services' Department suggests that, of nearly 2,000 boarders questioned during inspection work in the county, about 20 per cent reported bullying at least at the "I sometimes get bullied" level (unpublished work). These figures, and those of the in-service course, are significantly higher than those reported in the Scandinavian day schools. The figures quoted for boarding are not far removed, however, from those obtained by the use of a questionnaire by Ahmad and Smith in seven middle and four secondary day schools in South Yorkshire (20 per cent and 18 per cent respectively)[28]. It would, however, be unwise to make direct comparisons because the nature of the environment and the length of time children are present in the school are so different.

In *School Life*[29], Roger Morgan comments that bullying, like illness, will inevitably occur in a community; even so it needs to be identified and minimised. He adds:

> "*Victims of bullying wrote on their questionnaires of how they could not escape the bully in the house, or especially the dormitory, and it was clear that pupils differed in how much they could stand of verbal teasing, physical*

confrontations, theft or destruction of their property, or being 'sent to Coventry'. A few saw bullying as an inevitable part of school life; 'we don't have it, except at a natural level', 'it does toughen you up a bit'; others needed to escape; 'I need to go and cry it out'."

In another boarding school, with good care practice and very few reported incidences of bullying, a confidential survey revealed that about 16 per cent of the pupils in Year 9 (the first year of entry) had been bullied over the previous eight months. The perpetrators had, significantly, been almost entirely within their own year. Interviews with these pupils indicated a great reticence to share with any member of staff, and they were not at all keen to telephone their parents. The pupils felt that reporting an incident could result in some form of unpleasant feedback from their peers – if not retribution. Many felt that they could not contact their parents in case they were the cause of extreme anxiety, and that mum or dad might even telephone the headmaster, which would be most embarrassing and the cause of more trouble that the level of bullying warranted.

Closer questioning revealed that going to an adult was also seen as an admission of failure and, worse still, it would be a failure made public to their peers. A further significant comment, made by a boy who had been bullied, was:

> *"I am afraid to talk to the teachers because I know that the school will take it very seriously and last year a boy in Year 10 was expelled for bullying, and I don't want that hanging over me."*

This school had few notified incidences of bullying and the standards of care and welfare were judged in a recent inspection to be excellent. The previous term, a boy had been expelled from Year 10 for persistent bullying within his year group.

It is difficult to escape from the conclusion that an underlying incident level of about 15 per cent over a year (even in the best of boarding schools) may represent a form of 'tolerance level'; a horizon or boundary that even the best of practice would find it difficult to penetrate. This would be the level victims would tolerate because of their perception of the consequences of admitting to being bullied. Such a level, for whatever reason, should not be accepted as pupils will still be damaged, and severe cases may develop as a result of the incidences occurring covertly. Such an endemic occurrence of bullying, even in very good provision, has important implications for boarding staff and their management of boarding.

In boarding, bullies and victims live in close proximity for the full 24 hours a day and often seven days a week, and there is no home respite. It is clear that possibilities for bullying are more easily developed in boarding than in day schools. Adult supervision *may* be more effective, but there are long periods when boarders are not being directly supervised.

Bullies, bullying and victims

We all know of the stereotype of the large, domineering 'bully-boy' who is academically and personally inadequate and an anxious coward at heart. If we expect this, we are likely to be wrong in recognising bullies. No research supports this view. In general, bullies (boys) appear to have a combination of an aggressive behaviour pattern with physical strength and do not show signs of insecurity or anxiety. That is not to say that there are no bullies who are both insecure and anxious.

Boys may well bully more than girls; we know that girls are less likely to admit to bullying than boys. It is socially more acceptable for boys to admit bullying. But this does not imply that boys are more likely to be bullies than girls. Evidence exists that certain types of bullying are gender-linked; more of this shortly.

Olweus[30] usefully distinguishes between a large group of 'passive' or 'submissive' victims and a small group of 'provocative' victims. Passive victims may be physically weak, cautious, sensitive, and afraid of being hurt; they may have difficulty in asserting themselves with their peers; they may be anxious, insecure and unhappy with a negative view of themselves; they are not aggressive and often relate better to adults than to their fellows. They are likely to be generally unpopular.

Provocative victims are also likely to be anxious, insecure and unhappy, but they may be hot-tempered and fight back in a temper when provoked; they may be hyperactive, offensive, tension-creating and clumsy; they may be disliked by adults and may themselves bully weaker pupils.

Almost two-thirds of the callers to ChildLine's Bullying Line[31] were girls; this proportion was also reflected in the calls to ChildLine's Boarding School Line[32]. Why a bias towards girls should occur is not clear; they may suffer more from bullying than boys, although evidence from other sources suggests this is not so. The pattern of calls to the main ChildLine helpline seems to indicate that girls are more likely than boys to wish to talk to someone in confidence about a problem area. This is mirrored in calls to the Samaritans and counselling agencies generally, including Relate.

Evidence from both the Bullying Line and the Boarding School Line suggests that girls seem to be more involved in psychological bullying. This includes isolation, having character defamed and being picked upon for no obvious reason. Girls also report more incidents of theft while more boys reported being assaulted. Boys also appeared to be far more likely to be involved in violent incidents. Where there were problems with peers, many more girls made complaints than boys did.

Bullying by groups may be more 'visible' than bullying by an individual, and bullies are particularly difficult to deal with as a group. In day schools this may result in a transference of their activities to outside the school, or they may become disruptive and take up increasingly anti-school attitudes. In boarding, groups may be more concerned with exclusion, teasing and defamation but this is no less hurtful or damaging.

It is common to find in boarding, as in day schools, groups of pupils who participate as followers, some at the fringe, some rather more actively, but not initiating the bullying activity itself. All bear some degree of responsibility for bullying.

Factors affecting bullying

Factors associated with family upbringing are likely to have an important effect on whether a child develops aggressive attitudes and bullying traits. There is evidence[33] (Olweus 1993) that a lack of parental warmth and involvement are conducive to developing aggressive tendencies in offspring. Children from such homes may learn that aggression and violence are appropriate and effective means of getting their own way. They learn, perhaps quite sub-consciously, that this is a means to dominate others.

Many highly complex and interacting factors are likely to affect bullying within the house or school. The considerable variation in the incidence of bullying among houses and between schools probably reflects the complexity of these institutions and the human relationships within them.

Discussions[34] with both boarders and staff suggest that bullying tends to thrive where:

- there is inadequate presence of staff around the house, in the bedrooms and around the grounds;

- there is boredom, often bred of lack of purpose within the house or school;

- there is crowding in dormitories and bedrooms, or lack of common room space or lack of space for boarders to withdraw from the hurly-burly of boarding life;

- there is lack of appropriate supervision of toilet areas, showers and washing facilities;

- there is not an open and trusting society;

- boarders feel unable to share their problems with staff;

- there is a tradition of not disclosing or reporting on 'uneasy' situations or individuals;

- there is, in respect to a prefect body or senior boarders:

  - a near complete delegation of house duties and control to them;

  - little supervision of their duties;

  - little or no training or preparation for such responsibilities;

  - little realisation on the part of the staff of the broader pastoral context of the role of prefects.

Difficulties in adapting to rapidly changing circumstances may bring increased difficulties and strains in boarding. Changes in staff or in pupil intake can greatly alter the atmosphere in a house.

A change in boarding schools in recent years has been a shift in emphasis from primarily a policing role for prefects to one that is less defined and significantly more pastoral. Where this change is accompanied by a relatively rapid reduction in senior pupils' powers, considerable difficulties may occur. Senior pupils, who now carry diminished responsibilities, may feel that their authority has been undermined and that they have lost status and privilege (see Chapter 12).

This produces a major cultural change for senior boarders. Where they have not yet developed sufficient pastoral and welfare skills to handle changing relationships with younger pupils, they feel both ambivalent and confused about their relationships with them. In these cases, senior boarders may be wary of asserting disciplinary authority for fear of being accused of bullying. They may even become the victims of 'reverse' bullying. They feel that they have to tolerate a greater degree of unruliness from juniors before reacting, and sometimes react too strongly with a loss of temper. The house may become less disciplined overall, and this results in an increasing risk of bullying within the younger peer-groups.

In these circumstances, staff need to:

❖ clarify the tariff of sanctions seniors may apply;

❖ supervise and monitor the prefects more effectively;

❖ increase the level of overall supervision in the house;

❖ prepare senior boarders carefully for change;

❖ widen senior boarders' responsibilities to include a role complementing the house staff in pastoral and welfare matters.

Preventive measures

The most important preventive measure is for the school to have a clearly stated and effective anti-bullying policy. The policy must receive the wholehearted support of all staff, and it must be seen to do so.

The school's attitudes toward bullying must be clearly understood by parents, and strong anti-bullying statements are appearing in some school prospectuses. The one for Millfield, a coeducational 13–18 boarding school in Somerset, states[35]:

> *"Millfield regards the right of every child to enjoy all aspects of his or her education here, without interference from other pupils, as being of paramount importance. Any incident where a pupil's conduct adversely affects another's ability to enjoy this right is deplored. However, when a pupil persistently or repeatedly acts in such a way that another's happiness is directly and seriously affected, we are likely to regard this conduct as bullying. We take such cases*

very seriously. Pupils are told and regularly reminded that allegations of bullying will always be investigated thoroughly."

Such a statement makes a school's anti-bullying policy very plain to all parents and prospective parents. It has the effect of making them, effectively, subscribe to the school's fundamental belief that a pupil has a right to pursue his or her education free from adverse interference from other pupils.

The school's anti-bullying policy and associated guidance should give due emphasis to prevention and be a part of the school's overall discipline and social education polices. In boarding schools, it is necessary to indicate how and by whom the school's policy should be implemented at house level.

The policy needs to include a clear definition of bullying. It should state the importance of monitoring bullying and require the keeping of records of incidents. The policy should include information on how to record 'alleged' incidents and resulting teacher intervention, and indicate the need for these to be closely monitored. There should be a clearly stated and agreed course of action that teachers should take in the event of allegation or proved incident.

Clear and effective statements on training for boarding staff and senior pupils need to be provided. Senior pupils should have their responsibilities clearly defined, including a pastoral and welfare role that complements that of the house staff.

It is important that staff are fully aware of the incidence and nature of bullying in the house and across the school generally. Organising a confidential survey of pupils' views on these matters is an essential start. An example of such a questionnaire is given at the end of Chapter 3 of **Training Issues for Boarding Schools**[36], published by the Boarding Schools' Association, together with further information about writing anti-bullying policies.

Monitoring the incidence of bullying is important, and surveys done in subsequent years can provide useful evidence on the effectiveness of any anti-bullying initiative and of the general standard of welfare in the house or school.

The statistics obtained from using such a survey need to be used with considerable caution. Causes of inaccuracy or unreliability may arise for a number of reasons. These include: some or all pupils not understanding what bullying is, even when a definition is given; the incidence of bullying appearing very large because one incident was witnessed by a large number of pupils; a varying time span between surveys rendering comparisons unreliable. Commonly, 'one off' incidences of fighting are mistakenly seen as bullying.

The adequacy of supervision is an important element in prevention. Valerie Besag, in **Bullies and Victims in Schools**[37], states that:

> *"Good supervision coverage is one of the most efficient and economical preventative strategies which can be applied in schools to prevent bullying. . . . It is a sub-curricular activity in that it goes on underground in that 'curriculum' organised by the pupils themselves which runs parallel with that offered by the staff and which can, at any one time, be more important to the individual child."*

Good supervision need not be obtrusive and can be highly constructive in building rapport with pupils around the school or about the house. Duty rotas need to be constructed with this in mind. During periods of duty, tutors or house staff need to tour around the house when pupils or boarders are relaxing. This is good pastoral practice: it helps to create a good rapport with pupils and favourable conditions for an individual pupil to talk with an adult. Teachers must always be prepared to talk about bullying with pupils, and take action whenever they come across cases of isolation, harassment or physical bullying.

It is worth mentioning the pupils' views about prevention at this point. In **School Life**[38], the boarders' responses indicated that they felt the major preventive factor was its unacceptability to the older and influential pupils in the school. This, of course, has implications for the training and support given to older pupils in taking responsibility for younger. It is also of considerable significance that boarders often reported that they saw the well-run, all-age house, where different age-groups mixed healthily and socially as a good basis for the rejection of bullying.

Dealing with bullying

Any incident of bullying must be taken seriously. Action must be speedy, and thought needs to be given to whether action needs to be private or public. In all cases, sensitivity in response to bullying is important, particularly in boarding where the bully and victim live in such close proximity. In all cases, house tutors will need to talk seriously with both victim and bully.

When action is taken, victims must not be made to feel foolish or inadequate, as this may only serve to compound already existing feelings of inadequacy. But they must be given tangible support and their class group or tutorial may need professional counselling in the more extreme cases. It is important to guarantee, as far as humanly possible, efficient protection against harassment.

The bully must plainly see that the teacher and the school strongly disapprove of his or her actions. Where parents of bullies are to be involved, they too should be seen to disapprove. The message to bullies must be clear:

> *"We don't accept bullying in our house (or school) and will see to it that it comes to an end."*

It is helpful to identify any 'trigger factor'; this will inform other colleagues about possible parallel incidents and may help prevent a recurrence. At the very least, it will help to suggest why the incident occurred.

It is important to try to get the bully to see the victim's point of view. Empathetic thinking and feeling for others is often something that appears to be missing in a bully's emotional make-up.

Teachers who have to deal with an incident must inform those who need to know – and this must be stated in the school's policy document about bullying. Those to be informed should include the tutors of both the victim and the bully, the guidance staff and the head. There is also a need to inform both sets of parents in a calm, clear and reassuring manner.

Group bullying presents particular problems. It is important to know something of the dynamics of the group. It is likely that the best approach is to deal with individual members of the group separately. Here the role of staff with pastoral or guidance responsibilities for individuals is important. In many cases, this may be the house tutor. Bullies who belong to a group are usually quite willing to talk, and one-to-one discussion with a skilled tutor or counsellor can often prove very effective. It can often be counter-productive to make an example of the leader or any individual member of the group: it will cause resentment and is likely to bind the group more closely together.

Counteracting bullying

A number of strategies may be used to prevent and counteract bullying. Such guidance should be used as part of an overall school policy and introduced to suit the particular circumstances of the house or school

Improving the environment

The nature of the buildings and grounds in which boarders work and take their leisure may have a significant effect on the incidence and form of bullying. The nature of the environment itself is also likely to have an effect on the incidence and form of bullying. An inhospitable set of dormitories with no personalisation and crowded conditions, or a small, bleak playground as the only hard play surface for young boarders, may create tensions, unhealthy competition and lessen co-operation and concern for others.

Peer counselling

Some schools have introduced 'peer counselling' as part of their strategy to counteract bullying. Sonia Sharp and Helen Cowie in **School Bullying**[39] described the use of such a service in two of the Sheffield Project secondary schools. The use of peer counsellors implies the need for training in the art of active listening, support and supervision of those pupils involved. Such training needs to be carried out by a qualified counsellor. The pupils involved need also to be very clear about the responsibility that is vested in them; they need clear guidelines about confidentiality and how they should carry out their role.

Assertiveness training

Assertiveness techniques encourage the use of clear, direct and honest messages and avoid interactions that are deliberately manipulative, threatening, intimidating or dishonest[40]. Such training can provide a sense of security for pupils in which they feel more control over their situation and less despair. They are encouraged to react in ways that are neutral and less likely to escalate a difficult situation when threatened.

'Buddying' and support groups

The quality of relationships between older and younger pupils is an important element of the well-being of a school community. Schools may consider training older pupils to counsel and befriend younger ones who have been the victims of more persistent bullying. This could be particularly useful as a strategy where bullying is particularly entrenched in the school's culture. A senior pupil, held in high esteem by other children, chatting informally with a victim in the playground at break-time or by the tuck shop in the evening can increase a victim's confidence and self-esteem and deter bullies from taking further action.

Bully boxes and complaints procedures

Bully boxes have been used in a number of schools, and can be an important preventive measure, but their introduction can also be a very effective means of tackling bullying when problems suddenly come to the surface. They consist of boxes into which pupils may 'post' comments or accounts of bullying incidents they have seen or of which they have been the victims. Bullies also have been known to write about their very real concerns about their own behaviour. The sensitive nature of the information requires that they be kept securely.

'Common Concern' and 'No Blame' approaches

These are two similar approaches to dealing with bullying, the first being devised by the Swedish psychologist Anatole Pikas[41] and the second by Maires and Robinson. Both involve three-stage interview techniques whereby teachers talk with the victim and bully separately to begin with, according to a prescribed script of four questions or statements such as these for interviewing the alleged bully:

(*a*) "I hear you have been nasty to Jane; tell me about it."

(*b*) "So, it sounds as though Jane is having a bad time at school."

(*c*) "OK, so I am wondering what you could do to help Jane in this situation."

(*d*) "That's very good; try that for a week, and we will meet again a week today, and see how far you have got. Goodbye."

A similar interview is held with the victim. The second stage is the follow-up with the bully and victim separately to see how things are going. The third stage is a meeting with the bully at which he or she is invited to make positive statements about the victim. The victim is then invited to join the meeting, sits next to the teacher, and the positive comments are repeated. This meeting concludes with a review of the degree of success in improving the situation and how such a change can be maintained.

This is a non-confrontational approach and a difficult one to handle without some training. It is quite costly in teacher time.

Parental contact

Good schools emphasise the excellence of their relationship with parents and see them as partners working with them to the betterment of the welfare and education of their children[42]. In a boarding school, contact between the house tutor and parents is not generally as frequent as it can be in a day school. Nevertheless, the nature of such contact is frequently friendly and informal. At its best, the relationship is a close partnership and is supportive to the boarder, the parents and the tutor. Despite the best of intentions, the very separation of the boarder from his or her family is a crucial element when problems of bullying arise.

If a crisis occurs, particular problems are exacerbated by distance and physical separation. Parents can feel frustrated and helpless by their inability to be on the spot to provide support for their child. They may also feel apprehensive about talking to their child's housemaster or housemistress lest this is seen as an admission of weakness on their part or of failure on the part of their child.

Training issues

The school's senior management team should see awareness-raising and in-service training as important issues and plan accordingly. It is important to involve governors and parents in aspects of the training where this is possible. Senior management need to tap existing staff expertise, make use of existing training and discussion documents, and make use of local training initiatives. Ideas for training materials on prevention and protection as well as case studies for workshop sessions are not hard to come by. Besag, in *Bullies and Victims in Schools*[43] has separate chapters on prevention, protection, case studies and workshops. Training initiatives to counteract bullying need to be seen as preventive and should be a part of a broader programme of in-service work on pastoral care and welfare.

It is also important for the school to provide in-service training for older boarders in managing younger ones. This is especially so if peer counselling is being used. In general, training should indicate how boarders could contribute positively towards promoting the welfare of those for whom they have responsibility. It is important that all prefects understand that they have a crucial pastoral role complementing that of the house staff. Preparing pupils to take on appropriate responsibilities for others should be a key element in all boarders' personal and social development from the time they arrive in the house. Developing these skills further should be made a specific part of preparation for monitorial responsibility.

References and Notes

24. Olweus, Dan (1993), **Bullying at School**, page 9, Blackwell, Oxford.

25. Department for Education (1994), **Bullying: don't suffer in silence**, page 7, HMSO.

26. In **Bullying at School**, page 13, *op cit.*

27. Morgan, Roger (1993), **School Life – Pupils' Views on Boarding**, para. 14, London, HMSO.

28. Ahmad and Smith (1990) quoted in **Practical Approaches to Bullying** edited by Peter Smith and David Thompson, David Fulton (1993), Chapter 1. Details also given in **Bullying: don't suffer in silence**, page 25, DFE-funded Sheffield University project, HMSO (1994).

29. Morgan, Roger, **School Life – Pupils' Views on Boarding**, para 6.15, *op cit.*

30. Olweus, Dan, **Bullying at School**, pages 56–58, *op cit.*

31. **Bullying – the Child's View**, *op cit.*

32. **Boarding School Line**, A summary of the results of the experimental help line for boarding school pupils; January–July 1991, DES, London (1991).

33. Olweus, Dan, **Bullying at School**, page 40, *op cit.*

34. **The Welfare of Children in Boarding Schools Practice Guide** (Children Act 1989), Social Services Inspectorate, HMSO, London (1991). Paragraph 6.51 with small additions.

35. Quoted in **Countering Bullying**, page 114, *op cit.*

36. FitzGerald, Brian (1999), **Training Issues for Boarding Schools**, available from BSA.

37. Besag, Valerie E. (1989), **Bullies and Victims in Schools**, page 133, Open University Press.

38. Morgan, Roger, **School Life – Pupils' Views on Boarding**, para 6.20, *op cit.*

39. In Chapter 5, *Empowering Pupils* (pages 115–121) in **School Bullying: Insights and Perspectives**, *op cit.*

40. From **Bullying: don't suffer in silence**, paragraph 21, page 52, *op cit.*

41. Pikas, A. (1989), 'A pure concept of mobbing gives the best results for treatment', *School Psychology International*, 10, pp. 95–104, quoted in *Effective Action Against Bullying*, David Thompson and Peter Smith, in *Practical Approaches to Bullying*, *op cit.*

42. Besag, Valerie, *Bullies and Victims in Schools*, chapter 9, *op cit.* deals with parents as partners in dealing with and preventing bullying.

43. Besag, Valerie, *Bullies and Victims in Schools*, *op cit.* (chapters 7, 8, 10 and appendix).

CHAPTER
8

Conflict Resolution
Marigold Bentley

Conflict resolution has become a relatively new discipline during the 1990s. As with all new disciplines, it carries with it a range of new definitions, premises and theories. Like other disciplines, there are overlaps and similarities with other applied practices. In order to hold on to the purpose of conflict resolution as a developed discipline, it is important to be mindful of some of its roots.

Brief background

Although, during the latter part of the 1990s, conflict resolution has become a commodity for use by business alongside a range of skills, much comes from the peace movement. The skills and tools of applied violence are well known and well practised. For centuries, the human race has been carefully developing them. Since the Second World War in particular, there has been a growth in the exploration of alternatives to war and violence at many levels. It is this exploration which has given us the wide range of materials and skills which are now an established part of conflict resolution. Peace education has been a particularly rich source of material. With its basis on the premise that violence is not only wrong but unacceptable, peace education has contributed a great deal to conflict resolution. Peace educators have long been convinced that if people are to be taught the knowledge and skills required for applied violence, then they must also be taught the skills required for peace-making. These, then, are the skills of conflict resolution.

Sadly, during the Cold War in particular, peace education became closely associated with political movements and, as a result, much good peace education practice was rejected from schools and from curricula, and its development became inhibited. The end of the Cold War at the end of the 1980s and early 1990s enabled educators to take a fresh look at peace education in all its facets. Free from political labelling, parts of this discipline could be freely applied where it was most useful. Thus, the 1990s have witnessed a growth in the application of conflict resolution.

The most important aspect to remember is that it is meant to be applied and used. It is a discipline which comes from practice and process and has never been intended to be anything other than useful in many situations. The terminology often used is explained briefly below.

Problem solving

(Most active workshops on conflict resolution are based on a problem-solving model.)

Taking a problem-solving approach to dealing with difficulties assumes that efforts are made to find mutually satisfactory agreements to all parties involved. This is done through analysing the problem, identifying the needs, interests and purposes involved, seeking creative solutions or courses of action and negotiating which of those solutions will be implemented.

Mediation

This is a particular form of problem solving in which an uninvolved person or party helps disputants through a process to bring them to some mutually acceptable agreement. The importance of mediation is that the disputants retain responsibility for any solution suggested or applied. It is different from arbitration, in which a third party makes a decision on behalf of others which they have to agree to. (There are presently many peer mediation schemes in schools across the country. These schemes train young people in mediation skills, which are then used for problem solving in the school setting. These schemes are supervised by an adult in the school and that adult takes the role of trainer and facilitator of the scheme. These schemes often run hand in hand with an anti-bullying programme and with other peer-led methods.)

Reconciliation

This is the inward emotional healing that enables us to reach out to our opponent. It may be the role of counsellors or therapists. There is a need for reconciliation after a particularly severe fight or confrontation, especially where parties involved are deeply hurt. Deep-seated hurt can be a source of future confrontations if not dealt with appropriately.

Reparation

This is commonly used in most discipline policies in schools. It is where parties in dispute agree to some form of payment in recognition of damage caused. The examples we are mostly familiar with are picking up litter, cleaning requirements or apologies. Ideally, reparation needs to be directly connected with the incident, for example cleaning up graffiti or doing a service for the person who has been wronged.

Conciliation

This involves persuading people to come to the table to discuss differences and attempting to make them see the value of communicating and negotiating. It tends to be applied in long-standing disputes but can also be used, for example, to encourage disputants to approach mediation.

Peacekeeping

This is a non-violent alternative where trained individuals keep disputants apart and maintain order and calm – sometimes the role of the teacher on playground duty!

Exploring conflict

Conflict is an inescapable part of life. It is constantly with us and is a result of the varying needs, aims and perspectives of individuals and communities. Everyone experiences it and sees it both in and through their lives. All witness the many ways in which conflict is dealt with – many of these methods openly contradict one another. Invariably some rules – assumed or named – are known for handling conflicts and there are official and unofficial ways of dealing with it. Pressures towards dealing with conflict in a particular way can cloud the choices open to those responding. For young people, peer pressure in particular can present challenges to an ethos which seeks to encourage consideration of alternatives.

There have been few systematic approaches to educate young people in handling conflict constructively. Left to adopt models presented in society at large, the most pervasive ones tend to be those which are essentially destructive.

> *"From an early age, people are led to think that conflicts should be settled by someone in authority: the parent, the teacher, the headteacher, the gang-leader, the policeman, the judge, the boss, the president. If there is nobody to arbitrate, then the 'strongest' will 'win' and the 'weaker' will 'lose'. Traditionally, little encouragement has been given to young people to take responsibility for resolving conflicts, to look for 'win-win' solutions. Yet the way in which young people learn to respond to conflict will have a pervasive effect both on the quality of their personal lives and on the prospects for society as a whole. Affirming the personal value of each individual, encouraging mutual respect and consciously developing the skills and attitudes involved in creative conflict resolution must be regarded as an important educational priority[44]."*

This priority not only relates to curriculum requirements but also to relationships within the whole school environment. Adults should model that which they expect the young people around them to emulate.

Bringing your own experience in dealing with conflict creatively

Conflict resolution does not seek to prescribe a single method. Nor does it deny the experiences which we all bring to dealing with conflict. Creative approaches seek to draw on the whole range of experiences from any group of people. Everyone has coping strategies which are drawn on in times of direct conflict or simple problem solving. Consequently, the starting point for this type of approach is always to explore the skills we already have and make them more conscious. Once identified, named and discussed, most people are astonished at just how skilled they are at dealing with conflict creatively. A process which draws on experience of those participating can be both educative and empowering. It is educative because it helps to identify gaps in knowledge and skill, and empowering because it acknowledges the skills and abilities which people have already developed. Self-awareness is a key part of working creatively. We all need to be aware of possible triggers for poor response to disputes and confrontations. Opportunities to explore how we feel about situations as a starting point for determining and then choosing responses to disputes are essential. (See Chapter 5.)

Successful conflict resolution cannot be approached as if it were an academic problem, because it relies on personal relationships, feelings, hopes and fears. It is multi-dimensional and draws on the whole self – not on a set of theories. The building of self-confidence and trust are essential pre-requisites for a creative approach in all institutions.

Essentials

The essential skills and attitudes can be grouped under three main headings: affirmation, communication and co-operation. A conflict cannot be resolved without co-operation. Co-operation depends on communication, and people only communicate effectively when they feel affirmative about themselves and others.

Affirmation – of one's own intrinsic personal value and that of other people; a fundamental belief that all bring something to the situation. You may have your own views about them or their behaviour, but that does not alter your acknowledgement of their contribution. "If you are part of the problem, you are part of the solution." Developing affirmation or self-esteem skills may be the starting point for developing an affirmative approach to problem solving and conflict resolution.

Communication – through which you can communicate your own viewpoint and feelings clearly and assert them without aggression which denies the right of others. It demands development of listening skills and the ability to hear people in a non-judgemental way.

Co-operation – being able to work co-operatively with individuals and groups of people on shared tasks aiming to achieve a common goal.

Other skills linked with successful conflict resolution:

* Imagination and creative thinking – exploring a range of alternative or new approaches from a variety of perspectives, considering possible positive outcomes.

* Analysis and critical thinking – making a conscious attempt to approach problems with an open mind; exploring thoroughly the roots of the conflict; changing opinions in the face of new evidence; being aware of possible bias and propaganda.

* Empathy – imagining sensitively the viewpoints of other people including those of the opposite sex, other races, faiths and other cultures, and those whose life experience is different from ours.

* Commitment to justice – a respect for genuinely democratic principles and an understanding of how those should be applied.

Many levels of conflict

Few problems between individuals or groups are resolved through one gesture. A conflict resolution approach thus requires long-term commitment to identifying problems, analysing them, dealing with them through some kind of action and evaluating that action. Ideally, the long-term approach engenders increasing understanding, trust and empathy between all those involved. This in turn may result in more opportunities for constructive ways forward.

There are always links between levels of conflict. Personal problems have an impact on the way people relate to one another in their organisations and institutions. Difficulties in institutions have a direct effect on all involved, as do community or ethnically based disputes. We need to be mindful of those possibilities and work on identifying all these sources when applying a conflict resolution approach. Knowledge gained this way may have an impact on which method we seek to apply. We need to be aware that there are many factors outside our control which we may have to deal with.

Applying a problem-solving approach

In order to explore what happens in conflict situations, there is a simple procedure which can be used. Two examples will follow this through.

Firstly, ask what happened. What is the problem? At this point, it is important to encourage participants to state the facts so that everyone involved can agree with the definition of the problem. Invariably, those directly involved have difficulty with this, and it may become the responsibility of the facilitator to describe the situation in a non-judgemental way, taking care to separate feelings and value judgements from facts.

EXAMPLE 1(A)

> *A: She stole my stapler.*

> *B: She let me borrow her stapler.*

> *The facilitator works on a statement on which both A and B can agree. For example, "B took the stapler from A without asking and used it, then didn't return it".*

EXAMPLE 2(A)

> *School nurse*

> *The student had badly strained his ankle and was required to rest it for a specified period. The sports teacher did not listen to medical advice and encouraged the pupil to return to games too soon.*

> *Sports teacher*

> *The student had strained his ankle, but was keen to get back on the field. He said that his ankle was fine, and that he was ready to return, so I allowed him to do so after a short period of rest.*

> *Facilitator*

> *The student had sprained his ankle. The medical advice given did not seem to fit in with what he wanted to do. The sports teacher allowed the student to return to games before the time period recommended by the nurse had elapsed. There was an important match in which the student in question was to play.*

Secondly, participants should be asked "How do you feel about it?". This is an essential part of acknowledging that the whole person is involved with disputes and their emotions may have had a direct bearing on their behaviour and, consequently, on the outcome of the dispute.

EXAMPLE 1(B)

A: *I feel hurt that I can't trust the other students here, especially B who I thought was a friend of mine.*

B: *I feel hurt that I have been accused of stealing, when A had said earlier that I could borrow her things. I don't like being gossiped about and being called a thief.*

Facilitator

You are both hurt by what has happened here and you each recognise a problem in the way you communicated with one another.

EXAMPLE 2(B)

School nurse

I feel insulted that my professional advice has been ignored by a colleague, and that a student, with support from a staff member, has been allowed to undermine my position here in the school. I expect to be supported by my colleagues.

Sports teacher

I feel frustrated that the students are not allowed to judge some of their health needs themselves and that they are treated like babies too often. I respect the opinions of my students and, in this instance, the reputation of the school was at stake because of this match. This student is a key player.

Facilitator

You each feel undermined in your professional positions, with each of you stating that you have the best interests of the students at heart. You both have frustrations about the way this incident has occurred.

Thirdly, "What would you like to happen? In an ideal world, what would you like to happen now?". At this point, participants are encouraged to think laterally in order to name a range of possible actions and outcomes. There may be a lot of discussion here and, ideally, this part indicates possible ways forward which the facilitator can pick up on in the last session.

EXAMPLE 1(C)

A: *I would like anyone who takes my things to ask me first; then return them unbroken to me as soon as possible.*

B: *I would like to be trusted to borrow things from other people without them making a fuss all the time.*

Facilitator

It sounds as if you are friends, but that you need to communicate more clearly with one another.

EXAMPLE 2(C)

School nurse

I would like the school to pay less attention to its sports record, particularly the obsession with winning everything, and more to the actual needs of the students. However, we need to be aware that students do not necessarily know what is best for them, particularly with regard to their health. I would like my position in the school to be equal in status to that of the teaching staff, and I want my advice to be taken seriously.

Sports teacher

I would like the school to stop the gradual creep towards constant nannying of pupils and return to how it was. It used to be that sport was the most important aspect of life here, and that is still why parents choose to send their children here. I approve of the trend towards consulting students more about their needs, and this incident was a good example of my application of this.

Facilitator

You both indicate that you feel the school does not have the right priorities. You both recognise that the school may be changing in its approach to students, but you interpret that differently from one another.

Finally, "What could you actually do?". Drawing on some of the more acceptable suggestions made in response to the previous question, a suitable way forward may be identified.

EXAMPLE 1(D)

A and B: We can agree that, each time we want to borrow something or lend it, we ask first. We must try not to get cross if the other person says "no". We should not take anything without asking and getting a clear response. We agree that, if only one of us has an item which we both could use, such as a stapler, we can put it on the desk space between us and use it as necessary.

Facilitator

Well done! Would you like to meet again in a few weeks to see whether this arrangement is working out?

EXAMPLE 2(D)

School nurse

It would help me to attend staff meetings in school, where I can formally report to all the staff about particular health problems of students which might be affecting their performance. I suggest that the sports teacher goes on a course so that he can learn a little more about the medical issues involved.

Sports teacher

The sprained ankle was caused by poor maintenance of the sports field. I would like more of our budget to be spent on maintaining the grounds, so that we have fewer accidents. I will look into types of sports which stretch muscles and prepare students more appropriately for sports, as research indicates that this helps. I still don't think I was wrong to do what I did, but I am prepared to go along with other suggestions.

Facilitator

Thank you. You each have constructive ideas about possible ways forward which we can suggest to the management. Would you also consider some whole staff / whole school training on student-centred learning or team-building perhaps? I will talk to the head about these suggestions, and I recommend that you do too.

The two examples

The first was relatively simple; the other was not, which is fairly true to life. The situation which caused Example 2 to be a confrontation is more likely to be dealt with gradually through staff development and communication than through a 'quick fix'.

Ideally, this is a co-operative exercise, working towards practical action steps, no matter how small, which will help to identify a constructive way forward. If a thoroughly systematic approach is taken, it is useful to return to the chosen way forward some time after the process, to evaluate whether it was indeed useful.

The aim of this process is to find courses of action which modify attitudes and behaviour, so as to turn a destructive conflict into a constructive one.

Conflict is destructive when it:

- ❖ diverts energy from more important activities/issues;
- ❖ destroys morale, reinforces poor self-image and causes stress;
- ❖ polarises groups and hardens attitudes within those groups;
- ❖ deepens differences in values;
- ❖ produces irresponsible and regrettable behaviour or violence.

Conflict is constructive when it:

- ❖ opens up issues of importance;
- ❖ results in encountering real problems;
- ❖ increases the involvement of individuals in problem solving;
- ❖ causes authentic communication to occur;
- ❖ releases pent-up emotion, anxiety, stress;
- ❖ helps recognition of interdependence, builds cohesiveness;
- ❖ helps individuals to grow personally and apply what has been learnt.

Conflict resolution in schools

Conflict resolution can only be taught through the skills and processes involved; thus it requires experiential learning and process-centred activities. Although not necessarily required by the curriculum as such, they can be introduced through any learning situation. The processes described above can be used in order to create a more co-operative atmosphere in the classroom and in the institution as a whole. It is particularly useful for identifying commonly agreed action steps when there are difficult disputes between individuals, or when controversial issues arise in the school community as a whole. A simulated conflict can also be a teaching aid, as it encourages independent thought and applied problem solving.

With every generation, there come new ideas and methods of dealing with conflict. Some methods may not be acceptable from one generation to another. Similarly, institutions, particularly those with long-held and cherished traditions, may have difficulties in applying new methods. In the boarding school setting, this has its own particular problems. Some parents may have particularly chosen a school because of its reputation with regard to strict discipline or 'no-nonsense' practices. The emphasis here needs to be made on the encouragement of self-discipline rather than on externally imposed discipline. Conflict resolution approaches do not replace clear rules and guidelines on behaviour required by a school. What these processes can offer are means through which all members of the institution are involved in creating the rules and codes of behaviour which they then live by.

One of the reasons why this type of activity can be viewed as threatening is that some school authority structures and disciplinary procedures may not be designed to encourage pupils to take a responsible role in dealing with their own disputes. The common assumption is that the adults will have the answer to any conflict situation, whether it is between young people or between a teacher and a pupil. The assumption is that the adults have the authority to impose a 'solution'. If the authority structure is rigidly hierarchical, involvement of pupils in seeking creative responses to conflict may be seen as subversive. If the methods of conflict resolution that young people are being encouraged to apply to one another are in direct contradiction to the application of rules and codes of behaviour in the school as a whole, the approach will be unsustainable.

In an institutional setting, unless the adults in the community have themselves learnt to seek creative responses to conflict and have come to terms with an ethos in which they can exercise their responsibility and authority without being threatened by the active participation of pupils, the introduction of conflict resolution techniques will generate new conflicts. A sensitive and flexible approach is required.

The wider questions which may need to be addressed in the institution as a whole may be to do with the quality of relationships, the assumptions made about roles, hierarchy, responsibility and authority. Ideally, the parents of young people in the institution, as well as governors, teachers and pupils, need to be involved in these discussions. Although these discussions and processes used to be on the fringes of educational debate, they are now a central feature of all institutions seeking to reduce violence at many levels.

Reference

44. Bowers, Sue and Leimdorfer, Tom (1988), "Creative Responses to Conflict" from ***Affirmation, Communication and Co-operation*** – Report on a Quaker Conference on Education in July 1988.

CHAPTER

9

Ensuring A Safe Environment

Roger Morgan and Tim Holgate

Risks and risk assessment

The statutory duty to safeguard and promote boarders' welfare requires staff to protect boarders from suffering what the Children Act terms 'significant harm'. Everyday school life, however, presents risks of various kinds – of accidents and injuries through perfectly appropriate educational, sporting and recreational activities, of harm through bullying – which no school can fully eliminate, and of rare but extreme events such as abuse, or fires at school. Then there are possible 'acts of God' that no one could reasonably have been expected to foresee, but which if they do occur can bring disastrous consequences and recriminations about whether adequate precautions had in fact been taken. Litigation and the media are unforgiving commentators with the luxury of hindsight after the event.

Increasingly, the need for risk assessment is being recognised as a key requirement in safeguarding boarders' welfare. Risks exist, and sometimes they will incur injury and harm; they cannot be eliminated and, even if they could, both education and life in general would hardly gain. What is important is to identify risks and then to act reasonably to minimise them – particularly to avoid exposing pupils to risks that most people would regard as excessive or unnecessary, and to avoid harm that most people would say should have been foreseen by a responsible staff member. Identifying and assessing risks and taking reasonable action to minimise them both protect pupils and also provide staff with the means of demonstrating, should the worst come to the worst, that they had been responsible and had taken informed decisions in relation to reducing risks. When harm does occur, we would clearly all wish we had eliminated the risk concerned – but, as we do not have the power to foresee the future, the next thing is to use our best present information to plan the reduction of foreseeable risk. This is the process of risk assessment.

Activities and the management of risk

There are three main considerations. Firstly, you need to be satisfied that the activities are suitable for the children – including activities you let children take part in rather than organise yourself (*e.g.* outings, activity centres, cadet camps, at other schools, or organised by outside instructors you invite in). This requires you to take into account factors such as the age, number, competence, behaviour, skills and mix of children, and to recognise that what may be suitable for one group of children of a similar age may not be suitable for another. It also requires you to keep reviewing the suitability of the activities in practice, and to make changes if they appear to be becoming unsuitable for any reason – something that has never caused a problem before or with other groups may well start doing so.

Secondly, you need to take positive steps to minimise risks to both children and other people from the activities you organise or allow children take part in. You need to identify possible risks and to take action to counter them, as well as not taking (or letting children take) unnecessary or unreasonable risks (always taking their age, abilities and characteristics into account). Guidance on carrying out risk assessments is given below. You need to make sure that something that is suitable for older children, or for children who have reached a level of skill or responsibility, does not present any significant risks to younger or other children. In minimising risks, you also need to take into account the fact that children may be expected to go into places and to try activities that are attractive, even if they have been told not to. Proper safety precautions must be taken for any activity that needs them. The responsibility ultimately rests on the school, but also needs to be exercised by the person in charge of the activity (whether a staff member or not) and every member of staff or helper involved. Activities may well involve some elements of risk, but it is necessary to minimise risks to children – you should not therefore take the line that high levels of risk simply contribute to the fun or challenge of a particular activity.

Thirdly, you need to satisfy yourself that every member of staff, helper or instructor (including any outside instructor coming in for the activity) is competent to supervise or instruct the activities you are entrusting to their supervision or instruction. You need, therefore, to be sure that your staff, helpers and instructors (including any prefects, parents or senior pupils helping) are suitably responsible people, are properly skilled at the activity itself, and are able to lead or supervise that activity safely (which may require more knowledge and skill than simply being good at the activity themselves).

Where you run activities that involve a significant risk (*i.e.* that a reasonable person would see as involving a significant risk), as well as ensuring that staff are competent for such activities, you need to check that those leading the activity concerned hold the relevant qualification to supervise or instruct children in that activity. Such activities will usually be governed by a recognised national body or association, and you should check with that body what qualifications are needed to supervise or instruct young children taking part in the activity, and ask the relevant staff or instructors to show you proof of that qualification. DfEE guidance lists national bodies for commonly encountered activities. You also need to be satisfied that, if you take children (*e.g.* on an outing) to take part in an activity involving a significant level of risk, they are going to be instructed or supervised by suitably qualified people. Where the national body for the activity concerned specifies the number of qualified instructors or supervisors required, you should meet this number.

You should only provide activities which require special equipment, clothing or safety precautions, if you are able to provide these. Qualified instructors should know what special provisions are needed, and you should take their advice, and never require them to provide or give instruction in an activity without the required clothing, equipment or precautions. Note that extra precautions may be needed for children which adults may not require, and that the precautions and equipment may need to be different if the children taking part are unskilled novices rather than children skilled in the activity. Again, the national body for the activity concerned can usually advise.

The DfEE guidelines[45] on organisation of school expeditions and visits provide useful information on planning, supervision, checklists and sample forms.

The assessment of risk

It is wise to carry out a risk assessment in relation to your boarding accommodation, school grounds and recreational areas (official and unofficial), school journeys and travel arrangements, and accommodation (*e.g.* exchanges, cadet camps, field trips, skiing or leadership courses) away from school, as well as to any activity involving significant or unusual risk. This needs to relate to what pupils do, as well as to the physical health and safety characteristics of buildings and 'plant'. It is good practice to make a written record of your risk assessments.

A *significant risk* is one that a reasonable person would regard as significant rather than negligible, taking into account the ages, mix and characteristics of the children involved. An *unusual risk* is one that a reasonable person would be likely to regard as 'out of the ordinary', or part of a seemingly risky activity. You cannot be expected to foresee everything that might possibly occur – but, to meet the requirement to safeguard the welfare of boarders, you need to identify the hazards and risks that a reasonable person would regard as 'foreseeable'.

As a general rule, you need to identify and record those risks that a reasonable person could be expected to regard as an identifiable risk to children or others – and then to take, and record that you have taken, all reasonable and practicable steps to reduce that risk to a level that a reasonable person would regard as acceptable and appropriate for a recreation activity for children of the relevant age and characteristics.

'Risk' includes:

- ❖ risk of accident or injury to children you are looking after;

- ❖ risk of children being abused, being bullied, becoming lost or being taken by someone;

- ❖ risk of children suffering any form of harm that a reasonable person would consider significant rather than negligible;

- ❖ risk of children becoming significantly distressed or upset.

You should also identify, record and counteract any significant risks to your staff, helpers, instructors or members of the public arising from any activity you are running. Note that you do have legal responsibilities under health and safety legislation for the safety of children, staff and visitors, and carrying out risk assessments will contribute towards meeting those responsibilities.

Risk assessment:

❖ is simply a careful examination of what, in your activities, premises, outdoor areas and outings, could cause harm to children (or other people), so that you can weigh up whether you have taken enough precautions or should do more to prevent harm;

❖ is a protection for children, and your written records of it may one day be vital to you in demonstrating how you have considered and minimised risks, should a child suffer harm (or worse) in your care;

❖ involves 'hunting out' foreseeable risks, and taking reasonable action to avoid or minimise them;

❖ may appear complicated or time consuming in prospect – but in practice it is a matter of applying systematic common sense to the protection of vulnerable pupils from risks that could have been minimised or averted;

❖ will usually involve identifying the hazards present in any undertaking, and then considering the level of the risk involved; risk reflects both the **likelihood** that harm will occur, and the **severity** of its impact;

❖ should be carried out periodically, and all areas of the boarding house and each type of activity should be reviewed on a regular basis, particularly when changes to boarding accommodation or types of activity are taking place, or where different groups of pupils are involved.

Guidance is given below on carrying out risk assessments. You also need to take particular care to ensure that your staff know about risk factors and the action to be taken to minimise risks – decisions on action to reduce risks are only as effective as the steps taken by preoccupied staff under pressure all the time they are with children.

The level of risk

St Bede's School has a clearly stated analysis[46] of the scale of risk associated with different hazards. They point out that trivial risks may be ignored, as will risks arising from routine activities associated with life in general, unless the activity compounds those risks, or there is evidence of significant relevance to the particular activity. The process will enable the school to identify and prioritise the measures that need to be taken to provide a safe working environment. This will enable the risk assessment and findings to be used positively, such as to change working procedures or to introduce medium to long-term controls. Classifications of probability and severity in a school could be made as follows:

Probability

High   *Probability of an occurrence once per term;*

Medium *Probability of an occurrence once per year;*

Low   *An occurrence could occur but is unlikely to do so.*

Severity

Major   *An incident or school-related illness which could cause the death of a person, or serious illness or injury requiring hospital treatment of ten or more persons;*

Serious *An incident or school-related illness which could cause the absence from work or study of one or more persons for more than three days;*

Minor   *An incident or school-related illness which could cause the absence from work or study of one or more persons for more than a day but less than three days.*

Risk assessment matrix

The combination of probability and severity can be used to prioritise risks associated with any particular environment or activity. The following matrix illustrates one possible means of prioritisation. An alternative method is given at the end of the chapter, in one of the sample risk assessment report forms.

Figure 9.1

Probability Severity	High	Medium	Low
Major	Significant Risk (1)	Significant Risk (1)	Moderate Risk (2)
Serious	Significant Risk (1)	Moderate Risk (2)	Insignificant Risk (3)
Minor	Moderate Risk (2)	Insignificant Risk (3)	Insignificant Risk (3)

The risk assessment should be used to guide the school's judgement as to the measures that should be taken to provide a safe environment for work, living and activities, and to comply with the school's duties under the relevant statutory provisions. Those systems or activities with significant risk, if any, should be an immediate priority; those with a moderate risk should be considered in due course; whilst those with insignificant risks may not require further action other than monitoring and re-assessment in due course.

Carrying out risk assessments

Step 1 – Identify and list all the significant or unusual hazards to children and others that you can foresee while you or your staff are looking after those children. In doing this for your boarding house, you need to tour all indoor and outdoor areas, noting in writing any existing new possible hazards to children. It is helpful to do this with someone else, so that you can compare notes. Bear in mind that children can often 'discover' hazards that are not immediately apparent to an adult – it may sometimes be helpful to take an older child with you on your tour. In identifying hazards for your activities, go through all your planned daily programmes, again ideally with someone else, and write down all the foreseeable hazards and risks you can identify – *e.g.* from what the children will be doing, from where they are doing it, from the equipment or materials they may be using, from what the staff will be doing, and from what may happen if the children misbehave, go where they should not or fail to follow staff rules or instructions. Identify any particularly risky times or places, as well as considering the activities themselves, and consider risks to children not taking part in activities (*e.g.* walking to and from activities, or just wandering around), as well as those taking part. Do the same for planned outings and activities you are taking children to visit rather than providing yourself. Use the experience of similar activities run before by you and your staff, particularly over anything that actually led to an accident or a 'near miss' – but do not assume that something that has not caused problems before or with a different group of children cannot do so in the future. Take the advice of any specialist leaders or instructors you will be using. Take into account the age, numbers, skills, mix and characteristics of the children in deciding what might be a hazard. Figure 9.2 summarises the different aspects of hazard hunting.

Figure 9.2 – Identification of hazards during risk assessment

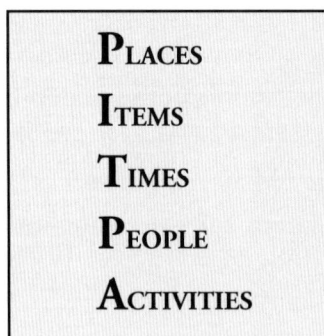

PLACES

ITEMS

TIMES

PEOPLE

ACTIVITIES

Step 2 – Write down exactly what harm or accident each of your listed hazards might foreseeably lead to. There may be more than one for each hazard on the list. Write against each foreseeable accident or harm what you estimate the likelihood and consequent level of risk of that accident or harm to be – *e.g.* 'very likely to happen', 'likely to happen', or 'unlikely to happen', and have a category for recording the worst that you could foresee as happening if things went badly wrong, under 'worst risk'.

Step 3 – Decide what action (or additional action) you can take to minimise each of the risks you have identified (note that the word is 'minimise' not 'eliminate' – reasonableness and care are expected, not unattainable total absence of all risks). You should not however provide activities or use accommodation or facilities which present an unreasonable risk to children. Possible actions to minimise risks might include removing hazards altogether, measures to prevent children (or certain age groups) from contact with those hazards, increased staff supervision, training and instructions, procedures such as regularly monitoring particular activities or areas, use of different equipment or materials, provision of safety measures such as protective clothing, safety equipment, or safety mats, relocation or separation of particular activities, changing your activity programme.

Step 4 – Write your action plan to take all reasonable steps that you have identified to minimise risks, allocating tasks clearly to people who need to carry them out. Take the action required in good time, and check and record that action has been taken.

Step 5 – Decide how you and your staff should respond if the identified accident or harm happens despite your action to minimise the risk, including how to respond to each item on your 'worst risk' list coming about. This is effectively your local 'disaster plan' – and the way you respond to serious incidents in order to prevent further harm and minimise the effects for individuals of what has happened (including getting medical help promptly) is as much a part of your responsibilities as are protective measures.

Step 6 – Regularly check that your risk-minimising actions are being carried out, and recheck your premises, outdoor areas, equipment, activities and outings to see whether your actions to minimise risks need changing or strengthening, or if any new risks have emerged (children may well have 'discovered' some since your initial assessment!). If so, carry out the above assessment and action steps for those too. Figure 9.3 summarises the essential steps in a risk assessment.

Figure 9.3 – The stages of a risk assessment

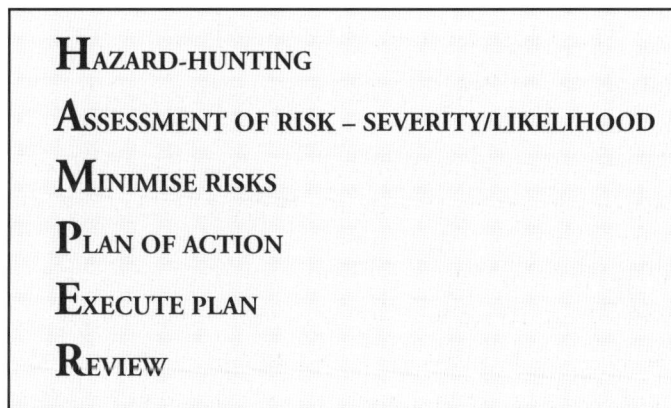

HAZARD-HUNTING

ASSESSMENT OF RISK – SEVERITY/LIKELIHOOD

MINIMISE RISKS

PLAN OF ACTION

EXECUTE PLAN

REVIEW

Two possible forms for recording your risk assessments are shown in Figures 9.4 and 9.5.

Figure 9.4 – Sample risk assessment form for activities

LOCATION   ACTIVITY   AGE RANGE   NUMBER TAKING PART

HAZARDS IDENTIFIED	POSSIBLE HARM OR ACCIDENT	LIKELY? Tick one			ACTION PLAN TO MINIMISE RISK	Person Responsible	Confirmed Action Taken	ACTION IF HARM/ ACCIDENT OCCURS	WORST CASE SCENARIO AND NECESSARY ACTION
		Very	Yes	No					
1.									
2.									
3.									
4.									
5.									

SIGNATURE OF RISK ASSESSOR ....   DATE ....

Figure 9.5 – Sample risk assessment form

BRIEF DESCRIPTION OF VENUE, EQUIPMENT OR ACTIVITY, AND THE POSSIBLE RISK INVOLVED

....

....

ASSESSMENT OF RISKS INVOLVED (Circle appropriate number in each column below)

PROBABILITY	+	**SEVERITY**	=	**RISK FACTOR**
Probable = 3		Critical/Life Threatening = 3		HIGH 5–6
Possible = 2		Serious/Major = 2		MEDIUM 4
Unlikely = 1		Minor = 1		LOW 1–3

ADEQUATE CONTROLS IN PLACE?   YES / NO

Detail ....

....

ADDITIONAL CONTROLS, MODIFICATIONS OR IMPROVEMENTS REQUIRED?   YES / NO

Detail ....

....

MAINTENANCE WORK REQUIRED?   YES / NO

Detail ....

....

SIGNED .... POSITION .... DATE ....

Health and safety

As part of their statutory duty to provide and maintain a safe and hazard-free environment, all members of the house staff team will need, as well as carrying out periodic and specific risk assessments, to review regularly and monitor the general health and safety provision around the boarding house, and be vigilant in spotting hazards when going about their day-to-day life and work. Pupils can also be expected to report any health and safety concerns to staff.

House staff are likely to focus on areas such as the following:

❖ Where relevant, food handling and hygiene arrangements will need to be in line with current statutory regulations, and will be liable to inspection by the relevant authorities.

❖ Adequate hand-washing and drying facilities need to be provided for all toilets around the house.

❖ The security of the house and its residents needs to have the highest priority. Coded security locks on external doors are now in common use, but the codes need to be changed periodically, and the doors to close efficiently after use.

❖ Appropriate signing-out and signing-in arrangements need to be in place, and the recording system monitored for its effective use. A case can be made for a separate book for overnight absence. It goes without saying that this must be quickly available to the responsible adult member of staff in the event of a night-time evacuation of the building.

❖ Hazards in individual studies and bed-sits can often be hard to spot, but trailing flexes, multiple use of electric sockets and cooking in rooms are possibly the most common.

❖ Electrical equipment, both provided by the house or school, and brought to school by pupils, should be subject to the statutory checks and records kept.

❖ House staff need to be quite clear about those who are entitled to visit and take boarders out. Are there any custody orders, court orders or restrictions of access in place, in the case of split families (see Chapter 3)?

- ❖ Does your staff guidance (see Chapter 11) provide clear cut procedures for pupils travelling in cars driven by staff, pupils or other parents?

- ❖ Fire practices and checks on fire exits are probably the most familiar health and safety functions of many staff. The bursar will be able to advise on any changing requirements of the local fire officer. Your house rules and procedures will obviously document clearly the day time and night time evacuation procedures. However, it is surprisingly easy to forget that the occasional pupils accommodated overnight will be unfamiliar with routines. They and new boarders should be talked through the procedure by a responsible adult.

- ❖ The location of first aid kits should be clearly known, and the contents regularly checked. The identity of the qualified first-aiders in the house should be known by all.

Above all, the whole house staff team needs to be familiar with the school's code of practice for health and safety, and particularly with those areas delegated to the individual boarding house and their particular responsibilities within it.

References and Notes

45. Department for Education and Employment (1998), *Health and Safety of Pupils on Educational Visits*, DfEE Publication HSPV2.

46. St Bede's School, East Sussex, Health and Safety Policy.

CHAPTER
10

Organisation and Communication in the Boarding House

Gill Dixon and Clive Thorpe

THE HOUSEMISTRESS'S VIEWPOINT – Gill Dixon

To be a housemistress and to lead and manage a successful house is probably the most challenging and most rewarding job in teaching, yet it is more than just a job: it is a way of life. It requires vision, drive, a lightness of touch and a willingness to work almost all hours.

The success of a house is not founded upon the traditions and reputations of times gone by: it reflects directly and immediately the leadership and management skills of the housemaster or housemistress. Paramount here is the way in which a house is organised and how communication is managed within it. These two themes will be brought into focus in this chapter by considering different experiences drawn from running an integrated day and boarding girls' house which caters for some 90 senior students all in their final A-level year at school.

It is the business of a housemistress to lead the house and, to do this successfully, you need a very clear vision of what your house should be. My vision was to provide a house for all girls in their final year at school which would act as a 'stepping stone' to help bridge the gap between school life and university. The young women have a less restrictive routine and a lighter structure imposed upon them, are no longer required to wear school uniform and are expected and encouraged to show greater independence and individual responsibility. My vision was also of a house that would fully integrate all day and boarding students. The day students could then enjoy and experience the benefits and facilities that full boarding life offered. This can give a greater sense of breadth and balance to the institutionalised life of the boarding student, which can sometimes be narrow and intense – a daily breath of fresh air.

In determining this vision, the housemistress must really spend some time looking at the physical structure of her house and must consider how to make the best use of the facilities within it. A simple rethink of room usage can have a big impact on the life of the students. In our house, each student shares a room with one other. Senior students often need to work late into the night, and many were having difficulty in finding a quiet space to work after evening lock-up, without disturbing their sleeping room-mate. A simple and relatively inexpensive door was created by knocking through a wall to an adjoining study centre giving the house access throughout the night which instantly relieved these considerable pressures. (It is also interesting to note how well students respond to having two separate spaces of their own, one to work in and the other to relax, socialise and sleep in.)

The biggest conflicts that arise in an integrated house often stem from the different needs of day students and boarders. The day students' demands are relatively straight-forward, typically a study space and a common room. The boarders' requirements are for much more of a 'home' environment. The housemistress must carefully plan and manage the space available and must consider issues such as privacy and personal space.

One simple fact is that the quality of the environment plays a significant part in determining the culture and atmosphere. If facilities are clean and well cared for, with plants and fresh flowers around, then students respond by looking after the place and graffiti or wilful damage is very unlikely. However, a house that is shabby and uncared for will be treated with no respect.

With students being part of my house for only one year before leaving school, my vision was also for the young women to experience a sense of development and growth through the year. The house was to act as a 'decompression chamber' with, as the year progresses, less and less institutional structure and routine, reducing numbers of meetings and roll calls and with a gradual withdrawal of staff into the background as the students begin to stand more on their own. Simple things can be introduced to soften the institutionalised edge of house life. For example, instead of reading out a long list of 90 names to register the morning roll call, students can be quietly checked off as they arrive in the main common room each morning, making the following house meeting much more relaxed and informal.

It is important to note here that a new housemistress does not necessarily have to invent a vision for her house, indeed it may well be inherited from times long past, but it is vital that one really believes and 'owns' it.

A particular problem that you are likely to face if you are taking over a house from another is the comparison which inevitably will be made, an endless echo of "we've always done it that way" from all those who have been there longer. It is comforting to note that tradition is often only that which was done last year and such comments do quickly fade.

With a clear vision in place, one must have good communication with the whole house. A housemistress can delegate many responsibilities and tasks to other staff, but the one thing which should never be delegated is communication. One must have frequent and direct contact with all individuals and must not be tempted to run the house remotely, communicating only through notices or through other staff or prefects.

With such a big house to run, and one in which day students and boarders are integrated, communicating with every individual is one of the biggest challenges I have faced. Whole meetings are not practical with such a number of students and the morning meeting is purely a means of registration and for passing on quick notices and information. Real communication can only take place in small groups and thus it is vital that a housemistress spends significant time with small groups and individuals, taking great care not to exclude any from the discussions. I have certainly found the best times to be during late afternoons with the whole house around and late in the evenings with the boarders. Often at midnight we have put the world to rights, and issues, which may have been difficult to resolve in a meeting of 90 students, have been quickly accepted and considered their own.

Delegation is a vital skill to develop. Rarely are roles clearly defined for the house staff, and it is all too easy to find yourself buried beneath a mass of paperwork, checking that the duty students have done their job, organising the catering for a house event and then picking up the litter around the bike sheds. The golden rule here is "only do what only you can do". One must be able to step back from administrative and domestic chores and be in the house with the students as their housemistress. The reality and demands of house life, however, often work against this. With letters to write home, endless phone calls to make, reports and references to draft, problems with the domestic staff to sort out, not to mention the lessons to prepare and the books to mark for the next morning's teaching, finding the time and setting the priorities prove to be the big challenge. Simple time management skills may help a little.

❖ Make use of an answerphone to help screen and prioritise phone calls.

❖ If a job will only take five or ten minutes, then do it immediately and don't add it to a list of things to do later.

❖ Open your mail when you have time to respond to it, and aim to deal with each piece of paper only once, rather than let it build up into a pile. It is often a good idea to open your mail standing up, on the move, and close to a waste paper bin!

❖ Don't under-estimate what you can do in ten minutes; use the small gaps of time which appear though each day.

The quality of life within the house is not only dependent upon your commitment and skill, but depends upon the whole team. The resident staff, the domestic staff and the academic tutors all play a significant part in the running of a successful house. Managing this team effectively is one of the most important tasks.

It is important that every member of the team knows clearly what is expected of them and that, once they do, you then trust and allow them to get on with it. Nothing can be more frustrating than for a resident or duty tutor, having been given the responsibility of looking after the house for an evening, continually finding that the housemistress is in the background checking that all is well.

In my experience, creating a hierarchy among the house staff does little for team spirit and, although the staff have different roles, it is vital that you value each one. Often small tokens of thanks and the odd treat are all that is needed to give the over-worked duty tutor or the weary matron a much-needed boost and make them feel appreciated.

The resident staff, which may include an assistant, resident tutor and matron, must meet together frequently if the house is to run well. We all tend to meet early each morning for five or ten minutes to share information and concerns. Also, each evening, it is important to have some handover/takeover procedure between the duty tutor and resident staff so that all are fully involved and aware of situations. To strengthen communication further, we also operate a house diary that acts as an *aide-mémoire* through each day and in which all staff write notes to each other.

The tutor is a much valued member of the house, and every successful house is built upon a strong tutorial team. Yet a good tutor defies definition, since much has to do with individuality and personality. Often the good tutor is simply the teacher who enjoys talking and really listening to students. He or she perseveres through the initial and often awkward small talk with a student and slowly builds up a real relationship of mutual respect and trust. During the evening, a tutor has the time to develop and strengthen these individual contacts, and one of the joys of tutoring is in knowing that sometimes the odd nudge or well-timed word can really change a decision and direction in the students' lives. A skilful housemistress is one who can recognise the individual strengths within her tutorial team and allow these to have an impact in house.

Dealing with a weak tutor is an even greater challenge. In my experience, some teachers can clearly operate well within the formal structure of the classroom but are uncomfortable in the role of tutor within a house. Such tutors need to be supported by the house staff if they are to grow in skill and confidence. If tutors are uncomfortable with the students, then they must be accompanied in house until they begin to feel less pressured and more comfortable with what is expected of them. It is also important that the weak tutor feels useful and needed, even if this means that you have to find some specific or perhaps artificial task which the tutor can handle well. Examples here may include such things as asking them to help organise a house event, cooking for the barbecue, driving the mini-bus, house administration, etc. It is true that weak tutors generally get better not worse if given lots of time, support and guidance.

A key player is the matron. Not only does she provide the vital medical support and management of domestic duties in house, but she is also often around at times when other staff are not, and consequently sees all sorts of things at source. Constant daily contact and a trusting relationship need to develop between the housemistress and matron, with both being prepared to share confidential details with discretion. A good matron is one capable of making decisions and showing initiative and, more so, a good housemistress is one who recognises and encourages this.

School rules are often clearly stated in black and white and, in every successful house, discipline must be seen to be firm and fair. Yet the good housemistress recognises that the reality of a situation means that discipline has, at times, to be a little grey. Most schools operate a fine or tariff system for smoking and drinking, which escalates as the severity of the crime increases. One knows that this system can only work if exceptions are made. Teenagers will break rules and will make mistakes for all sorts of reasons, and you must be able to show compassion and discretion to judge the best option for each individual. The priority here is to try to keep such students on track and to allow them to learn and develop within the school community. Of course, there will be some students who will not make it, and the housemistress, with the head, must also be able to judge when enough is enough.

It is important, particularly in a middle or senior house, that students are given real responsibilities and not just chores that need to be done. Within my single year group we have no house prefects but have a group of seven or eight elected representatives who meet frequently, with or without staff present, and who contribute a great deal to the day-to-day running of the house. They help sort out some of the personal problems that arise between students; they plan and co-ordinate all social events; they administer all drama and chapel activity; they advise staff on routine and structure. The obvious advantage for me is the seniority of the students, but I am convinced that younger girls and boys really can rise to an appropriate challenge and handle real responsibility well.

The relationship between you and the parent is an important one to get right. Not so many years ago, parents may only have contacted the boarding house once or twice a term, to arrange to drop off or collect their son or daughter. The situation is now very different and you will have to handle many letters, phone calls, e-mail and faxes from parents throughout the term. The relationship between a school and its parents is now much more collaborative. The housemistress and parent must now consider themselves partners – an education professional assisting fathers and mothers to bring up their children as best they can. This partnership can be put under considerable strain if both parties have different and conflicting perceptions of a child's needs. Through such difficulties, you must always keep in mind that you have gained experience, with 60 or so children in house at a time, and that you are being paid for this experience and expertise. It is also vital that the interest and welfare of the child must always be the focus of all discussions. The child is not the product: the child is the client.

Certainly the most awkward conversations with parents arise when their daughter has been involved in some disciplinary problem at school. The immediate reaction on the phone is usually one of shock and disbelief. "It couldn't possibly be my daughter. What proof do you have? Who has encouraged such behaviour?" The next reaction is normally one of anger, which may be directed at the daughter herself, or her friends, or indeed the school. The final reaction is normally one of an acceptance of the situation. "What have we done wrong? Should we withdraw her from school?" Each of these stages may last a minute or may last a month depending upon the parent, the child and the misdemeanour, but the pattern and progression seems fairly set. As a housemistress, when dealing with such situations, the most important thing is to let the parents quickly see throughout the discussion that you are looking to do the best thing for their child. The conversation must be a positive one, even if the punishment is to be very harsh, and the aim must always be to help their child back on track and to allow her to learn from her mistakes.

One point to stress here is the importance of having early contact with parents. It should never be the case that the first contact between you and the child's parents is when something has gone wrong, when the 'wheels have already come off'. You must try to establish a relationship with parents as soon as possible and must continue to work hard to develop this so that, if and when a problem arises, there is a base from which to work.

If the approach of a housemistress is calm and helpful, parents will come and seek advice. You often see a child in a much broader range of circumstances than parents do and, as there is a distance between a child and a housemistress, your judgement can often be more objective and well founded.

To lead a house is a privilege and an opportunity to make a real difference in young people's lives. The measure of success for me seems most clear when, after a few years, one meets up with the once nervous young girl who has grown into the well-balanced, confident, independent and successful young woman. With many happy reminiscences of her years in house and incidents recounted that were of great significance to her (though often long since forgotten by me), the rewards of this job are brought sharply to focus.

There cannot be many jobs that are more worthwhile.

THE HOUSEMASTER'S VIEWPOINT – Clive Thorpe

Boarding houses in a school are very much like ships in the navy. They are each following the same sort of course and bound by an overall structure of discipline and procedure. Each ship, however, has its own traditions and ethos which is very much a reflection of the captain's personality. Each house in a school will have its own ethos and atmosphere, which will complement that of the school's mission statement. Everyone working and living within a house ought to feel comfortable with the atmosphere and management structure within it, and should feel that they are able to contribute to the development of that special atmosphere. The ethos and atmosphere should not be imposed, but should develop from the way in which staff and students interact with one another.

There are, however, certain legal parameters within which we all have to operate (see Chapter 3). These include the Children Act 1989 and legislation governing occupiers' liability, health and safety at work, fire precautions, handling of food, and transport.

Whatever structure and ethos you wish to create, you have to ensure that procedures are within the parameters mentioned above. The 21st century boarding school is very different from its portrayal in films and on television. John Le Carré's novels are seeded with dysfunctional individuals whose distorted lives have been influenced by a boarding school education. It is natural, therefore, that a juicy 'boarding school story' is highly sought after by the British press.

House structure

Each school will have a different template for the way in which houses are run. Just as the ethos of the house should be organic, so should the management structure. The structure will reflect the school's development plan and logistics but, more importantly, will reflect the strengths of the personnel involved. Those who manage ought to ensure that the structure is clear to their house teams, to students and also to parents. Although 'job descriptions' in a boarding house can be a contradiction in terms, as we all pitch in doing different jobs as and when required, each person in a pastoral team should have a clear idea of their broad areas of responsibility. In some cases it might be easy to distribute defined roles, such as tutor to Year 9.

It is always a good idea to re-negotiate roles annually. The teaching profession is becoming more fluid anyway and so there is a greater turnover of staff than in the past. Doing the same thing, year on year, can lead to inertia and, more importantly, stunt professional growth. In some cases, there might be good reasons for certain colleagues continuing in the same role in the house – for example, a Year 10 tutor taking the group into Year 11. In many other cases, a change of role might help reduce or even avoid conflict and breathe a freshness into the house.

Meetings of the house team ought to be both structured and unstructured. A structured meeting allows you to go through the house methodically, identifying quickly where there might be problems. Structured meetings which are minuted give you the opportunity to refer back to a concern raised which might become a problem in the future. The housemaster should not be the only one to chair a meeting, nor take the minutes. You will develop your team professionally if others are involved directing discussion. Very often one chairs a meeting for the first time after becoming a head of department or a housemaster.

An unstructured meeting allows you to challenge policies which are in place and to explore new practices. In the latter case, radical ideas may be generated which can then, by further discussion, be refined and included in a policy revision or in the implementation of a new policy.

The academic–pastoral link

Each establishment will have its own links between these two very important aspects of school life. The worst position, in which any team can find itself, is one where the academic and pastoral staff snipe at one another from behind covered wagons. You must try to keep the dialogue open between the two groups. Be positive and always try to exploit one another's strengths rather than concentrating on weaknesses. Be open, and give as much information as possible to other tutors or members of the house team. There may, however, be some information that you cannot or would prefer not to pass on. Professionals should be able to respect the 'need to know' principle.

Examinations are now exerting a greater pressure over a longer period of time on more year groups in a school. At primary/preparatory level, children face a barrage of assessment tests, Common Entrance, Scholarship and bespoke entrance tests from an early age. At secondary level, Key Stage 3 tests, GCSE and A-levels and an examining period which can stretch from the beginning of Year 10 to the end of the upper sixth impact on the way in which students lead their lives. Gone are the days when the summer term in Years 11 and 13 were the only pressure points. If you read graduate advertisements in the broadsheets, you will find that more and more employers are asking for a specified number of UCAS points plus degree category from potential job applicants. Employers, too, are tracking back through CVs and are looking at A-level grades when considering candidates for second or third jobs. Students who are aware of this know that any mistakes made at school, academically, can have serious knock on effects for the rest of their lives. Links between academic and pastoral tutors must aim to help pupils through a very long ordeal during what is, emotionally, a very difficult stage of their lives.

The role of the matron

The role of the matron will vary from school to school. The matron is an essential part of the house team as she is probably the one who knows exactly what is going on. Parents need to be introduced to the matron as soon as possible, so that they can put a face to the person who will play a vital role in their children's lives and, more importantly, when the children are feeling at their lowest.

One crucial role is that of being the eyes and ears of the housemaster. This is not supposed to be seen as playing the role of chief sneak or quisling, but much more as an early warning role or providing information to pre-empt something which, if indeed were to take place, would have major consequences.

A matron can sum up the mood of the house and provide essential feedback on how certain policies might (or might not) be working. Because of her, information might come her way that would have remained 'underground' or would have only been revealed after a long period of time. Some information might remain confidential between the matron and the child. Other confidential information, such as a child's disclosure of abuse, will have to be passed on. One method to establish at which stage or for what reasons a matron might disclose a confidence is to work through case studies as part of an in-house training programme during team meetings. Matrons need to have a working knowledge of the Children Act and of the school procedure concerning referral to social services. (See Chapter 3.)

Matrons have a right to be in house meetings and invited to all house events. Both housemaster and matron ought to regard one another as critical friends. Matrons are like the wise retainers in Molière's plays – they speak their minds and tell you the truth. There is one caveat, however: the housemaster might have information which only he can know. There might be occasions when a 'need to know' policy has to be implemented and that certain information does not come matron's way. She needs to respect that. Fortunately, such situations only rarely happen.

Communications with parents

Before pupils come into the house

As soon as you know who is coming to your house, it is always quite nice to send a letter of welcome to the child concerned. It does not have to be too long nor should you overburden them with too much information. The same is true regarding communication with parents. We can fall into the trap of communication overload where the information that you send resembles a Haynes workshop manual, where every specification and scenario is covered. Be honest – how many colleagues religiously read the staff or departmental handbook from cover to cover? Parents (and students) will neither have the time nor the inclination to read everything, and too much information can appear frightening. Don't make the experience of changing schools more daunting than it ought to be. Keep it simple!

When the pupil is at school

Give parents some feedback at the first weekend. What you might have to say may not be a lot, but some good news is better than nothing. Try and pick out something positive that the child has done.

If you are not a housemaster or housemistress, it is always best to check before you give parents a ring. In many cases there will be no problem, but there may be occasions, however, when a phone call might not be appropriate or, if a phone call is made, there might be areas that are best avoided. It is always useful, after a phone call, to make notes for later reference.

Links with the bursarial department

Once again, each school will have different departments within this area. My heading would consist of the sanatorium, cleaning staff, maintenance and catering personnel. One should treat, and encourage others to treat, such staff as colleagues who are in the same team and whose major aim is, as yours is, the welfare of the students. As they often come from the local community, they are very important in the unconscious marketing of the school. Should they be unhappy, then the local community will soon become aware of it.

If there are to be any changes of routine, such as building work, then it is only polite to let your cleaning staff know. Often, particularly in holidays, they like to get ahead in order to save some time towards the beginning of the school term. Imagine how they feel if they see that they have wasted time cleaning rooms, only to find that a refit means that the work has to be done again. Catering staff, too, need to be aware of changes both in routine and numbers. They have to run to a budget and there can be cost implications if catering staff have to stay at work in order to accommodate a group of students of whose arrival they were unaware. Trying to manage a catering budget is difficult enough in normal conditions – the price of a box of bananas can seriously upset how much has been budgeted for food. It is therefore essential that they are told when numbers requiring meals are less than normal in order that they can save on food. Weekend exeats are a good example of this. Although the savings to you might not appear much, they might be quite significant when spread over a year.

Links with outside agencies

At some time during your career in a boarding house, you are likely to have some dealings with an outside agency of one sort or another. If you are unsure about speaking, for example, to the Social Services, then see your line manager and discuss the procedure. If you adopt the habit of documenting what measures have been taken when managing students – rewards, sanctions and so on – then you will find such communications easier, as you will have all the necessary information to hand.

You should clarify the school's policy for dealing with the police before you take up your appointment. When such an issue arises, events will run their course very swiftly, and you cannot afford to spend time checking what you have to do. If you have to contact the police then let your line manager know immediately.

Situations in which you and students have to be interviewed by the police can be worrying and emotionally draining for all concerned. It is important that the house team reassures and provides a source of comfort for students and colleagues concerned.

Communication with families

Although it can be time consuming and at times exhausting, it is best to try to establish as open a relationship as you can with all parents in your house. You will find that it is easier to establish such a relationship with some than with others. Keep information flowing both ways and remember it is important to tell parents both good and bad things that have happened at school. Too often we fall into the trap of communicating only the bad, and only rarely do we celebrate successes.

It is always easier to pass a firecracker than to launch a rocket-propelled grenade. Small problems can build up and become more serious. If you have worked together with parents when a problem is small, then the bigger problems will not come like a bolt out of the blue.

Success with parents can be measured by how many keep in contact with you once their child has left school. Some parents might well become friends. There are, however, particular areas that are problematic. Where there is a split family, with bitterness between the two parties, then there is a possibility that one or other party might attempt to draw you into their conflict. Become a listener (as you will acquire useful information about the environment in which one of your students has to live), but don't take sides. As some parents become friends and you see them socially, be circumspect in what you say about your school and colleagues. Should the friendship turn sour for whatever reason, you do not want to have to defend yourself against unprofessionalism.

Parents can be generous, and it is always welcome to receive gifts of one form or another and, in Asian cultures, giving is a very important part in establishing and continuing a relationship with someone. Do make note of what you are given and, if necessary, tell your line manager. In today's litigious society, businesses have compliance officers who ensure that staff cannot be compromised as a result of gifts received. It makes sense to protect yourself.

Communications with your own families and partners

Remember that what you do is a job, and ensure that you protect yourself and those close to you from the vicissitudes of life in the house. It is all too easy to be very patient with someone whom you know might, for example, run away should you be harsh with them, and then at the same time snap at your own husband, wife, partner or child because they are close to you. Try not to let the mood of the house affect you at home and avoid, if you can, the deadly "I haven't got time" with your own children when you might be spending inordinate amounts of time with other people's children.

Your personal life will change over time, as well as your professional life. The average toddler might develop into an excellent player or performer whose needs, too, will have to be met. Your partner's attitude to work and to your work might change and thus add a different dimension. Steven Covey[47, 48], a management guru from the USA, has much to say about this issue, and sees personal development and refreshment very much as "sharpening the saw".

Working in a boarding house at any level is one of the most demanding jobs in education. Unless one has done it, one has very little idea of what it is like. It is also very rewarding. You are often saving young adults from themselves and helping them to reduce the number of times they might go round saying "If only I had . . ." in their future lives. Keep things in perspective. If things go wrong it will not, in most cases, be your fault; and remember to look after yourself and those around you.

References and Notes

47. Covey, S. (1989), *The Seven Habits of Highly Effective People*, Simon & Schuster.

48. Covey, S. *et. al.* (1994), *First Things First*, Simon & Schuster.

CHAPTER

11

Coping with Policies and Procedures

Tim Holgate

Developing documentation and staff guidance

It is a fact of life that hard-pressed and busy boarding staff can sometimes regard policy statements and other written documentation as a tiresome nuisance, to be consigned to the filing cabinet once completed and resurrected when the inspector calls. However, a properly considered and well-understood procedure can save time and perhaps even lives in an emergency, and a well-constructed policy can help significantly to ensure a smooth-running boarding house.

It is recognised that policies and procedures are usually written:

❖ to ensure clarity of information and purpose;

❖ to ensure consistency where needed between staff within a house, and between different houses;

❖ to enable welfare provision and standards to be monitored, evaluated and reviewed at regular intervals;

* to ensure that staff can be guided towards an appropriate response to the many situations they face;

* to narrow the range of different interpretations and responses made by staff.

They can also help to translate aims and objectives into actions, and assist in the induction of new staff. Modern boarding schools not only need to achieve the highest standards of welfare and care, but also to be seen to have the structures and procedures for maintaining them.

Documentation and policies are likely to be of three types:

* **Policy statements,** requiring specific action to be followed as and when necessary (*e.g.* child protection policy);

* **Statements of principle,** which may be relatively short (*e.g.* an equal opportunities statement);

* **Guidance to staff,** to provide a framework for action (*e.g.* dealing with home-sickness, confidentiality issues), or to guide staff through the unexpected (management of crises). Policy statements will often have appropriate staff guidance associated with them.

The documentation provided for a boarding house will inevitably include many whole-school policies and procedures, but will also contain aspects which are unique and special for the house. Some aspects of this written guidance are likely to be related to staff needs, others to pupils' needs, and some to both.

Most schools publish a specific boarding handbook and, in larger boarding schools, individual house handbooks, enabling the different style and 'flavour' of each house to be expressed. Such a handbook may be primarily aimed at staff, but may also contain sections for use by pupils, or versions for the information of both pupils and parents. In some schools, separate handbooks are provided for boarders, often written with a lighter touch for younger pupils, perhaps suitably illustrated. Some schools state clearly the expectations that a pupil or parent should have of the school, and the expectations that the house/school should have of its parents and pupils. For example, it may be appropriate to state that parents can expect the house to look into and deal promptly with any concerns and complaints, and that the boarding staff should expect parents to inform them of any illness suffered during the school holidays.

Whatever its style or tone, an induction handbook for new boarders and their parents is likely to be the first communication the new family will receive from the prospective housemistress or housemaster and, together with a covering letter (perhaps from matron, too), can greatly help to allay the anxieties and worries (of both pupils and parents) for the first-time boarder. The pupil/parent version of the boarding house handbook will reassure, provide basic information and set out clearly the tone and 'feel' of the house community which the pupil is about to join.

There is, obviously, no single format for a house handbook, and its content and the stress placed on its different items will be a matter of individual needs and preference, and related to the type of school and house involved.

A boarding handbook might contain:

❖ principles on which boarding is based;

❖ a statement of boarding aims;

❖ policy statements;

❖ boarding staff personnel, responsibilities and contact details;

❖ a map or plan showing the layout of the house;

❖ structure and organisation of the house;

❖ day-to-day organisation and routines, times and daily arrangements;

❖ domestic arrangements (medical, health, clothing);

❖ leave-out/absence arrangements;

❖ code of conduct/expectations of behaviour;

❖ rules, regulations, rewards/sanctions tariff;

❖ duties and responsibilities of boarders; the use of prefects and monitors;

❖ academic/homework arrangements, tutoring and support provision;

❖ complaints procedure (more often couched in terms like 'what to do if you have a problem'); details of contact with school counsellor, chaplain, independent listener, etc.;

- contact with home; mobile phones and e-mail;

- a policy statement on bullying and procedure for 'what to do if . . .'.

It is a matter for debate whether it is appropriate to include complete policies and statements on major whole-school areas such as child protection and countering bullying. In any case, these two policies are likely to appear in school in two versions – one appropriate for staff, in terms of awareness, identification, responding to concerns; and one written for pupils, setting out their rights and expectations, and how to respond if they, or someone they know, are being treated badly.

In developing and reviewing their child protection procedures, schools and houses will need to study the latest government guidance[49].

At this point, it is worth stressing how important it is that all boarding staff are familiar with the agreed procedures, and aware of their roles in responding to possible child protection and bullying situations. This should include non-teaching staff, domestic staff and Gap students, all of whom are in positions where they are as likely (or even more so) to detect problems as the teaching house staff. Failure on the part of these important non-teaching staff to respond to a potential problem situation or, through ignorance, handling it inappropriately, could have tragic consequences for a troubled and unhappy child. (See Chapters 3 and 7.)

Such staff, therefore, need clear and sensitive guidance and training in understanding what to look out for and how to respond. A case can be made, at a suitable level, for enlisting the help of senior (secondary age) pupils and prefects as well. Such pupils will also need careful preparation and guidance for what to do if a pupil confides in them. A recent report of Her Majesty's Chief Inspector of Schools, and other welfare inspection evidence, highlight the fact that many junior staff in boarding schools do not clearly understand their roles and responsibilities in these two crucial areas.

The handbook for staff will probably include the suggested contents listed above, with amplification and explanation where necessary, in an enlarged boarding staff manual. Some of the guidance may be attached to key policy statements, such as countering bullying and child protection as mentioned; other items may not warrant a policy statement, but would be free-standing in order to help staff deal with issues that can arise. The involvement and support of boarding staff in drawing up these guidance statements is, in itself, an important part of the development of the boarding staff role.

Guidance provided to help the house staff team might include:

❖ child protection – guidance on how to respond to suspicion or allegation of abuse;

❖ reducing the occurrence of and reacting to bullying incidents or harassment;

❖ staff supervision arrangements/rotas/back-up cover;

❖ guidance on the school's position on one-to-one contact with pupils;

❖ handling confidential issues and disclosures; contact with medical staff;

❖ the security of the house and its occupants;

❖ health and safety arrangements and risk assessment;

❖ transport of pupils in private cars (staff, parents and pupils);

❖ reacting to unexpected incidents and crises.

Crisis management

This aspect of guidance is especially important for non-teaching staff, newly appointed staff and Gap students. It may depend on the age range and structure of the house, but it would be wise to have discussed and agreed the way in which staff should react in the event of unexpected situations or critical incidents.

Much has been written about crisis management, and there is a growing number of consultancy firms keen to provide a tailor-made policy and procedure for schools.

It must be acknowledged that spending time drawing up contingency plans for events that have not yet happened, and might never happen, is probably not a priority activity for many schools. Nevertheless, those schools which have had crisis response measures in place when the unthinkable has occurred have been grateful for their foresight and the time invested in drawing up reaction plans and allocating responsibilities in advance.

Many schools will possibly have procedures in place for those crises which are likely to have a major impact on the life and work of the school. On a smaller scale, many aspects of the measures in place will be relevant to individual boarding houses. It is obvious that one cannot start thinking about a range of possible responses when quick action is needed in an emergency. The strengths and talents of individual staff members need to be recognised and utilised early on. Channels of communication, between staff, between staff and pupils, and between house and parents need to be established in advance. (And, incidentally, the mechanism by which British Telecom can quickly install additional telephone lines – perhaps dedicating one for out-going calls only – needs to be explored in advance of need.) Prevention methods and pre-planning of responses are clearly better than reaction after the event, and much of the staff guidance listed earlier can go some way to anticipating possible problems in advance. The school may well have already explored, for example, the provision of additional counselling and support help in the event of a tragedy affecting large numbers of pupils, and it will certainly have thought about the issue of dealing with the press. It is highly likely, in a crisis situation affecting a boarding house, especially if the incident is news-worthy, that the press will contact the house directly, and whoever happens to be on duty and answers the phone will not wish to regret a hasty remark made in the heat of the moment, or the equally damning "no comment".

It would be wise, then, to check on what school-wide contingency plans have been drawn up by the school. It should be quite feasible to adapt some aspects of these for generic crises affecting the house, in terms of:

- ❖ significant damage to the physical environment;

- ❖ a critical incident affecting pupils;

- ❖ disruption of (and return to) normal school operation.

For example, a burst water-main flooding an entire dormitory, a leaking gas main requiring evacuation of the entire house for 24 hours, a severe school minibus accident, or (as happened recently) the gutting of an entire boarding house by fire, are all scenarios which could be discussed in advance.

It would be helpful to have a set of building plans for the house. For older buildings, it may well have been brought up to date during a recent refurbishment or the installation of new fire alarm systems. It should be regularly kept up to date when, for example, dormitories are sub-divided, or new electrical circuits are installed. It should show all zoning of fire-alarm systems, the location of gas/water stop-cocks, electrical isolation switches and panels, break-glass fire-alarms, fire-extinguishers and central-heating isolation valves.

Critical incidents or traumatic experiences involving groups of pupils or individual children clearly need sensitive and sympathetic handling, and are likely to resolve themselves in a way not easily suited to generic contingency plans. Children and young people will react to family bereavement, a fatal or major accident involving a friend or loved one, contact with violence or a major accident in many different ways. Communication between boarding staff and teaching staff is vital, and psychological reaction to shock will happen after varying lengths of time. Changes in a pupil's behaviour, emotional stability and relationships with others, and a disinclination or inability to discuss feelings, may need to be tolerated and treated with understanding. The traditional need for treating difficult pupils firmly and consistently may need to be waived in favour of helping the rehabilitation of a child experiencing crisis. Classroom and academic performance may well be affected adversely.

The reaction to and handling of a crisis occurring during a school outing or expedition, especially one overseas, will obviously be affected by separation from the school's administrative machinery, geographical isolation, time differences and limited availability of back-up staff. Planning for a school expedition and the need for risk assessment and for anticipating worst-case scenarios are dealt with in Chapter 9. Guidance on planning of expeditions is available from DfEE[50] and ATL[51].

Here, then, is a checklist of some possible areas to be clarified in setting up the framework for handling major incidents effectively:

* obtaining accurate information and briefing key staff as an immediate response;

* making notes and keeping records for a possible subsequent enquiry;

* ensuring telephone access for out-going calls;

* procedures for handling the press and limiting potential media damage;

* ensuring that communication to anxious parents provides accurate information; dealing with genuine enquirers;

* keeping concerned and worried pupils in the picture;

* ensuring that normal school routine is preserved as far as possible;

* providing professional support for pupils and staff affected by a traumatic event;

- ❖ ensuring that any computer-held house records are regularly backed up;

- ❖ establishing what emergency overnight accommodation arrangements the school may have in place (*e.g.* members of staff, other boarding houses, local bed and breakfast, classroom blocks).

Once normal routine appears to have been re-established, there is still a need for certain staff to continue the response strategy. The necessary de-briefing after a crisis or major incident will, no doubt, pinpoint possible causes and contributory factors to the event, as well as any failures on the part of the school or house to respond in expected ways. Such information should be evaluated and used to influence the preparation and response plans for a future event. This evaluation may highlight deficiencies in existing procedures or failures of the physical environment, and these should be remedied. Finally, we need to ensure that the impact of the incident on those affected (both pupils and staff) is monitored long after normal life has been resumed.

The re-integration back into normal school routine of those affected by a traumatic event is particularly important, especially if the person concerned has been absent for some time. This is crucial for resident boarding staff involved, who may carry a heavy physical and emotional burden at the best of times. Support and understanding from the whole house community is vital.

One clearly cannot legislate or plan for each and every crisis or unexpected incident, especially minor events, but house parents will probably find it worthwhile considering how they would wish their house staff teams (again not forgetting matrons and Gap students) to react and respond to various kinds of situation. It should not be overlooked that crises often have a habit of occurring when the housemaster or housemistress is off duty or away from school!

How, then, would your house staff react to the following?

- ❖ fire/emergency evacuation;

- ❖ intruders in the house;

- ❖ severe accident or injury to pupils;

- ❖ a steadily worsening flu epidemic;

- ❖ a meningitis scare;

- missing pupils;

- parental custody disputes;

- request for access to a pupil by an unexpected adult;

- minibus breakdown or accident during a trip or outing;

- major theft;

- dealing with outside agencies (*e.g.* police, press);

- bereavement;

- irate or threatening parents;

- suspicion or evidence of drug taking or sexual misconduct.

Whether or not the house and school have specific written documentation on the above areas, it is clearly good practice for all staff, experienced and inexperienced, new and old, to have discussed their implications, and to be quite clear about their responsibilities and the necessary action to be taken.

Particularly important is the need for staff to be clear about who to contact and how, in the event of an emergency. Let us take the case of John or Mary, aged 22 and straight from college, relatively new to boarding and on their first full night on duty in a new school. It is nearly midnight, and the housemaster or housemistress has been badly delayed by severe weather from returning from a rare and well-deserved evening out. A crisis occurs – say a nocturnal break-in or intruder, a gas leak, or a pupil needing to be taken to hospital.

- Are the contact numbers for senior staff, any school estate staff on call, the emergency numbers for gas, plumbers and electricity quickly to hand? When were they last updated?

- Has John or Mary been briefed on whether to call the head or deputy head if needed? Has the head indicated those situations when he or she would expect to be notified immediately?

- Does John or Mary know how to get back-up cover in order to take a pupil to hospital?

❖ If needed, do they know how to get access to details of parents/guardians or next of kin for a pupil in your absence?

It is impossible to have policies and written procedures for every eventuality. Ultimately, a good deal depends on the vigilance, initiative and common sense of the house staff. Obviously, the more they are involved in sharing responsibility for the day-to-day well-being of the boarders, the more they are likely to get things right. In the final reckoning, if things went badly wrong, could you say, with the advantage of hindsight, that you and your team had made provision for everything that was reasonably foreseeable?

References and Notes

49. Department of Health (1999), *Working Together to Safeguard Children*, The Stationery Office.

50. Department for Education and Employment (1998), *Health and Safety of Pupils on Educational Visits*, The Stationery Office.

51. Association of Teachers and Lecturers (2000), *Taking Students Off-site*.

CHAPTER

12

Leadership and Management of Senior Pupils

Angus McPhail

When I was appointed a housemaster, my father gave me a copy of Ian Hay's masterpiece ***The Lighter Side of School Life***[52], published in 1912. The picture it painted of prefects and their peers was one familiar to my experience of boarding in the early '70s. At the beginning of the chapter entitled 'Boys', Jackson says farewell to his housemaster at the end of the summer term. They shake hands and the housemaster, almost as an afterthought, says "*. . . by the way, I shall want you to join the prefects next year*". There follows a brief homily, and a request to "*. . . get accustomed to the idea in the holidays*", and Jackson returns to his study mate Blake, only to discover that he has not been favoured with a similar invitation. Blake is polite in his congratulations, but there follows "*. . . an unhappy silence*", and he leaves "*. . . to join the proletariat round the Hall fire. The worst of getting up in the world is that you have to leave so many comrades behind you. And worse still, the comrades frequently persist in believing that you are glad to do so*".

In Hay's day – not greatly different in the early '70s – prefects were crucial in providing free help (we now look for cheap help from Gap students) in the running of the school, and they were given power and privilege – character forming – that went beyond anything teaching staff enjoy nowadays. Their role has changed hugely in the last 30 years and the reasons for this are legion. John Rae comments that "... *sometime in the 1960s and 1970s school prefects threw their hand in*[53]", and there is no doubt that the greater questioning of authority, suspicion about hierarchy and belief in individuality present in the '80s and '90s has made senior boys and girls uncomfortable about the traditional role. The spread of coeducation has also played a part, because girls have challenged the views of senior boys and male staff, and the pressure of exams has led them – often supported by their parents – to consider the opportunity cost of unpaid duties.

Schools have had to respond to these changes and have, inevitably, become more defensive when faced by health, safety and welfare concerns and the pressures of litigious parents and alert media.

A greater focus on co-operation, consideration and consultation has resulted but, at the same time, the championing of entrepreneurship and leadership that has characterised the last two decades has led schools to consider how best to train these skills, often outwith the prefectorial system. It is against this shifting and increasingly demanding background that staff in boarding schools have had to consider how best to educate and manage their senior pupils. The sections that follow offer some thought about this.

Defining the role

With the possible exception of headship, positions of responsibility in boarding schools carry with them job descriptions, and there is a strong argument for giving all pupils with particular responsibilities a written statement of what they are expected to do. The principal danger of such an approach – that pupils will have too limited a view of their role – can be avoided, and there is great benefit in having a clear statement of objectives and responsibilities that can be revisited.

It is a truism that boys and girls like to know where they stand and a pupil given a particular role will be grateful for a list of routine duties he or she will be expected to perform. It should be stressed that such a list will evolve over time and it should be discussed prior to agreement. It is also beneficial to stress that **any** position of responsibility carries with it an expectation for the pupil concerned to set a good example. Anyone entrusted with responsibility should show:

❖ concern for the interests of other pupils;

❖ commitment towards and support for a broad range of school activities;

❖ good work habits;

❖ smart appearance;

❖ respect for school rules.

In the case of prefects, a job description will also concern their responsibility (along with staff) for good order in the school and an explanation of formal channels of communication and the use of sanctions. Such a job description can accompany a letter of appointment.

Selecting senior pupils for positions of responsibility

Most senior pupils want to be given responsibility, whether as a prefect or in some other post. Amongst Ian Hay's troop of sixth formers, there were different reasons for this: Hulkins relished the power and the ability to punish; Meakins hoped it would stop him being ragged and Flabb cherished the perks. The contemporary senior pupils cannot expect many perks, and are unlikely to have much power, but they do want to feel that staff believe they have something to contribute, and they do want to help to improve the school.

At Strathallan we asked all the new prefects why they had accepted the responsibility offered. They had little interest in being able to impose punishments and they also realised that it was not going to be a huge asset on the UCAS form. They were keen to help other pupils by listening to their problems and representing their concerns to staff, but they were not very interested in privileges. They recognised their importance in creating the right atmosphere, and were anxious about the possible confrontation and conflict of interest that the position would bring.

If the principal role of prefects is to be a channel of communication, there is a strong argument for not *selecting* prefects at all, as communication could be maximised by all senior pupils taking on the role. The principal arguments against such an approach arise when prefects are required also to help with the day-to-day running of the house and school, to encourage, cajole and if necessary put pressure on others to do things that do not appeal. Under such circumstances there are likely to be some who do not want the responsibility, some who would find it a miserable experience, and others who, through setting a poor example, would adversely affect the performance of the other prefects.

Pupils electing prefects is another option and, as long as you are willing to live with the choice, it has attractions. It may be that staff and pupils in their penultimate year constitute the electorate, or you may wish to have appointed prefects electing the school and house captain(s). You must judge how important democracy is, to what extent the school will be a happier and more productive place as a result and whether you can work well with those elected.

If you decide to select and appoint yourself, then you should have a clear idea what you want from those appointed, and you should consult with those who understand the demands of the job, notably staff and senior pupils currently in post. You should also be prepared for the questioning of your selection by pupils, staff and parents. If you are lucky, this will be explicit – a letter, or meeting – but it is just as likely to be indirect. I know of a headmaster's wife who, taking the dog for its regular morning walk, had been shunned by a friend whose son had not been made a prefect.

Whether you appoint or elect pupils to post, you will need to agree the duration of the responsibility, and the most obvious consideration here is whether the role continues during the final exam term. Parents are much more inclined to apply pressure about this nowadays, citing the possibly adverse effect the duties can have on the work of their son or daughter. It is, however, very difficult to have senior pupils who are recognised to be in a position of responsibility enjoying a sabbatical on site during their final term. It undermines the notion of responsibility in the school or house and can make the job of the heirs apparent very difficult. A compromise is a reduction in workload for those in their last term, but no early retirement or abdication!

The opportunities for responsibility go well beyond being a prefect. Boys and girls can learn much about the joys and difficulties associated with responsibility and leadership in many spheres. They can develop their interests and talents through positions of responsibility associated with, for example, games, societies, music, drama, the Duke of Edinburgh scheme, community service, combined cadet force, chapel and Scripture Union, social events, school tours, library, school council.

Some pupils unsuited to the demands of being a prefect may relish the challenge of organising, advertising, or recruiting for such activities. In doing so they will learn very useful skills and grow in confidence. Consideration should be given to the recognition of service in such areas, in the way that excellence in games is generally rewarded.

Training senior pupils to cope with responsibility

It is ironic that the curtailing of senior pupils' powers and responsibilities in the last decade has been accompanied by a mushrooming of training. It is understandable given the prudence (fear?) of schools faced by a plethora of health, safety and welfare regulations and increasingly litigious and unreasonable parents. It is not true that someone is unable to do a job unless they have been given specific training but, nonetheless, training – even for those who are 'naturals' – is a good thing.

All pupils given specific responsibilities should be clear about the abilities they will need to develop, but it is particularly important for prefects, whose impact within the house and across the school can be profound. Training should build confidence and a sense of teamwork, and focus on the need to use one's imagination. Prefects should aim to arrive at a shared set of objectives and may be helped by trying to draw up a list of do's and don'ts. Prefects who have punishments at their disposal should be led to think about suitable and consistent sanctions and they should be encouraged to discuss difficulties with peers and staff. There is no doubt that the consideration of case studies is beneficial and these should involve incidents involving peers, staff, junior pupils and parents.

There are many professional groups and companies who offer to run such training courses and it may be worth getting some to visit the school and discuss what they have done for other schools – check this with the schools themselves – and how they would tailor their programme to the particular circumstances of your school. Whether the decision is to use an external company or arrange training 'in house', there is much to commend working with groups that cross boarding house divisions. This can promote greater consistency and also dispel the often misplaced beliefs about differences between houses.

Good training will lead to closer co-operation with staff, a reinforcement of a positive atmosphere and a happier year. Consideration should be given to the training of all pupils as to the role of prefects. It is important that they understand the importance of prefects to the smooth running of the school and happiness of the community. All pupils should be aware of the powers that prefects have and the need to support them by acting on suitable and fair instructions. Last, but by no means least, parents should be given a statement of what prefects can and cannot do through the medium of house or school handbooks.

Monitoring and guiding performance

In **The Naughtiest Girl is a Monitor**, written by Enid Blyton in 1945, the central character, Elizabeth, is, much to her surprise, made a monitor. It is the sort of gamble most in managerial positions will have taken at some time in the hope that the sparkiness, energy and 'street cred' of an individual can be harnessed to their benefit and that of the community. Elizabeth makes some errors, but is eager to do well. Then something rather serious blows up and she is called to explain herself.

> *". . . Elizabeth, why did you think you could put these matters right yourself? . . . You should have come straight to us and let us deal with it."*

> *"Oh" said Elizabeth, surprised. "Oh I somehow thought that as a monitor I could settle things myself – and I thought it would be nice to put things right without worrying you."*

> *"Elizabeth you must learn to see the difference between big things and little things. . . ."*

Pupils placed in positions of responsibility need guidance and support. They will, despite this, get things wrong and it is unrealistic always to expect them to show mature judgement. This said, their performance will be measured against an ideal, informally and formally, by staff, parents and other pupils.

In monitoring and guiding senior pupils coping with responsibilities, the three key questions identified by HMIs involved in welfare inspections in Scotland may be useful. You should consider:

- ❖ **How are they doing?**

- ❖ **How do we know how they are doing?**

- ❖ **What are we going to do now we know?**

Informal assessment of performance will involve observation and discussion with junior pupils, staff, parents and the senior pupils themselves. Not everything has to be written down! More formal assessment may take place through regular meetings, through appraisal, or questionnaires. It may be helpful to consider the performance indicators provided by those who will inspect the school. Whilst you will want to talk to individuals, it is also helpful to get all those involved, together, to discuss their performance.

A review of performance after half-term in the autumn will allow those in positions of responsibility to consider their performance as a team. This will encourage boys and girls to air concerns in a detached way and strengthen the idea of working together. The difficulties will quickly be seen to be shared and an attempt can be made to develop greater consistency. I have found prefects in particular to be very honest in their assessment of strengths and weaknesses, and house staff – who should, I think, be present – can do much to suggest solutions.

Within houses, time needs to be put aside with senior pupils to listen to their views on how things are going and this may benefit from being an informal occasion. It will afford an opportunity to pass on concerns, or praise, expressed by junior pupils, staff or parents. This said, it is terribly important for all staff to congratulate and thank senior pupils for their work, where relevant – too often this is left to house staff.

From time to time problems will occur with senior pupils failing to fulfil their responsibilities and this must be followed up. It is good to go back to the statement of aims discussed with the pupil on appointment to highlight what has gone wrong. It may be that they have become uninterested, idle, inefficient or disloyal, or that they are breaking school rules. The severity of the situation will determine how best to deal with this and, in the case of prefects, there will be the question of whether they should remain in a privileged position. It is very unsettling when prefects are demoted, but retaining someone who does not want to work within the system can weaken the prefectorial body greatly.

Senior pupils' responsibilities and inspection

I do not believe that a school should design the way it gives responsibility to senior pupils simply in order to meet the performance indicators or boarding standards set out by those who will inspect the school, but it would be naive not to consider how your system will match up to the measures that will be applied.

Inevitably there are differences in the guidelines in England and Wales and in Scotland. In England and Wales, the National Boarding Standards (see Appendix 2) provides two standards (12 and 13) of particular relevance, the latter being designated as a core standard. Standard 12 calls on schools to provide formal opportunities for pupils to express their views on boarding provision and indicates that there should be evidence that these views are being taken into account.

Core Standard 13 says :

> *"Any prefect system (or equivalent) should give prefects (or equivalent) appropriate specific duties and responsibilities with adequate staff supervision and measures to counter possible abuses of the role."*

It goes on to list the expectations that inspectors will have with regard to selection, job description, training, supervision and monitoring, and stresses the need to provide opportunities for leadership and responsibility outside a prefectorial system.

In Scotland, the role of prefects is covered in several performance indicators listed in ***Improving the Care and Welfare of Residential Pupils***[54], namely 4.1, 4.2 and 5.1. Again there is a concern that pupils understand their role and the limitations to their power, and also a belief that responsibility should be available outside the prefectorial system. In Scotland, there is a more overt call on pupils in positions of responsibility to help new pupils settle in, to be sensitive to the needs of particular groups – those most at risk – and to combat prejudice and bullying.

Inspectors believe that senior pupils can play a key role in supporting and strengthening the ethos of the school. They are, however, very concerned about senior pupils being given unsuitable and unfettered powers – they should be '*appropriate . . . and specific*' – and they are suspicious of hierarchical systems that may inhibit or adversely affect the weaker members of the school. They want to see openness and expect senior pupils to support this.

Responsibilities in junior and preparatory schools

Giving pupils responsibilities in the years before senior school has in the past been seen as both assistance with the day-to-day running of the school and a part of the learning experience for the child. Today, children in their last years at preparatory or junior school are given responsibilities – *e.g.* being a prefect, taking a table at lunch, showing parents round, captaining a side – to give them experience of the demands involved. Discipline is no longer the remit and privileges have diminished, but there is much to be gained from allowing pupils at an early age to look after their juniors or to represent the school on formal occasions. (See Chapter 13.)

In schools where pupils are appointed prefects, this generally results from appointment by the head in consultation with other staff, but there are instances of pupils voting. Training is of benefit for those given responsibility and it is worth considering offering this training to all pupils in their penultimate year, as outlined by A. J. P. Nott in his article for **Prep School**[55]. This serves the dual purpose of identifying those best able to cope with the role and providing training for all senior pupils, be they prefects or not.

Responsibility and risk

There is no doubt that the concern with apportioning blame and avoiding mistakes that affects much in education and other walks of life has meant that schools are increasingly concerned about pupils making mistakes, and increasingly wary about allocating duties. This shows itself in fewer powers and responsibilities and more checks and balances. Staff – 'they are paid to do it' – are asked to do more and more, and a challenge for the next decade will be to reverse this trend. I hope that boys and girls will be given more opportunities to experience genuine responsibility in the future. In most cases this will not be a preparation for tomorrow's leaders, but rather the development of social conscience and a sense of duty. Ian Hay thought that the country had been well served by schools who prepared pupils to be "*. . . conscientious, generally efficient and never, never tyrannical or corrupt*" and, 90 years on, we could do worse than establish similar objectives for the management of our senior pupils.

References and Notes

52. Hay, Ian (1914), **The Lighter Side of School Life**, T. N. Foulis.

53. Rae, John (1998), **Letters to Parents**, Harper Collins.

54. Scottish Office (1998), **Improving the Care and Welfare of Residential Pupils**.

55. Nott, AJP, 'How to make sure you have the perfect prefects' in **Prep School**, No. 38 (2000).

Preparatory School Issues
Peter Dix

Introduction and background

What fun I have trumping the horror stories of my friends as we sit around the dinner table recalling our early days boarding at prep. school! I have the advantage of having been 'sent away' to school in the 1950s in South Africa – a time and a place when any hint of gentleness to children was the first step on the slippery slope to Communism or, at the very least, the unthinkable prospects of democratic government and the introduction of television. No – men had to be men, and preparatory school was where the toughening up really began. Dormitories were uncomfortable and furnishings sparse; matrons breathed fire and brandished razor-sharp claws, and any contact with home was frowned upon as a serious threat to the boot-camp regime that was in operation. In fact, in all things, the purpose was to get as far away from the comforts of home, both physical and emotional, as was humanly possible. With this went, of course, the received wisdom that you got the best out of children in their work and in their conduct by dint of threat, rules and plenty of punishment. As a result, generations of children had the message communicated to them, at the most formative time of their lives, that you worked hard to avoid being kept in during break and behaved well to avoid the lash of the headmaster's cane.

In Britain, too, the boarding experience was meant to be uncomfortable. Boys had to become men quickly and harshly, and girls had to become wives and mothers who were strong and resourceful. After all, there was an Empire to govern and to defend. Or was there? Almost overnight the world map lost its smear of pink and the boarding school premise was drastically changed. Some schools moved more quickly than others but, long before the Children Act of 1989, which presupposed the continuing existence of Dotheboys Hall, most boarding schools in Britain had recognised that children no longer needed cruelty and hardship to prepare them for life, and that parents no longer expected it nor wanted it. A fundamental revolution had taken place which changed completely the nature and purpose of boarding. Pastoral Care became the watchword: "comfortable, cosy, cosseted" were the epithets that characterised the boarding schools of the '80s and '90s, and with recession sharpening the scrutiny of prospective parents, schools began to compete in lushness of carpet and luxury of facility.

Modern boarding

Today, as we settle into a new century, we find 'modern boarding' very much the key phrase in every prospectus and, with the advent of the National Boarding Standards, a new inspectorate and BSA training courses in full swing, it seems the old notion that discomfort and hardship are somehow good for children has finally been put to the sword – and not before time. The whole rationale of boarding has turned through 180 degrees. The aim now is to get as close as we can to the model of really good home life: to provide children with comfortable accommodation in which they can relax, feel genuinely contented and happy, and even look forward to coming back to school! If we add in the advantages of developing in children a degree of independence as well as consideration for the well-being of the others with whom they are sharing living space, the benefits of the extended day, and also the fun of a 'sleepover' every night, we have something which can be extremely attractive to families, especially children.

We should be driven hard by the idea of a 'home from home' for young children, not just as something to tell prospective parents or to add warmth to the prospectus, but as something that characterises everything about the boarding environment. This is a home to the children for long periods at a time, and it must be comfortable just as it must be fun. After supper it will be time for showers, teeth and general romp, and then, half an hour before 'lights out' perhaps, the overhead light goes off and the children read by their own bedside lamp. If they feel sleepy early, they can turn it out and drift off . . . just as they do at home. Despite what one still hears from some about children not noticing or not minding about scruffy dormitories, uncomfortable beds, cold showers and peeling paint, give them something as close as possible to what they have at home, and then sit back and listen . . . both to them and their parents! And please do not believe those who tell you that children will only wreck a nicely appointed boarding house. Give children a barrack room and they will respond accordingly – give them something like their own homes, and they will treat it with respect and even pride.

The new preparatory school boarder

Nevertheless, these children will still be living away from their own homes and families for some of the year, and there is bound to be some homesickness for all but the most resilient. It is crucial, therefore, that before young children start boarding both they and their parents are prepared.

Here are some ideas on what you might say to parents:

❖ You should be reassured that you have chosen the best and that your children will have a wonderfully rewarding and fulfilling time at this school. To help achieve this it is vital that school and parents communicate, trust each other and work as a team.

❖ Make sure you have talked through with your children why they are going to boarding school. Play down any reasons which are to do with parental convenience, unless they are very good ones, and explain that the experience will be a happy one but also one that "could take a little getting used to". (This is a key phrase!)

❖ There is a good chance that all children will be homesick at some stage – not necessarily during the first few weeks – so try to explain how they might feel. Explain that this is nothing to be ashamed of and that we have all been there at some stage in our lives. It is also a good idea to try to arrange some 'sleepovers' with friends during the summer holidays.

❖ You must not tell your children that they can leave if they are unhappy, (even though you, of course, retain the right to withdraw the child if things do go wrong). Not only is this negative, but they will bring it up the very next time they are feeling a bit low.

❖ Make a plan with them before you come to school next term as to when you will first take them out . . . and then stick to it, for it is all-important that the children feel they can trust you in such things. Get them a diary and write it down for them, as they can become confused with dates.

❖ You should also provide them with an address-cum-telephone book. This is very important.

❖ Let them bring lots of teddies and cuddly toys, and during the holidays help them make a collage of their favourite photos of family and pets. It is not wise to do this at the last minute, as it can cause the child to panic that time is running out. Likewise with packing the trunk: do this together so they can see how to do it, perhaps a week or so before the beginning of term. Make a game of it. Perhaps you may want to hide a little surprise in a package for them to find when they unpack but, please, not tuck!

❖ . . . and, speaking of tuck . . . we, like most preparatory boarding schools, recognise that allowing children to bring in tuck is an invitation to litter, theft, tooth-decay, vermin and meals not eaten! It is also invidious that weekly boarders and day children should be able to bring in quantities supplied by parents whereas the full boarders are denied the same. The school tuck shop should be the only source and at certain times. Please co-operate with the school on this and do not smuggle sweets in or sew them into teddies or the linings of dressing gowns. Yes – it happens! We know you want to make it easier when you bring your children back from exeat but, if you conspire with the children against the school in this way now, will you be tucking cans of beer into their overnight bags in a few years' time when they are at senior school? Don't undermine the staff – be part of the team.

❖ It is important that you do what you can to help the children feel confident about some of the new things they will be expected to do on arrival, and so make sure that your son knows how to tie his tie, your daughter knows how to do her hair in the style she is used to, and that they can tie their shoelaces and clean their shoes, brush their teeth properly, put on and take off a duvet cover, carry a tray with food and a drink on it, and take meat off a chop or chicken bone.

- Make sure you have acquired everything that is on the clothes and equipment list, and then help the children become familiar with their new school uniform. Have a practice run so it is not so daunting when they put it on to come here on their first day.

- Please warn your children about nits. Schools do their very best over this, and every child should be checked weekly. It is not a stigma and they must not be embarrassed. Assure your children that regular brushing and combing minimises the risk of catching nits and then keeps them nit-free. (You may want to mention that most doctors advise against the effectiveness, and even safety, of the lotions.)

- Please name everything, including CDs, books, toys and teddies. Boots and shoes are particularly vulnerable to loss when they are not named. (The stick-on insole type for shoes is excellent). Please name all sports clothes on the outside. This not only helps the staff learn names quickly, it also helps them identify children not wearing their own clothes.

- Stick to the school's deadline for departure, say your goodbyes and then go as swiftly as you can. Have some hankies handy, as you have the hardest part. The school will ring you during the first 48 hours and, if you can bear to wait to hear, it makes it easier. But most of all, do not worry. They will be fine – the big tears will come when they have to leave us!

. . . and once they have started . . .

- Keep up the communication with your children. Plenty of fun cards and cheerful letters are great tonics, and make regular use of both fax and e-mail. Do not, however, let the convenience of e-mail bring to an end your letter-writing. Children love to receive a real letter in your own handwriting in a real envelope! There is also the telephone, but try to discourage the children from ringing just before bed-time and, if at all possible, try not to ring them on a Sunday evening – it is a time when they can be at their most wobbly.

- And speaking of telephones . . . every child likes to dump on Mummy – seldom on Daddy for some reason! – and then, having achieved the objectives of (*a*) cleansing the system, (*b*) getting oodles of concerned attention and (*c*) making Mummy feel guilty or whatever, the child puts down the phone and skips down the corridor to the waiting friends and another game of Murder in the Dark. Mummy puts the phone down and feels just awful. Most of them do it, so don't be too alarmed by it and, if the house staff tell you that this is happening, you should probably believe them!

❖ Children's easy access to telephones is, of course, something of a double-edged sword, and if you feel you are receiving too many calls, speak to the house staff and agree on a schedule which can then be sold to the child.

❖ Your children will always have someone they can talk to – their shadow, tutor, form teacher, houseparent, matron, dormitory captain, other children, head and spouse – so please encourage them to talk to us first. We are the people most likely to be able to sort out the little hiccups, which will undoubtedly seem major issues to them. The urge to call Mummy is strong, but you probably won't be able to help with the lost pen or trainer!

❖ Please tell the school if there is a problem at home with a relative, friend or pet. If the staff don't know, they cannot help or make allowances. Again, communication is the key word.

❖ Indeed, good communication between home and school is of vital importance all the way through the child's time at school in every area. So, too, is clarity of instruction: if the school calendar says boarders should return in 'best' uniform or by 7 p.m. or on the night before school starts, parents should adhere to this and help the children learn what is expected of them. If you encourage them to think that these things do not matter, you will find them becoming first confused and then selective themselves as to what rules they obey or not. Remember, we are in this together, so be part of the team!

Much of this (and the several other points specific to your school) you may want to put in a booklet, which you send out with joining instructions during the summer term prior to entry. You may also want to hold an 'Experience Day' during that term when you invite families due to join in September to spend a day with you acclimatising and starting the bonding process. The children find this especially helpful as it reduces much of the anxiety which accompanies the start of a new year at a new school. It may be worthwhile gathering all the parents together during this day and running through the sort of advice contained above and giving them the opportunity to ask the head questions.

He should give them all the reassurance he can muster: how cosy the children are in their dormitories and what fun they have at weekends; how well you attend to travel arrangements; how important healthy eating and good table manners are to you; how ready you are to listen to their concerns and how determined you are to get things right.

You do not want ever to over-sell and under-deliver. On the contrary, the head should be poised with his staff to exceed expectation and aim for what the marketing people call 'customer delight' rather than just 'customer satisfaction'. Always try to go the extra mile and get those contented parents telling their friends round the dinner table how happy their children are and what a wonderful school you have!

Responsibility

It is a well-worn truism that transfer from preparatory to senior school is all about sizes of fish and ponds. Fortunately, preparatory schools nowadays do not give senior pupils too much authority over younger ones nor encourage the sort of swagger that leads to nemesis on day one at the next school! Older pupils nevertheless benefit from a taste of responsibility when they reach the top of their preparatory schools, though I would not advocate giving a pupil any responsibility, the value of which you wish to retain, just because you think it will do him or her good. I believe these things should be earned and aspired to. Dormitory captaincy is the best example in the boarding context, but it is imperative that you explain very carefully to each captain exactly what is expected of her and how far her authority extends, just as one does in any school with the senior children in whom one is vesting responsibility and trust. The days of little Hitlers lording it over miserable dormites is, I hope in every boarding school, a thing of the past. Indeed, I suggest dormitory captains should have no punitive authority at all – they should refer naughty children, who will not do as the captain is requesting, to house staff.

Punishment of all sorts should be kept to a minimum and used only as a last resort. Treat children with affection and kindness, and they will respond to reasonable requests and behave in a civilised way – just as they do at home. The dormitory captains should, however, have pastoral responsibility, and it is in this that they can be of great benefit to younger children and learn a great deal both about leadership and themselves. Naturally, the captains will expect some sort of recognition and reward for what they are doing – the excitement of the appointment and novelty of the post will soon wear off – and the attentive houseparent will have the captains in regularly for hot chocolate and a team talk!

Independence and supervision

As the children grow older and become increasingly used to being away from home for some of their time, so they will generally become more independent and more adventurous. This is, of course, very much to be desired, but we must try to strike the proper balance between this and continuing supervision and attention to their welfare. Each school will have its own style and its own emphases. Both common sense and the law will provide guidance in most things, but we must remember that we are 'preparatory' schools and we bear a heavy weight of responsibility to equip our children for what lies ahead. If we err too much either side of the golden mean in this, we will be doing those children a disservice.

Show the children how to organise themselves. There will be significantly less sympathy shown them at their senior schools if they leave their books in the house, turn up late for things or forget to make their beds. The scale of the operation there is likely to be much larger and less centralised, with the scope for bewilderment and general shambles correspondingly greater. Let them also have genuine free time in which they can learn to prioritise and manage their time, and do not let them become over-dependent on adult assistance in all that they do. Show them how to amuse themselves without something being organised for them every second of the day. Can they sit for three-quarters of an hour with a book; are they in the habit of reading a newspaper; do they have hobbies which they can pursue without a member of staff fussing round them?

Adolescent culture

A new culture embraces boys and girls soon after they arrive at their senior schools, and some aspects of it give us all cause for concern. The occasional cigarette behind the bike shed and the can of beer swigged in the grounds by the sixth-former has given way to the 13-year-old swallowing half a bottle of vodka, the ever-increasing menace of drugs in schools and the culture of 'The Party'. Drink has sadly now become almost a rite of adolescent passage, and there can hardly be a teenager in the land who has not had illegal drugs at least within his grasp. A preparatory boarding school is, I suspect, the best environment for helping children develop the resources to deal with all this – there are no drug peddlers at the school gates and far fewer social opportunities for experimentation of this kind. We should take full advantage of this shield and try to ensure that our children emerge into adolescence reasonably well equipped. Some schools use scare tactics and bring in police and ex-drug addicts to frighten the children. I am not so sure about this and feel we should rather be concentrating on promoting decision-making skills in PSE classes and teaching the children how to say "no" to any number of temptations and insidious influences.

Pastoral care policy

PSE classes are, of course, just one element in your overall policy on pastoral care. I am sure you will have a detailed document in your school dealing with all topics of children's physical and emotional welfare, and offering the staff guidance on such things as child protection procedures, physical contact with children and counselling. I suspect, however, that all pastoral policy documents will be revised in the light of the National Boarding Standards, and it would be wise for all boarding staff to be expected to read the NBS document and have a copy of the school's pastoral care policy close to hand at all times.

Weekends and evenings

The success of preparatory school boarding depends to a large extent on what happens at weekends. With a large boarding population, some can afford to offer flexible arrangements at weekends (with no restrictions on exeats) and still be assured of good numbers in every weekend. Others may not enjoy this luxury, but the weekend programme either way is of huge importance. Gap year students can contribute substantially to the weekend activities. Here for just one year, their enthusiasm is boundless (but they, like other staff, must be chosen with the greatest of care). Ponder the fact that you get six Gaps for the price of one full-time member of staff, but be ready to offer them accommodation and provide them with responsible supervision and support.

Be aware, though, that weekday evenings are also of vital importance. You should have a really worthwhile and varied hobby programme in the evenings to supplement whatever you are doing about 'prep', for this is a crucial part of the boarding 'value added' and without it you will have children wandering about on dark winter's evenings starting to feel homesick – and then phoning their parents.

Staff

The most important element in the success or otherwise of a boarding school is the staff. Obviously they must be responsible, kind, fun and caring (in any order you like) and they will ensure a 'homelike' atmosphere and approach. There must also be enough of them to guarantee that the children are treated with all the care and time that they need: birthday tables organised and cards presented, hair washed and nails cut, shoes cleaned and lost clothing found, stories read and games played. They must also have the time to talk with the children: to talk about their day, their sport, their music, their successes and their failures. They have a tremendously important role in helping these children develop motivation and self-esteem and in shaping their attitudes to learning and to life in general.

Boarding in the new millennium

Running a boarding school is not easy. We do not say goodbye to the children and their myriad problems and needs each afternoon – we have an extraordinary and wonderful responsibility. In our boarding schools the role of the house staff is pivotal, crucial to the well-being of the children and of the schools themselves. Boarding will continue to be an extremely attractive option to thousands and thousands of families for the foreseeable future, and it is we who are entrusted with the responsibility of ensuring that we continue to provide those children with the very best care and guidance that we have at our disposal, and the very finest education, in the fullest sense of that word, that is available to any children anywhere in the world. I am hugely confident.

CHAPTER

14

The Needs of Overseas Students
Philip Hardaker

The changing scene

As independent boarding schools move into the new millennium and establishments take on a more global perspective, the number of students from abroad whose first language is not English will continue to increase. No longer will a few international students be assimilated into a school's culture by a simple mix of initial care and attention. Neither can the emphasis be placed on developing a knowledge of British culture in general, and boarding school culture in particular, by the students simply "being there long enough to understand". A more structured and far-reaching system needs to be developed to ensure that students from abroad not only survive but also thrive in the modern boarding school environment. Both inside and outside the classroom situation it is of prime importance that schools raise the awareness of the academic, cultural and linguistic problems faced by overseas students and are well-equipped at all levels to deal with them.

Tony Hubbard – the first Director of the unified Independent Schools' Inspectorate – recently commented: *"rarely do ISC (Independent Schools' Council) schools fall below the minimum standards of instruction, but one or two do, and a few more sail very close to the wind in what they provide for minority groups such as pupils from overseas"*.

This comment clearly indicates that the question of quality provision for international students has been raised at Inspectorate level. The fear of failing an element of an inspection, however, should not be seen as the driving force in dealing with this issue. Schools need to adopt a genuine desire to embrace fully the exciting challenge of integrating students from all over the globe into their schools, to allow them to experience our society, to perform well academically and socially, and yet retain the values, beliefs and customs from their own cultures. Indeed, the enlightened school will see the full integration of overseas students as a symbiotic relationship, a marvellous opportunity for the school to be enriched by a full understanding of other cultures, and in particular the values of students from other parts of the world.

Culture – what do we mean?

A much-used – indeed much over-used – word but what exactly does 'culture' mean? The following definition implies that the problems of moving from one culture to another are as much related to the individual as to the main elements of the culture itself.

Culture "... *has many definitions as well as being an all-inclusive term. It takes into account values, beliefs, norms, rationalisations and symbols*" (Pederson, 1991). In education, we must extend our perception of cultural problems to include previous classroom experience in the student's homeland and objectively compare this with classroom experience in the UK. We must remember that a unique mix of expected standards, norms and learning techniques exists in any school, whether in the UK or abroad.

I hesitate before considering the next related phrase. Although 'culture shock' should be acknowledged and dealt with sympathetically, effectively and positively, it must not be allowed to lead a school into a state of inertia (particularly if we accept that culture is as much an individual concept as that of a group) where there seems to be so many problems that the whole process becomes too daunting, and no clear procedures can be drawn up.

Culture Shock "... *is the phrase often used to describe the feelings of confusion on encountering a new and unfamiliar cultural experience*[56]". There are, however, varying levels of adjustment to be made to such confusion by individuals. Adjustment, both in terms of its effect and its speed, is connected not only to the student's personality and determination but also to how far removed the student is from the British culture.

This chapter cannot, therefore, simply provide a prescriptive list of 'off-the-peg' solutions but will, hopefully, raise awareness and provide pointers to the way forward for schools, as living institutions dealing with international students as individuals.

As stated above, it is important to realise that both culture shock and cultural differences occur not only in the boarding house but also in the classroom.

A student writes:

> *"In the Chinese culture, youngsters have to show respect for elders, obeying parents at home and listening to teachers at school. We usually have to render a salute to teachers and call them "teacher" in Chinese. However, instead of doing so to the teachers here, students simply say "hello" and smile at them. I remember there was once a Taiwanese guy in my ESL class who had a question to ask. He tried to catch the teacher's attention and, as respectfully as he could, called out "teacher". Unfortunately she did not realise that someone was calling her and continued writing on the whiteboard. At that time, I thought it funny and wondered why she would rather respond to someone calling her by her last name, which was an impolite way of calling a teacher in the Chinese culture. It made me dare not call any teacher for a whole semester. Needless to say, I thought I was an impolite student during that period of time[57]."*

The implications of a student not asking for help for a whole term are obvious and provide a clear example of the problems teachers face when attempting to integrate international students into the classroom learning experience.

Student difficulties

Having outlined the increasing importance of full integration of international students into British boarding school life, I would now like to reflect on practical considerations. Again, I must emphasise that neither the list nor, where applicable, suggested approaches to dealing with cultural issues are either fool-proof or prescriptive. Each school must carefully consider its own issues and act accordingly. The list below is also in no particular order of priority.

❖ **Climate**

The British climate could be either significantly warmer or cooler than that experienced in the student's own country.

❖ **Dress**

Some students will come from countries where uniform is the expected norm; others come from countries where there is no school uniform.

❖ **Food**

The British cuisine (and its perceived fascination with the potato) will not match 'mum's cooking', no matter where home happens to be!

❖ **Jet-lag**

This is often forgotten in the hurly-burly of the first few days of term. Remember that first impressions are significant – allow the students to settle, both academically and socially before making any initial judgements. Allow time for their ears to tune in to the English language and avoid too much testing in the first few days.

❖ **Language**

This is, invariably, one of the most crucial issues to address. Problems can be both academic (not understanding the lessons) and social (not making friends from other nationalities using the medium of English, and therefore gravitating towards students from their own country or those speaking the same language).

❖ **Non-verbal communication**

Different cultures will adopt different rules relating to eye contact, touching and general posture.

❖ **Homesickness**

This problem may continue well beyond the first few days of term and could be well hidden from adults and peer group alike. Schools should not assume it is a problem confined to younger students.

❖ **Study methods**

These differ from country to country – from those which expect students to display a passive role in the classroom, to those at the opposite end of the spectrum – and students could experience difficulty, not only in the classroom but also in any learning situation such as homework or coursework.

❖ **Status**

Students may experience difficulty as they leave one peer group at home, where they are invariably respected and well liked, and are then placed in another with students who may have been together for several years. The latter could, at worst, treat the international students with caution, even disdain, because they are perceived to be 'different'.

❖ **Religion**

This is an obvious area of concern for students, particularly in schools with traditional Christian beliefs and regular chapel services.

School difficulties

The cynics amongst us may comment that the above list provides sufficient 'problems' for a school to deal with but it would, nevertheless, be beneficial to consider the issues that more directly face schools when accepting overseas students:

❖ **Language**

Problems arise for the school, both inside and outside the classroom. Textbooks may be appropriate for all except those for whom English is not their first language. The level of the language used by the teacher may likewise not be appropriate to the teaching of overseas students. If students are removed from lessons to obtain EFL provision, are schools literally creating a secondary problem in relation to work missed in other subjects? In the house, how much do students understand? Are they able to write up their preparation and homework tasks without extra supervision? Is a lack of language isolating the student in the house? These are all issues a school must address.

❖ **Prior knowledge of the British system**

Many students, and particularly parents, although aware of the quality of the British independent education system, are equally unaware of both the academic system and boarding school requirements and philosophies that are central to an understanding of school life in Britain. This can cause problems both on arrival and at various stages throughout the student's time at the school.

❖ **Teaching methods**

Most boarding school teachers have little or no formal training in EFL and there are undoubtedly significant differences in the teaching style and pace required in teaching most overseas students. As a 'stand alone' problem, this should give rise for concern, but it is further compounded by the usual scenario of overseas students being asked to thrive (or survive) in the same classroom as native English speakers. It is often said that all teachers, irrespective of their subject discipline, are teachers of English. Nowhere is this more true than when dealing with overseas pupils.

❖ **Religious services**

A serious consideration for all independent boarding schools which insist on compulsory services. Schools must ask themselves whether it is acceptable to ask non-Christians to attend regular Christian services. Even if a school feels that it is an important part of the students' development, irrespective of their own spiritual background, to experience the religions of others, how much will an overseas student gain from hymns and prayers which are invariably couched in archaic English? Does a school open the gate to church absence for all its congregation if it makes an exception for its non-Christian populace? Should alternative arrangements be made, and should these be made compulsory?

❖ **Contact**

Even in a rapidly advancing technological society, where methods of communication seem to shrink the globe, the question of who to contact remains. It is frequently difficult to convince overseas parents of the need for a UK-based guardian and yet, because of the distance of this particular group of students from their parents, one could argue, and probably would, that their need is the greatest. Similarly, too frequently the 'paper guardian' is either non-existent, frequently abroad or little older than the student himself! This problem often only materialises when a school needs to contact a guardian quickly, for example, if a student has been injured or is in trouble. Contact with parents can also be a problem, as schools too often wrongly assume that parents speak fluent English and are able to understand reports and other important documents sent to them.

❖ **Travel and exeats**

Boarding schools must decide how far they are prepared to bend the rules over term dates, as many parents and guardians will book tickets for their children or wards to fly into and out of the UK on days which do not correspond to the beginning and end of term. Students are therefore liable to miss lessons and this, in turn, can cause class disruption. Similarly, the problem of where to send students on exeat weekends, particularly closed exeat weekends, is a very real one for housemasters and housemistresses to solve if the student does not have a genuine guardian. It may also be necessary, as the number of international students increases, for a school to consider the need for a travel office, as flights need to be organised up to twelve times a year. Schools must also take measures to ensure that important faxes and e-mails relating to travel can be dealt with outside office hours, as time differences will inevitably lead to such situations occurring. It is worth remembering, for example, that most of the Islamic world does not work on Thursday and Friday, but parents from that part of the globe may well wish to contact the school on Saturday and Sunday.

❖ **Medical information**

School medical forms can often be difficult enough for UK-based parents to fill in and are frequently too daunting for parents who send their son or daughter vast distances to be at a UK boarding school. Linguistically, they can be rendered of no value whatsoever and, even worse, can be misinterpreted so when returned they convey incorrect medical information to the school sanatorium – if they are returned at all. Schools must evaluate the risk they run in not possessing correct medical information on students from overseas.

❖ **Academic information**

A similar problem relates to the quality and quantity of academic information received from both schools abroad and the parents of the student about to enter the school. Often, school reports are badly translated into English at source or are presented in the native language which the school concerned may find difficult to translate. Entrance papers sent abroad to be taken by hopeful applicants (or their friends!) are notoriously bad indicators of ability.

❖ **Time**

All the issues raised above, and some of the suggestions that will be considered below, depend to a large degree on the school having sufficient time and manpower to deal with them effectively. Schools must not start to put in place procedures and systems that are flawed, incomplete or merely fade away as other important areas of school life are given priority.

Coeducational schools need also need to consider the difficulties of placing students from certain cultures into classes containing students of the opposite sex. Indeed, some students, and more particularly their parents, may even have problems with a coeducational teaching staff!

It is also worth being aware of what I would call 'the age trap'. Whilst we can now, more than ever, due to the National Curriculum, assume that UK students will have acquired certain skills and a body of knowledge at a particular age, these assumptions cannot necessarily be extended to include international students. Such students may be either in advance of or behind their UK counterparts in the development of such skills and knowledge. It is certainly of benefit for a school to have a rudimentary knowledge of the education systems of other countries and possess an idea of equivalence.

The way forward

If the above list seems daunting, then it should be remembered that many of the issues can be resolved by a simple mix of empathy and common sense. Raising staff awareness is central to coping with many problems. If the games teacher finds an international student shivering in the changing room in the middle of November, it should be considered whether he or she is being sensitive to the climatic needs of that student, and what can be done to help. When (rather than if!) the students complain about the 'Britishness' of the food, the school should consider what part the students can play on the dining-hall committee, and how they may help shape the menu on a particular day. Similarly, schools need to consider how they adapt their e-mail and internet policies to provide adequate provision to meet the needs of overseas pupils.

There are, however, more central issues that need considering and I will conclude with a brief consideration of three of these, which I believe are important to the full integration of international students into the British boarding school environment. These are:

- parent induction;
- student induction;
- language.

The word 'induction' is often linked to, or thought to be synonymous with, 'arrival' and yet, when considering the problems of integrating international students, this is simply not the case. Schools must provide a comprehensive parental induction system in order not only to inform them fully but also to allow much information to be passed on to the students themselves before arrival. The parents' handbook should be carefully considered, particularly in terms of its linguistic content. The school should ask itself whether such a document can be understood, or whether parts of it need either re-writing or translating into the mother tongue.

Similarly, consider whether the information provided is even applicable to overseas parents, remembering that they may not fully understand either the British educational system or the boarding school environment. Concepts and procedures that British parents take for granted may not be so obvious to overseas parents. Schools can also use a parent induction system to alleviate many problems before arrival. Issues surrounding the appointment of guardians, the need to complete and return medical and academic forms, as well as the requirement for attendance throughout the whole term, can all be resolved before the student arrives, by ensuring that overseas parents understand exactly what is expected of them. It is much easier to insist that school procedure is followed if one feels that parents have been fully informed. If school requirements are met, then many problems can be avoided. For example, if genuine guardians are in place before arrival and are able to accommodate their wards for a few days before the term starts, then jet-lag need not be a problem. Similarly, students need not leave before the end of term or arrive late back to school, as guardians can host their wards until a suitable flight can be caught.

Student induction needs careful planning, and the school must begin by deciding how much the induction procedure for overseas pupils should be held in tandem with that for new British students, and how much should be done separately. This is not an easy issue to resolve satisfactorily. The advantage of being part of the main induction group is undeniably a sense of belonging from the outset, and an avoidance of the feeling of being somehow different. The advantage of providing separate induction provision is that more appropriate language can be used and therefore better understanding achieved. Similarly, more personal attention can be given and cultural issues, such as those relating to teaching methods, attitude to preparation or homework and non-verbal language, can be explained. How many of us, when scolding a student, have uttered the immortal lines "Look at me when I'm talking to you, boy (or girl)!"? It is perhaps interesting to note that, in many parts of Asia, it is thought rude to look at a teacher when you are in trouble.

Careful consideration must also be given to the appropriateness of any written material given to overseas students – particularly any student handbook provided by the school. Do school rules and procedures need simplifying or translating? Does an existing student handbook need to be supplemented by information particularly aimed at integrating overseas students?

Finally, schools must understand that the induction procedure for overseas pupils may last much longer than that for their British counterparts, and must ultimately be replaced by a quality system of monitoring that continues throughout their stay at the school.

Probably the most obvious problem when discussing the challenge of overseas pupils is that of language. We have already touched upon this in the boarding house environment, but it is equally important, if not more so, in the classroom. Schools cannot merely accept international pupils into the classroom without giving careful thought as to how they will be provided with a quality education. A worst-case scenario of a teacher adopting a 'sink or swim' attitude must be avoided, and schools need to work out clear strategies to deal with this very real issue. Removing students from lessons to provide EFL support is common practice, but schools must ensure that this does not lead to a lack of continuity in other areas of the curriculum.

Schools need to raise the level of teachers' awareness of their duty of academic care for these students, even in a class where the majority have a sound if not excellent command of language. Text books may well have to be supplemented and separate preparation or homework tasks used, particularly in the early months. The teacher may have to repeat instructions using simplified English or adopt a less language-based approach to teaching. In essence, all teachers, whatever their discipline, must learn the basics of EFL teaching and accept that they have an important role to play in both the development of skills and understanding, and also the development of language.

It could be argued that many students will inevitably suffer in an environment that places them at such a linguistic disadvantage to their UK counterparts, and that maximising potential can only be achieved if they initially attend a specialist school that only accepts overseas students. These can therefore concentrate all their efforts into resolving the problems outlined above. Such institutions have evolved to complement British boarding schools, to act as educational, social and cultural 'bridges'; in short to allow overseas pupils to transfer as painlessly as possible to boarding schools and, on arrival, to thrive there. Class sizes are small (typically six to eight), and all teachers are fully aware of how to teach students for whom English is not their first language, thus maximising their potential. Similarly, more time outside the classroom can be given to adjusting students to the British way of life and ensuring that the transition into British boarding school life is as seamless as possible.

Each issue raised in this chapter needs to be considered by schools in relation to their individual strengths, circumstances and resources. In all schools, however, such issues must be considered and the finances made available so that these issues can not only be given high priority but can be dealt with properly. Not to do so would betray the trust placed in us by overseas parents, and tarnish the image of the British education system abroad.

I have concentrated on the issues surrounding the admission of an increasing number of international students to our schools. It is important that schools also remember that international students have much to offer by enriching our culture, and in allowing us to share and appreciate their philosophies and beliefs. They can, and already do, enrich boarding school life. It is up to us to ensure that we, in return, provide for our international students the quality of education, in its broadest sense, that we would wish to provide for British pupils.

References and Notes

56. *British Council Orientation Booklet For Overseas Students*, July 1999.

57. Gania and Powell, (1999), *Seeding Intercultural Sensitivity in the Classroom*.

CHAPTER
15

Managing Pastoral Issues
Emma McKendrick

Schools, and perhaps even more so boarding schools, are undoubtedly very complex institutions. They exist to provide a holistic education for children away from home and so must meet the needs of each individual girl or boy in their care, thus enabling them to flourish and develop.

Ten years ago, the then Department for Education and Science defined pastoral care as follows[58]:

> *". . . pastoral care is concerned with promoting pupils' personal and social development and fostering positive attitudes: through the quality of teaching and learning; through the nature of relationships amongst pupils, teachers and adults other than teachers; through arrangements for monitoring pupils' overall progress, academic, personal and social; through specific pastoral structures and support systems; and through extra-curricular activities and the school ethos."*

Looking at this list, there are virtually no areas of school life that do not contribute to successful pastoral care. When children are away from home, the importance of providing high-quality pastoral care is heightened as the direct and immediate parental pastoral input is less.

In essence, good pastoral care is delivered through an effective web of human relationships which exist around a pupil to support her and which are built up with her directly. Creating such a web takes time and there is no substitute for investing time in the relationships which form it. The housemistress who cares for the individual children finds herself in a central and unique position in this pastoral web. She may sometimes find herself in the position of being a pupil's housemistress, teacher and perhaps even tutor. She may be the first one to share in their moments of joy and upset, the disastrous examination, the failed driving test, the break up of a relationship; she is there to help them through some very formative and sometimes difficult moments. It is also her task to represent the interests of the pupils in her house to colleagues in the school. All this she must achieve whilst also enabling parents to play a very large part in their child's development and keeping them up to date without compromising the needs of the whole community.

The purpose of this chapter is to explore some of the pastoral issues that a housemistress might encounter and offer some suggestions for ways in which they may be managed, with particular focus on the pastoral web and communication networks in place for managing them.

The head's expectations

It may be a platitude to say, but the fact that every school is different is nonetheless relevant when considering the head's expectations of her house staff. The ethos of the school, its management structure, its size, its location, its communication structure (both explicit and implicit) as well as the type of boarders – full, weekly, flexi – are some of the many factors that will have a bearing on this. A good staff handbook, house handbook, policies, the job description and of course the school's induction process will all help to clarify what your head will expect, but there are perhaps one or two general points worth making.

The head is the person who has overall responsibility for the boarder; she is the one who is likely to have 'sold' a certain set of expectations on to the parents and yet she is often the person who has less if not little contact with the individual pupils than many others, especially the housemistress. She is, except in rare cases, the one from whom the pupil may feel at the greatest 'distance' and in whom she is least likely to confide directly when there is a problem. She is therefore dependent in particular on the relationship that the house staff establish within the house and school, in order to be sure that her promises to parents and obligations to the child can be fulfilled, and the aims and objectives of the school as set out in the prospectus, parents' handbook or other appropriate information are met. She is also dependent on the house staff for reinforcing to the pupils the school's expectations and values. It is the housemistress who builds the foundation or reinforces the base on which the head can build her relationship with the pupils. A housemistress who constantly refers to the head's displeasure and uses her as the 'stick' in conversations is likely to skew the relationship the head has with those pupils in one direction rather than another. Similarly the head who is presented as not really caring about them will be viewed in a different way by the pupils. The house-mistress thus forms a very important link between the head and the pupils.

Building an atmosphere of trust and a sense that the care given is unconditional in a house are perhaps two of the most important tasks of a housemistress. They are, without a doubt, two of the prerequisites to effective pastoral care. A child needs to know that, whatever she does, the housemistress will respond consistently, fairly and will still like and care for her no matter how angry or disappointed she is. Those who find themselves fulfilling the role of a pupil's houseparent, tutor and teacher, and thus accumulate a wealth of knowledge about the pupil that few parents would be able to, should not be surprised when, like parents after a parents' meeting, they find themselves wondering whether the child that others see is the same one that they have in their charge!

This level of knowledge makes the responsibility of the housemistress who carries it great. In order to build trust and create a feeling of security, she must make clear to her charges the guidelines within which she will operate and the code of conduct she will follow, as well as those which the pupils must operate within and follow. For example, the pupils have to feel that, when they make mistakes, as indeed they will, there will be an opportunity to move forward from them. They have to be secure in the knowledge that a mistake made at 'home' will not be the subject of staff room debate the next day – discretion is essential. In addition, if their parents need to be informed, a child needs to be secure that this will be done in a balanced way. When considering more serious incidents, the child must always be clear what needs to be passed on, and of course needs to know that confidentiality cannot ever be promised without first hearing the nature of the information that is given. It is only by establishing an atmosphere of trust and clear guidelines that pastoral concerns will readily come to the surface; there will be a spirit of openness, and children will have the confidence to share directly or give indirect signals to the housemistress that there are or may be problems afoot. It goes without saying that the problems have of course to be dealt with appropriately once evident. Every small problem dealt with will build a foundation of trust for future greater problems should they arise.

Keeping the head informed of what is happening in a house, so that she can carry out her role efficiently and effectively, is essential. A certain amount of professional judgement is of course necessary, and knowing your head and the style that she has is important. Whilst it may be very impressive to a parent that the head knows that his son's bike is broken, this may be more important to a younger pupil, member of the cycling team or for the pupil who has difficulty in building peer group relationships and transfers much of her energy into this, than for the pupil who simply keeps one because 'well, everybody does' and it is handy for getting about. There are, however, some issues about which it is likely that all heads would wish to or need to be informed. Sometimes information will be passed on for action, sometimes to elicit support, sometimes for discussion and sometimes purely so that the head has the knowledge of the situation and will, as a result, not be wrong-footed, or she will be able to tuck it away and keep it as an interest. She may also wish to or need to discuss with the housemistress who else needs to know in order that all staff are appropriately informed to carry out their roles effectively.

In short, the head's expectations of her house staff could be summarised as the person who provides an effective link between herself and the pupils, promotes the school's values, engenders an atmosphere of trust, sets clear guidelines, follows problems through, is consistent, represents the pupils in a balanced way, invests time in them and those who will support them, and provides unconditional care.

Who needs to know? (See also Chapter 6)

As the housemistress is at the centre of the pastoral web, promoting the child's welfare does, as already emphasised, mean keeping the head and other staff in touch with any matters relating to a child on a 'need to know' basis. Those who 'need to know' can perhaps best be defined as those who will not be able to carry out their role effectively without that information. In addition to passing information on, it may of course also be necessary to consult other staff for advice, verification or for further information.

The presentation of a balance of information and balanced reporting of incidents mentioned earlier should not be overlooked when considering the information that others need to have. The tutor or perhaps a particular teacher would really benefit from being able to comment on or discuss an outstanding achievement in a particular area of school life. The tutor, who is able to say to her tutee on Monday morning at registration that she is thrilled that their four won the regatta on Saturday, will through this simple action show the tutee that she has a real interest in them and, in doing that, the housemistress shows that she has a pride in her charge that complements or fills the gap of the parent who may be overseas or not able to express it first hand. Ensuring that positive information is passed on again can help to build trust and to pave the way when more difficult issues are to be tackled.

House staff like parents will often absorb the brunt of the day's injustices, how certain teachers have 'got them wrong', 'really do not understand them', 'do not like them' and similar. The pupils have to be able to off-load to someone when they get home and the housemistress, like the parent, skilfully guides them to the realisation that perhaps a certain situation is not as they feared, or provides a balancing argument to put things back in perspective. Very few of those conversations need to be passed on, and indeed should not be, unless they are symptomatic of some other pattern of behaviour or fit with another piece of information of which a housemistress is aware. Indeed to pass them on is likely to result in a clamming up from the pupil and a breach of trust, thus denying the pupil access to future help when it is really necessary.

Some of the situations, however, that might bear closer inspection when considering who needs to know what, in order to ensure effective pastoral care management, might include the following.

(a) A change to family circumstances

A child whose parents split up or go through difficulty needs to be protected from the member of staff who may inadvertently find themselves touching on the topic. Similarly, the member of staff needs to be protected from making a *faux pas* which could cause discomfort to the child. Unless there are specific reasons to avoid it, this sort of information needs to be available to all those who teach the child as well as the tutor, members of the house team and of course the head. It is helpful, too, for the staff to have guidance on whether to discuss the matter or to avoid any mention as far as possible.

This can often be agreed with the child and/or parents first. It is important to remember that the initial information may need to be followed with updates as the child comes to terms with the change and the situation evolves. The same is true for a child who loses a member of their family or a close friend. The information needs to be passed on quickly and, as the process of grieving is different for every person, the staff need to be made aware of an individual's journey through the grieving period. It is often months after the death when real vigilance is required.

(b) Eating disorders (see also Chapter 16)

Not always, but often, the physical manifestations of weight loss and associated symptoms of bulimia and anorexia, for example, mean that there may be many people within the school community who have concerns about a pupil's eating habits, health and welfare. Often it is the pupils themselves who will express concern first. The housemistress may find herself, together with medical staff, to be the repository of information and many concerns. Her role is primarily to help to manage these and ensure that, in consultation with the medical centre or equivalent staff, a plan of action is set down to address the problem and that staff are reassured of this. She will need to share this action plan with the members of the house team and the tutor and, if the action plan determines it, other staff (*e.g.* the PE staff), if there is to be restricted exercise. There are rarely easy solutions or quick fixes to such problems which can be frustrating for staff and pupils alike who may feel that nothing is being done. The promotion of a calm reassuring approach, with any helpful guidelines on how the pupil concerned or the other pupils should be supported, is very useful. The head will want to be fully appraised of the situation and may choose to co-ordinate the school's response to it with the medical centre and house staff. She may, for example, in the worst cases have to address with the parents whether the pupil can continue to remain resident at the school.

(c) Alcohol and substance abuse

The response to these situations will vary depending on an individual school's policies. If a pupil gets drunk on a Saturday evening, one has to question whether anybody apart from the head and those on the house team need to know. It is unlikely that the boy or girl who gets drunk at home on a Saturday will find their parents ringing in to tell the staff unless there are specific reasons for so doing. There is the same risk whether at home or at school that, if they were in the company of other pupils in the school, it may be discussed in front of staff the next day. However, there is no real reason why these sorts of one-off misdemeanours should become public knowledge or the subject of wider debate. If there is a chance that a greater problem exists and that it may spill into lessons then that is of course a different issue.

I have heard it argued that it is not necessary for the head to know of such incidents. I believe that the head will need to know for one of many reasons – there may be issues of under-age purchasing and drinking of alcohol; there may be a trend across the houses that she needs to consider; it may cause concern amongst parents; she should not hear it through the grapevine where information given is usually less accurate.

A housemistress who discovers that a pupil in her house is in possession of or has used illegal drugs should follow the school's policy and procedures. These are in place for her protection as much as the protection of the child. Everyone should be clear about who needs to know and how they will be told.

(d) Sexual abuse and rape

As with the use of illegal drugs each school will have a very clear child protection policy which sets down the procedure to be followed. This will cover who needs to know, in which order and how the information is to be dealt with. Rape, like sexual abuse, needs to be handled with great care. In each case, the head and/or the named child protection officer in the school will be informed and very careful and discreet handling of the case will be essential. For legal reasons or reasons of child protection, it may be impossible to tell the staff any more than that there is a problem and to 'bear with you and the pupil'. Where staff are confident that they will be given the information they need to know, they will be much more accepting of such situations.

(e) Abortion and pregnancy

If a housemistress is aware of such a situation then the involvement of the head is essential. She then has to consider very carefully after consultation who else needs to know depending on the circumstances, and decide upon and manage the school's response to the situation. Each situation will be unique and it is not useful to offer any specific further thoughts on this. Medical staff discovering such situations are, of course, bound by medical confidentiality, and a different code of practice comes into play, and is dealt with in Chapter 6.

(f) Suicide and self-harm

If a child attempts suicide then there should be no question that the head needs to be informed, as with a severe accident. The house team will also need to be taken into the housemistress's confidence if they have not been present. (This all presupposes that the medical staff have been contacted first!) Similarly, staff who may be immediately involved with the pupil's care will need to know – the tutor, for example. Depending on the circumstances and the context, it is possible that a whole-school statement will be necessary, for other staff may hear stories from the pupils and need reassurance themselves or appropriate information in order to help and support the child's friends or siblings. Guidance may need to be given immediately and, at a later stage, to staff on how to help the child to re-integrate and whether anything should be mentioned to the child or parents directly or not.

Self-harming, which may lead to suicide risk, needs also to be passed on to the head and of course to the medical centre staff. This is very important, as the head may wish to ask for an assessment of the level of risk and consider the impact on the other children in the house. They may sometimes carry a terrific burden of anxiety and believe that they will be responsible if something goes wrong. They may also be under pressure from the pupil who is self-harming 'not to tell', as it might make it worse. Consideration may need to be given to whether it is appropriate for that pupil to take part in certain activities and so on. It is unlikely that a wider audience for such information will be necessary.

(g) Patterns of behaviour

There will sometimes be patterns of behaviour that a housemistress notices within her house as a result of daily observation or as a result of looking through her day book and records. It could be that it is useful to share it with the head and with others. I remember being told of the drinks machine in a school that, in certain houses, was emptied on a Sunday night and a Monday morning after a whole-school exeat. This in itself is not noteworthy, but the fact that it happened every Sunday after a whole-school exeat across a certain range of houses, was eventually a clue that led the school to discover the regular use of ecstasy at parties, which led to the pupils being very dehydrated. There may be many other incidents which appear to be small in themselves, but when put together may or may not lead to something. One has to be very careful however not to put two and two together and make six and a half!

Dealing with the above of course presupposes that the housemistress has the knowledge. This comes back to building that relationship of trust and spirit of openness mentioned earlier, and underlines how important this is in promoting a child's welfare.

The medical centre

One of the key departments in any school is of course the medical centre. The staff will often hold vital pieces of information regarding the welfare of a pupil and be bound by medical confidentiality. Each school must work out its own *modus operandi* which is effective for it. The medical centre, like the chaplain, may be the first port of call for a pupil who needs help or a sounding board. The medical staff can guide the pupil and work with them to get them to the point where they will talk to the housemistress about problems with which they may be able to help. Similarly, they will be able to suggest children who might need a special eye keeping on them without going into further detail. This is one of the most difficult relationships which exists in a school community, and I come back to the need for trust. Time needs to be invested by the housemistress in learning more about the medical centre and how it works, as well as *vice versa*, so that both parties can settle into a working relationship which is effective for the pupils.

The best laid plans . . .

Whilst it is possible to offer all the above guidelines and suggestions, it is very difficult to control how much the other pupils might know and have discussed, and might mention to staff who do not 'need to know' but may find themselves knee deep in a conversation they find mystifying or difficult. This cannot be prevented and it must simply be stressed to staff that there is a difference between those who need to know and those who do not, and that we have to trust each other. The fact that not everybody knows should serve to reinforce positively the fact that staff are discreet and do keep their word!

Coping with difficult pupils

"In spite of all my best efforts and in spite of all the positive feedback I give and pass on to others, I still cannot get this girl to respond, show any enthusiasm or show any desire to play a positive part in school life. There are no particular problems I am aware of or can get her to admit. Her parents are baffled and they cannot do anything with her either."

I am afraid there will always be one or two pupils like this in our schools. There is no magic solution – some will simply appear to wake up one morning and have reached the end of their 'teenage tunnel' and normal service will be resumed; others will alight on something that makes everything fall into place for them, be it their first successful piece of coursework received back or their triumph in archery; some will be helped by their peers to realise that the adult world is not against them. I cannot offer any particular solutions except to come back to the points that, if the pupil knows you are fighting her corner in spite of the fact that she makes that difficult, you are prepared to give them your time and show an interest in them, you accept them unconditionally, you are consistent in your dealings with them and will not give up on them, there is a much greater chance of success.

Support for the housemistress

In establishing a good communication network and effective pastoral web, one enables not only the pupil to benefit from the best of care with each member of staff performing effectively, but it also means that the housemistress does not carry the whole pastoral burden. She will need support from time to time and discussion with other appropriate staff may often be useful. A child, too, may need to talk to someone else and she should expect this, for she cannot be 'all things to all men' all the time, although it may seem that that is required from time to time!

Some concluding points

1. Every school is different – know your school policies and structures.

2. Every situation is different – each individual and each individual situation needs careful consideration.

3. The housemistress has a unique knowledge of her pupils – more information means greater responsibility.

4. Effective pastoral care has its basis in trust, engendered by good working and caring relationships.

5. Clear guidelines within which pupils can expect you to operate, as well as those within which they must operate, are essential.

6. Information should be passed on a 'need to know' basis – those who need to know would be prevented from carrying out their role effectively if they did not know.

7. Pupils need to experience a consistent, balanced approach and feel that the pastoral care they receive is unconditional.

8. As much time as possible needs to be given to direct contact with the children and those who help to care for them in the pastoral web.

9. You cannot be 'all things to all men' all of the time; you are part of a wider pastoral team, all of whom are working together to meet the pupils' needs.

10. The challenge of managing pastoral issues in a boarding environment is difficult but the rewards are unsurpassed!

Footnote

58. Department of Education and Science (1989), *Report of HMI on Pastoral Care in Secondary Education: An Inspection of Some Aspects of Pastoral Care in 1987-8*, DES.

CHAPTER
16

Eating Disorders and Self-Esteem
Sue Mickleburgh

Introduction

Before we examine the link between eating disorders and self-esteem, it is necessary to consider what we mean by eating disorders, why people develop them and the signs and symptoms to look out for, along with some figures to show the prevalence of this illness. We also need to look at the devastating effects that eating disorders have on individuals, their families and the community. In order that we can help to minimise the problem, we will also outline some prevention models and intervention strategies.

What are eating disorders?

'Eating disorders' is the term used to describe specific illnesses that are physical in nature but have underlying emotional and psychological causes. They develop as outward signs of inner turmoil. By eating, or not eating, the eating disorder patient tries to block out painful feelings and, if appropriate help and treatment is not received, the eating problem may continue throughout life.

These illnesses are complex, and both the disturbed eating pattern and the psychological aspects need to be treated. Once a regular eating pattern can be restored then the patient needs to be helped to come to terms with the underlying emotional issues at the root of the eating disorder.

Eating disorders include the following:

(a) Anorexia nervosa

The literal translation of *anorexia nervosa* is 'loss of appetite for nervous reasons'. However, this is misleading in that eating disorder patients have lost the ability to allow themselves to satisfy their appetite. By restricting the amount that they eat and drink, they focus on food in an attempt to cope with life. Their intention is not to starve to death but to demonstrate that they are in control of their body weight and shape. However, once the illness takes hold, chemical changes in the brain affect the nervous function and distort thinking, making it impossible for the person to make rational decisions about food. As the illness progresses, many people suffer from the exhaustion of starvation and, occasionally, people may die from the effects of *anorexia nervosa*.

(b) Bulimia nervosa

The literal meaning of *bulimia nervosa* is 'the hunger of an ox' and the hunger, in this instance, is an emotional need that cannot be satisfied by food alone. The person will 'binge eat' a large quantity of food to satisfy their hunger, and then will immediately get rid of the food by vomiting or taking laxatives (or both), or they will work off the calories with exercise.

As these measures are taken to prevent weight gain, bulimia is more difficult to detect because a person's weight may appear to be relatively stable. Even people close to them may not recognise the illness and it, and their chronic lack of self-confidence, may continue for many years undetected. Many people with bulimia have high-powered jobs that demand them to appear to be self-assured and out-going and, as with people with anorexia, they rely on the control of food and eating as a way of coping with the emotional difficulties in their lives.

What is a binge?

A binge is a means of coping with emotional difficulties but this can get out of control. The person eats foods which are generally high in calories, full of carbohydrates and fat and, occasionally, they may even eat frozen food. As they start to feel full, they feel guilty, and in desperation they vomit or take laxatives in order to purge themselves of the food that they have consumed. At this point, some people feel emotionally relieved and light-headed. This cycle can keep emotional pain and unhappiness at bay, but only for a short time.

The frequency of these bulimic cycles varies from person to person, and ranges from once every few months to several times a day. Some people vomit automatically after eating food, while others appear to eat socially and then purge themselves in private. To some, the illness is not a problem as it becomes a way of life, but others despise and fear the vicious cycle in which they have been caught.

(c) Binge eating

Both binge eating and *bulimia nervosa* have only recently been recognised as distinct eating disorders. Binge eating is similar to bulimia in that the person 'binge eats' a large quantity of food but will not purge themselves afterwards.

(d) Other Eating Disorders

Other eating disorders exist which do not closely follow the above patterns. Some variations are more distinct such as 'chew and spit' behaviour, where a person chews food and spits it out, and regurgitation where food is swallowed and then brought back into the mouth for re-chewing. Other examples are where some people eat non-foods, such as paper tissues, to fill themselves up without taking in calories.

For an eating problem to be defined as an eating disorder, it must have a psychological basis. The term does not include problems such as food allergies or disorders of the digestive system.

Why do people develop eating disorders?

Anyone can develop an eating disorder, regardless of age, race, gender or background. However, young women are most vulnerable, particularly between the ages of 15 and 25 years. *Anorexia nervosa* may develop at a lower age than *bulimia nervosa*, which is most likely to develop in the late teens to early 20s. A person with *bulimia nervosa* may have had – or go on to develop – *anorexia*. This sometimes occurs because they believe that *bulimia* will help them to diet successfully, when other attempts to lose weight have failed.

Research suggests that a person's genetic make up may make them more vulnerable to developing an eating disorder. In addition, a key person may adversely influence other family members through their attitude to food. Where there are high academic expectations or social pressures, a person may focus on food and eating as a way of coping with these stresses. Traumatic events can trigger *anorexia* or *bulimia nervosa* and someone with another long-term illness or disability may also experience eating difficulties.

The most common causes of eating disorders are listed below:

❖ feelings of low self-esteem;

❖ a lack of self-worth;

❖ the need for control in a life that seems out of control;

❖ feelings of loss or grief:

- bereavement
- divorce
- relationship breakdown;

❖ relationship with siblings:

- rivalry
- competition
- feelings that they are receiving favouritism
- illness
- feelings of rejection
- feelings of guilt;

❖ abuse:

- sexual
- mental
- physical;

- body image problems or distorted body image;

- the need to achieve, either self-imposed or imposed by others;

- relationships with others, *e.g.* parents (over-possessiveness, controlling);

- high expectations, either self-imposed or imposed by others;

- stress;

- dieting.

Eating disorders, self-esteem and body image

At this point, it is worth considering self-esteem whose absence is at the root of many eating disorders. Self-esteem comes from a strong, rooted sense of self-worth which survives both failure and success. It survives mistakes, disappointment and, most importantly, acceptance and rejection from others. If a person is suffering from low self-esteem and something traumatic or stressful happens in their lives, they will find it extremely difficult to cope and may have to devise strategies for coping. Eating, or not eating, can become the coping mechanism.

Low self-esteem is a common characteristic of an eating disorder, whether this is *anorexia nervosa*, *bulimia nervosa*, obesity or another form of eating distress. In addition, people with eating disorders tend to have a very negative body image and feel unhappy with their bodies. The mental picture they have of their body is very different to reality, and they become convinced that their body looks as bad as it feels. For many people, body image and self-esteem are closely related. If they feel unhappy with their body, they feel unhappy with themselves. Self-worth becomes dependent on attaining or maintaining a particular body shape or size, which is an impossible ideal for most people.

Signs and symptoms of eating disorders

The signs and symptoms of *anorexia* and *bulimia nervosa* can be broken down into physical, behavioural and emotional or psychological. They can be summarised as shown in Figure 16.1.

Figure 16.1 – Signs and Symptoms

Anorexia Nervosa	Bulimia Nervosa
Physical ❖ in adults – severe weight loss; in children – often failure to gain weight ❖ loss of menstrual periods (women) and libido ❖ growth of downy hair (lanugo) all over the body – loss of hair on the head when recovering ❖ feeling cold and poor circulation ❖ difficulty in sleeping ❖ constipation and abdominal pains ❖ dizzy spells and fainting ❖ swollen stomach, face and ankles ❖ dry, rough, discoloured skin ❖ loss of bone mass and, eventually, osteoporosis (brittle bones)	**Physical** ❖ sore throat ❖ erosion of tooth enamel ❖ dehydration and poor skin condition ❖ lethargy ❖ erratic menstrual periods ❖ frequent weight changes ❖ disappearing to the toilet after meals in order to vomit food eaten ❖ swollen salivary glands making the face more round
Behavioural ❖ vomiting and/or purging ❖ excessive exercising ❖ perfectionism ❖ rituals attached to eating, such as cutting food into tiny pieces ❖ restlessness and hyperactivity ❖ secrecy	**Behavioural** ❖ 'binge eating' large amounts of food ❖ vomiting and/or purging after eating ❖ secretive and ritual behaviours ❖ devious and deceptive behaviours ❖ periods of fasting ❖ excessive exercise ❖ food disappearing unexpectedly ❖ reluctance to socialise ❖ shoplifting for food; abnormal amounts of money spent on food
Emotional/Psychological ❖ emotional and irritable behaviour ❖ depression ❖ isolation and loss of friends ❖ intense fear of gaining weight, even within the normal weight range according to height ❖ distorted perception of body shape or weight ❖ denial of the existence of a problem ❖ changes in personality and mood swings	**Emotional/Psychological** ❖ mood swings and emotional behaviour ❖ social isolation – feeling helpless and lonely ❖ uncontrollable urges to eat vast amounts of food ❖ an obsession with food ❖ distorted perception of body weight and shape ❖ anxiety and depression; low self-esteem, guilt and shame

In summary, the following elements generally apply to all eating disorders:

* Weight loss/gain;

* Fear of weight gain;

* Distorted view of body shape and size;

* Hormonal changes – loss of periods in women; loss of libido;

* Obsessional thoughts – control of weight and eating; recurrent thoughts about food and weight loss/gain.

Effects on the individual, families and the community

(a) The individual

The long-term effects of *anorexia nervosa* on the body and mind can be severe and alarming. Women with *anorexia* tend to find it more difficult to become pregnant and there is the possibility of developing osteoporosis in later life. However, once the body receives proper and regular nourishment, many of the effects can be reversed. When the person is recovering, it can take some weeks or months for the body and mind to readjust. Eating and drinking regularly again can cause the body to become bloated temporarily, and personality and mood swings may take some time to settle, depending on the underlying emotional difficulties.

Bulimia may take over the life of the person, making them feel trapped and desperate. Chaotic eating and loss of fluids can cause physical problems, but these can usually be corrected once the body is nourished correctly. *Bulimia* can in extreme cases be fatal, due to heart or organ failure, for instance. An imbalance, or dangerously low levels, of essential minerals in the body can significantly affect the working of vital internal organs. Other dangers include rupture of the stomach, choking, and erosion of tooth enamel.

Statistics

In 1992, the Royal College of Psychiatrists[59] estimated that about 60,000 people may be receiving treatment for *anorexia nervosa* and *bulimia nervosa* at any one time in the UK. However, EDA (Eating Disorders Association) currently believes the number to be nearer to 90,000 with many more people whose eating disorders have not been diagnosed, in particular those with *bulimia nervosa*[60] (EDA, 2000).

The incidence of new cases of *anorexia* and *bulimia nervosa* has been estimated[61] as:

❖ *anorexia nervosa*: up to 11 new cases per 100,000 population per year;

❖ *bulimia nervosa*: up to 18 new cases per 100,000 population per year.

The average age of onset for *anorexia nervosa* has been reported to be between 16·6 and 18·3 years (Theander[62], 1970; Halmi[63], 1974; Crisp[64] *et al.*, 1980) and, according to different reports, the average age of onset for *bulimia nervosa* is between 17·7 and 21 years (Russell[65], 1979; Fairburn and Cooper[66], 1984; Mitchell[67] et al., 1986). *Bulimia nervosa* is rare before the age of 13.

Anorexia and *bulimia nervosa* are most common amongst girls and young women. However, approximately 10 per cent of people with eating disorders are male, although among school children this may be as high as 25 per cent (Andersen[68] *et al.*, 1999).

Clinical problems and mortality rate

❖ One of the primary complications of *anorexia nervosa* is loss of fertility. Treatment of the malnutrition usually reverses this problem but difficulties can remain throughout life (Treasure[69], 1997).

❖ Osteoporosis, or brittle bones, is another major health problem. Women who have had *anorexia nervosa* are at risk of developing fractures spontaneously or following minor amounts of trauma.

❖ In addition to a range of health problems, *anorexia nervosa* presents itself as having one of the highest mortality rates for any psychiatric condition, estimated to run at around 13–20 per cent per annum (Howlett[70] *et al.*, 1995).

(b) The family

Anorexia and *bulimia nervosa* not only affect the person with the disorder – the whole family is affected. Each family is different, but the following common trends have been identified.

- People who develop an eating disorder have usually been compliant and obedient children.

- Such people would be less likely to become angry than their brothers or sisters and would have been eager to please.

- They would often have hidden their inner feelings and anxieties.

- They fear failure and have an overwhelming desire to please and care for others.

- They are committed to achieving high standards set, or believed to have been set, by parents or teachers. Often the high standards are self-imposed.

Eating disorders can develop in some families which are so close that the child finds it difficult to become independent. Eating, or not eating, demonstrates their independence through control over food.

(c) The community

The effects and social costs of eating disorders can be divided into five main areas:

(i) People with eating disorders can become anti-social in their behaviour which may manifest itself in drug addiction, alcohol abuse, shoplifting or other addictive behaviours which lead to increased police and court costs.

(ii) People with eating disorders cause family relationship problems which can manifest themselves as the break up of the home, increased social security payments and costs, and homelessness. These in turn can lead to higher taxes.

(iii) People with an eating disorder affect individuals, homes and families which, in turn, can affect friends, school, work, employees, general practitioners, psychiatrists, social workers, psychologists and police.

(iv) People with eating disorders are unable to reach their true potential and this can result in lost production through inefficiency, absenteeism and ineffective use of money spent on education and training which can result in higher prices.

(v) People with eating disorders have low self-esteem which can lead to psychiatric problems, tranquilliser addiction, long periods in hospital, physical health impairment and suicide, which result in increased NHS costs.

Prevention and intervention

People with an eating disorder have the following needs:

❖ help and support;

❖ information about:

- the illnesses
- treatment services and approaches or methods
- recovery;

❖ understanding;

❖ boundaries and responsibility for themselves;

❖ hope that recovery is possible;

❖ continuity and trust;

❖ time;

❖ care but not control.

The important thing is to take action as early as possible. Boarding schools, in particular, are advised to create a school policy on dealing with eating disorders as a priority and not wait until there is a problem before doing so.

When writing a policy, the following issues should be considered:

(*a*) Delegate a core team of people to deal with the matter (*i.e.* those who need to know, such as the head, houseparent, PE staff, school nurse and doctor).

(*b*) Information about the weight and height of a pupil is crucial for detecting any sort of problem with growth and development, including the onset of an eating disorder. Weighing all pupils at least once a term and ideally twice (*i.e.* at both the beginning and end) will ensure that a record is kept of each pupil's development. The weighing should be handled discreetly and sensitively.

(*c*) The issue of confidentiality is one that must also be dealt with carefully. It should be made clear to pupils who approach staff for help that the matter will be dealt with within the school's policy on confidentiality. They need to be advised that the core team may well need to know about the problem, but without all of the personal details. (See Chapter 6.)

(d) Often pupils will not want their parents to know that they have a problem. However, the parents have a contract with the school and may feel they have the right to know if their child is ill. It is useful to work with pupils and encourage them to tell their parents of the difficulties, preferably with the support of a member of staff. Again, parents do not necessarily need to know all of the personal details. It must be decided which member of staff will speak to the parents, and this must be handled carefully and sensitively in order not to alienate them at this stage.

(e) Be realistic about how much the school is able to do. Boundaries will need to be set and, if a pupil needs help and support, one member of staff alone may not be able to provide this. Staff can offer a great deal of support by being available to listen and supply information. If there is not a specialist eating disorders unit close to the school, the school nurse may well need to provide counselling in a calm environment in order to develop a continuous and trusting relationship with the pupil.

(f) Once the policy has been written, it will need to be explained to all staff (and possibly governors) so that everyone is clear about the school's approach. The policy will become both a guideline to staff and a clear indication to parents and pupils about how the school will deal with an eating disorder and what they can expect to happen.

Treatment and recovery

There are a number of different types of treatment available and it is important that it is tailored to the individual's specific needs, as each individual will respond differently to the various treatment approaches. In addition, there may be limited treatment resources available locally. However, treatment for people with eating disorders can include the following:

❖ inpatient – very severe cases

❖ day patient

❖ outpatient

❖ counselling

❖ cognitive behavioural therapy

❖ writing

❖ music

❖ hypnotherapy

❖ self-help groups

❖ self-help programmes

- motivational enhancement therapy
- drugs
- psychotherapy
- dramatherapy
- art therapy

- aromatherapy
- reflexology
- self-esteem/assertiveness training
- acupuncture
- massage

Bearing in mind the link between eating disorders and self-esteem, it is recommended that schools deal with the self-esteem issue by means of education for all.

Sources of help

(*a*) Self help is available through books on eating disorders, self-help groups and support by professional staff.

(*b*) Medical help is available by GP referral to a specialist eating disorder service (NHS or private), referral to general psychiatric services, referral to a dietician or referral to a counsellor (NHS or private).

(*c*) Talking therapies are available through private counselling.

(*d*) Alternative therapies, such as aromatherapy, reflexology and drama therapy are available either privately or through the NHS.

(*e*) Help is available from Eating Disorders Association (EDA) which is a UK-wide charity providing a range of services including:

- national telephone helplines;
- a UK-wide network of local self-help and support groups, postal and telephone contacts;
- a comprehensive range of information, including leaflets for young people;
- membership, which includes a quarterly magazine;
- lists of treatment available in your area;
- a helpline and support service for young people;

- ❖ an annual conference for members to learn about the latest developments;

- ❖ a telephone counselling programme for people with *bulimia*;

- ❖ training for professionals in health, education and social care;

- ❖ a professional journal, ***European Eating Disorders Review***, which provides information and practical help for professionals in all disciplines;

- ❖ Service Specifications guidelines for the treatment of *anorexia* and *bulimia nervosa*.

Telephone Helpline: 01603 621 414 (Weekdays, 9 a.m. – 6.30 p.m.)

Youthline: 01603 765 050 (Up to 18 years of age. Weekdays, 4 p.m. – 6 p.m.)

Recorded Information Service: 0906 302 0012

E-mail: info@edauk.com   Website: www.edauk.com

Summary

'Eating disorders' is a complex subject which needs careful handling. If a school can provide early help and support to somebody who has a problem, then the eating disorder may well not develop into a long-term, intractable health problem. The existence of a policy statement will make it clear to staff, governors, pupils and parents how the matter will be dealt with, should it arise. Information and training for staff and school nurses on eating disorders should be made available in order to remove any myths about the illness and to prepare people for action. Training in self-esteem and assertiveness is a useful means of building pupils' self-confidence. Finally, the following key points about eating disorders should be remembered.

- ❖ It is not about food, it is about feelings (*i.e.* me!)

- ❖ Share the responsibility when dealing with someone with an eating disorder

❖ Be clear about your personal and professional boundaries

❖ Maintain concern and support (long term) and trust

❖ People do recover from an eating disorder

❖ Support from a trusted source is beneficial

❖ Use setbacks as a way of moving forward.

References and Notes

59. Royal College of Psychiatrists (1992), 'Eating Disorders' in ***Family Doctor Publications***.

60. EDA (2000), Eating Disorders: The need for action in 2000 and beyond, EDA.

61. EDA (2000), Unpublished information.

62. Theander, S. (1970), '*Anorexia Nervosa* – A psychiatric investigation of 94 females' in ***Acta Psyciatricia Scandinavia Supplement***, **214**, 1–194.

63. Halmi, K. A. (1974), '*Anorexia Nervosa* – demographic and clinical features in 94 cases' in ***Psychosum.med***, **4**.36, 18–26.

64. Crisp, A. H. (1980), ***Anorexia Nervosa: 'Let me be'***, London, Academic Press.

65. Russell, G. F. M. (1979), '*Bulimia Nervosa*: an ominous variant of *Anorexia Nervosa*', in ***Psychological Medicine Disorders: Physiology, Psychology and Treatment of Obesity, Anorexia and Bulimia***, New York, Basic Books.

66. Fairburn, C. G. and Cooper, P. J. (1982), 'Self-induced vomiting and *Bulimia Nervosa*: an undetected problem' in ***British Journal of Medicine***, **284**, 1153–1155.

67. Mitchell, J. E. (1986), '*Anorexia Nervosa*: medical and physiological aspects' in K. D. Brownell and J. P. Foreyt, ***Handbook of Eating Disorders – Physiology, Psychology and Treatment of Obesity, Anorexia and Bulimia***, New York, Basic Books.

68. Andersen, E. A. and Bowers, W. A. (1999), 'Males, gender and eating disorders – risk bias and treatment outcome', Presentation to the Fourth London International Eating Disorders Conference, 20th–24th April 1999.

69. Treasure, J. (1997), Unpublished information.

70. Howlett, M., McClelland, L. and Crisp, A. H. (1995), 'The cost of the illness that defies' in ***Postgraduate Medical Journal***, **71**, 36–39.

CHAPTER

17

Raising Standards and Planning for the Future

Tim Holgate and Roger Morgan

We have seen that well-defined aims and principles for boarding can be used to inform and influence the provision of pastoral care, and produce a positive living and working environment (Chapter 2). We are in an age of significant and sometimes rapid change in boarding education, with greater accountability, increasing pressure to maintain boarding numbers, often responding to the demands for different types of boarding, and coming to terms with a changing inspection framework and climate. Because of this, it is even more important for boarding schools to be achieving high levels of welfare provision and pastoral care, and to be seen to have the systems and mechanism for reviewing and maintaining these high standards.

Education is firmly embedded in a strong culture for improvement and, while most will be heartily thankful that league tables for welfare and pastoral care are not with us, we need to be constantly and positively self-critical, acknowledging that things which work well will not necessarily do so for ever, reacting to the changing demands of parents and families, and responding to the changing needs of the pupils themselves. There is, thus, the need to take stock periodically of current practice and identify and agree possible new courses of action and changes of direction. This chapter will look at three areas – carrying out a welfare audit, designed to identify strengths and weaknesses and pinpoint possible areas for change; the use of National Boarding Standards (NBS) in the process of self-evaluation, to identify these improvements in provision, or refinements in procedures; and the task of action planning, to implement the desired priority areas.

The process of taking stock and moving forward can be summarised by three simple questions:

WHERE ARE WE NOW?

WHERE DO WE WANT TO BE?

HOW DO WE GET THERE?

The audit process

Why might we want to initiate this procedure and carry out a welfare audit?

❖ **Pre- or post-inspection activity**

The boarding house may wish to carry out some identified improvement or to be seen to have plans drawn up to do so, as part of the preparation for a welfare inspection, or one carried out by ISI or OFSTED. Alternatively, it may wish to use the results of the external inspection process to contribute to a wider audit of particular areas as a response to the inspection.

❖ **On-going issues**

There may well be areas of concern that have been identified during the routine life and work of the house staff, in their day-to-day contact with the pupils.

❖ **Managing change**

Significant changes in boarding provision that might be facing a house or school will have an impact on welfare arrangements in the house. Examples of these may include:

• moving to full coeducation;

• creation of a sixth form house;

- reorganisation of horizontal / vertical house structure;

- day pupils in boarding houses;

- major refurbishment;

- building new houses;

- major changes in composition of house staff team.

The creation of an upper sixth house, for instance, will have significant impact on the responsibility expected of the lower sixth year, which would now become the senior year group, and this would provide the opportunity to look at many other aspects of welfare provision.

❖ **Reassurance**

House staff might wish to reassure themselves that recently instituted changes or improvements are still working well and having the desired effect.

It would be unusual to embark on a welfare audit of most areas of the boarding house at once, across the whole welfare spectrum. House staff need to identify a small number of welfare areas to look at, perhaps as part of a termly rolling programme of audits. As indicated above, it is probable that specific areas of concern, worthy of more detailed investigation, may have already been identified. An examination of the 53 welfare areas included in the NBS (Figure 17.1, and see Appendix 2), as part of a preliminary 'broad brush' evaluation of current provision and practice, may suggest a manageable number of areas for audit treatment. These are likely to come under one or more of the following headings:

❖ human resources
   e.g. deployment of staff, training and use of prefects;

❖ physical environment
   e.g. standards of accommodation, health and safety issues;

❖ structures and systems
   e.g. ethos, tutoring opportunities, personal development;

❖ procedures and policies
   e.g. child protection, anti-bullying, good communication.

Figure 17.1 – National Boarding Standards: Welfare Topics

Boarding policy statement	Risk assessment
Anti-bullying policy/practice	Information provision to boarders
Child protection policy/practice	Staffing levels
Disciplinary policy/practice	Pupil access to supervising staff
Complaints policy/practice	Night staff cover in houses
Health policy/practice	Staff training and supervision
Pupil welfare records	Written guidelines for staff
Management of boarding	Staff/pupil relationships
Management of crises	Pupil privacy
Separation of ages and genders	Staff recruitment checks
Activities and free time	Restriction on unchecked adults
Pupil input to policy/practice	DfEE notifications of dismissals
Prefect system	Standard of boarding premises
Staff approachability for help	Access to boarding areas
First-aid and medical services	Standard of sleeping areas
Supervision of ill pupils	Study facilities
Support for personal problems	Toilet and washing facilities
Non-discrimination	Changing rooms
Contacting parents	Recreational areas – in and out
Safe keeping money/valuables	Safety hazards
Induction of new boarders	Accommodation for ill pupils
Checks on guardians	Laundry provision
Monitoring of incident records	Drinking-water and snacks
Catering provision	Purchase of personal items
Fire precautions	Use of lodgings
Any unusual demands/routines	Use of off-site accommodation
Accommodation of non-pupils	

Areas needing to be looked at may also be identified by analysing recent incidents in the house, or any 'near misses', any complaints or concerns raised by pupils or parents, and any targets already set as a result of wider school initiatives. Once these broad areas for investigation have been identified, the welfare audit process can begin, and this is summarised below.

The welfare audit process

❖ collect information

❖ compare with desired standards

❖ action taken for improvement

❖ follow up to check its effectiveness

Collecting evidence and data

The gathering of information about the welfare issues within the areas identified is a crucial first step in gaining a clear and accurate picture of the current situation. This can be done in a variety of ways.

(i) Detailed self-evaluation by house staff using the NBS format is likely to produce valuable evidence. Figure 17.2 shows a possible self-assessment grid, adapting a sample NBS statement and providing the opportunity to evaluate current provision against the various criteria connected with the standard concerned, together with the reasons for any minor or major shortfalls. This example shows the standard expected for countering bullying, and it will be seen that the criteria are, in part, hierarchical. The first specifies the need for a school to have a satisfactory policy to counter bullying. The second requires it to be available and known to staff and pupils. The third requires it not only to be known but for the measures in place to be effective in practice.

(ii) Pupils can also be asked to give an assessment of specific areas of boarding life, and cross-checking can often be achieved by staff simultaneously discussing the same issues in two randomly selected groups.

(iii) Surveys of house staff, pupils and parents can generate specific information on a range of issues, such as incidents of bullying, satisfaction with food and catering,

Figure 17.2 – Sample self-assessment sheet

2. CORE STANDARD

The school should have, and follow, an appropriate policy on countering bullying, which is known to pupils and staff and is effective in practice.

House:

Assessors:

Date:

Criteria	Assessment			
	Fully Met	Partly Met	Not Met/ Hardly Met	Reasons for Shortfall
The school has a satisfactory policy on countering bullying, covering both measures to prevent bullying and to respond to observed or reported bullying.				
This policy is available and known both to staff and pupils, including junior and recently-appointed staff.				
Discussion with pupils and staff confirms that suitable measures both to prevent and to respond to observed or reported bullying are being implemented in practice.				
No 'initiation ceremonies' intended to cause pain, anxiety or humiliation are reported by pupils or staff.				
Reported rates of bullying at the school (*e.g.* through pupil survey), as defined by pupils, do not significantly exceed the norms for comparable schools.				
ACTION	**TO START**	**DONE**	**RESPONSIBILITY**	

effectiveness of rewards and sanctions, and strengths and weaknesses of accommodation. This may lend itself to a semi-quantitative analysis using, say, a scale of 1 to 5. There is merit in using a questionnaire format which can be used again on future occasions, thus enabling trends and patterns to be identified over time. Norms for reported incidents of, for example, bullying in boarding schools are available to support the application of NBS in inspection and self-evaluation.

(iv) Examination and analysis of boarding house records of, for example, accidents, punishments and incidents can highlight trends and significant incidents associated with particular times, places and groups of pupils.

(v) Exit and entry interviews and debriefing of those (both pupils and staff) new to the boarding house, as well as those about to leave, can provide useful information about perceived strengths and weaknesses.

Staff need to be aware of the reliability of data collected by inference or second-hand, where no direct observation is possible, and that such evidence is likely to need corroboration. For example, where cases of bullying have been reported by one or two individuals, corroborative evidence in the form of discussions with other staff or by a survey of a larger number of pupils may well need to be undertaken. Evidence of a straightforward factual nature, made by direct observation such as the absence of window restraints on upper floors or inadequate shower arrangements, is of course much more reliable.

Evidence gathering, especially when it relies on feedback from pupils, can have its pitfalls, and certain limitations should be taken into account when looking for corroboration.

❖ Recent incidents are often fresh in the mind, but may not be typical of normal routines and provision: nevertheless, they may loom large in the minds of pupils (and staff!).

❖ In a similar way, past minor incidents may have, over time, been blown up out of proportion, and become part of folk lore.

❖ Some pupils, eager to please, may provide the answer that they think the questioner is hoping for or expecting.

❖ Pupils are particularly prone to the sweeping generalisation, as in "the hot water *always* runs out" or "my games kit *never* comes back in time from the laundry".

❖ Pupils are sometimes apt to treat hearsay as gospel truth.

❖ Over-familiarity with minor problems (*e.g.* a loose door handle or stair tread) may prevent pupils and staff recognising their existence.

❖ Pupils' loyalty to their friends and the house may cause a biased viewpoint being put forward.

By now, a clear picture of the current situation in those areas chosen for audit will have been built up. By no means all (or most) of this will be negative. Strengths in provision will obviously also emerge. At this stage, the data and evidence need to be sifted and summarised.

Hargreaves and Hopkins[71] (1998) identify five outcomes to a specific audit:

❖ **Strengths are revealed**, possibly in areas that were not regarded as strengths by some staff. A house may also choose to audit a perceived strength in order to learn more systematically from its own practice.

❖ **Some weaknesses may be remedied easily**, and can be solved quickly without an action plan.

❖ **A specific audit becomes a priority.** If an unusually detailed audit is felt to be needed in a particular area, this can become in itself a priority within the development plan, and an action plan drawn up for carrying it out.

❖ **The audit process provides the basis for action planning.** The report of the audit may identify the detailed work needed to be carried out as part of the action plan.

❖ **A list of potential priorities is identified** as a result of the audit, with a rough estimate of the work needing to be done.

> "*The audit paves the way for the identification of priorities for development[72].*"

Evaluation of evidence and data

The question now arises: "Is what we have seen good enough? Can it be improved further?". The next stage is to evaluate provision against desired standards and obtain a clear view of what we want to do. Figure 17.3 outlines possible sources of information for defining welfare standards, against which the current provision can be evaluated.

The NBS will probably provide the clearest detail for evaluation and comparison. Remember that these are *minimum* standards, and many schools and houses will wish to aim for higher standards in some areas. Staff will probably wish at this stage to refer back to the NBS self-evaluation grids, as shown in Figure 17.2.

Figure 17.3 Defining Welfare Standards

❖ **National Boarding Standards**

  (see Appendix 2)

❖ **Children Act Guidance**

  Department of Health publications

  The Children Act 1989: Guidance and Regulations (Volume 5 – Independent Schools)

  The Children Act 1989: The Welfare of Children in Boarding Schools (Practice Guide)

❖ **Legal Requirements and Statutory Obligations**

  (see Appendix 1 and the BSA publication *Running a School Boarding House: A legal guide for housemasters and housemistresses*)

❖ **School Development Plan**

  (targets already set, development areas for whole-school pastoral care)

❖ **Inspection Recommendations**

❖ **Aims/Objectives – House and School**

Planning for improvement

Shortfalls in provision and areas identified for development and improvement will now suggest welfare issues to be resolved, which will suggest in turn specific targets for action. Some issues may well need to be linked into the whole school development plan, where areas have a wider pastoral impact or where significant staffing or financial resources are involved.

However, a case can be made anyway for the construction of an individual house development plan, to shape and guide short- and long-term future developments within the boarding house. Depending on the number of areas audited, it is likely that a 'long list' of priorities will emerge, and will need to be put into some sort of order of importance before planning for action. This may be influenced by:

- ❖ the degree of urgency of the desired change;

- ❖ implications for statutory obligations;

- ❖ availability of funding and human resources;

- ❖ the size of the task, and its ease of implementation;

- ❖ any sequencing constraints necessitating the completion of one area before another can be started.

The emerging house development plan is likely to list:

- ❖ the issues arising from the audit;

- ❖ a review of the previous house development plan (if it already exists);

- ❖ proposed priorities with time scale;

- ❖ a justification of the priorities in terms of the context of the house and/or school;

- ❖ links with other whole school initiatives;

- ❖ links to school aims and objectives (especially for boarding).

The plan will need to focus more precisely on the year ahead, identifying perhaps three or more major priorities, each with a number of elements, manageable in number and scope. Resource and financial implications will need to be clarified.

Action planning

The next stage will be to draw up an action plan for the coming year, whereby the desired changes can actually be effected.

Hargreaves and Hopkins[73] define an action plan as *"a working document, which describes and summarises what needs to be done to implement and evaluate [the necessary change]"*. Each priority is assigned to an individual or a group, and the likely availability of boarding staff will emphasise the importance of not taking on too many priorities in any one year. One key priority may be quite enough for a small house team. The process leads to a series of targets outlining a set of more discrete tasks, timescales, allocation of responsibility, success criteria, time/dates to assess progress, and resource implications. This last aspect is important, since existing resources may be able to be used more effectively or re-deployed, as well as highlighting the need for new resources. Allocation of responsibilities should identify the person(s) responsible for making sure action is taken and for identifying others who may be asked to help within and outside school. It is also important to indicate how the programme will be monitored and who will be responsible for the evaluation process. Each action plan thus describes the progress of work to be carried out to achieve improvements or change.

A vital part is, thus, the monitoring of progress and evaluation of the success or otherwise of the intended outcomes. The action needs to be tested to see if has had the desired effect and achieved the improvements identified earlier at the audit stage as being necessary. Also, one needs to assess the impact of the change on the welfare of the boarding pupils. It can by no means be taken for granted that completion of the action will automatically have the desired effect. A time interval since the audit stage may mean that different groups of pupils are now involved, or the accommodation has been used differently.

Government guidance[74] explains success criteria as *"a form of school-generated performance indicators"*, providing the means for evaluating an action plan. They will state the evidence needed to judge successful implementation of the changes, and will influence the way that the target is designed and guide action needed to achieve agreed standards. They will help to distinguish between process and outcome, and help shape further action if the degree of success falls short of expectation. *"They emphasise success rather than failure, and refer to future rather than past performance[75]"*.

Targets set will need to be SMART, according to the acronym:

SPECIFIC

MEASURABLE

ACHIEVABLE

RELEVANT

TIME-RELATED

The action that needs to be specified in drawing up the action plan is shown below. The resulting action plan should not be a lengthy document.

Action planning sequence

❖ welfare issues identified

❖ priority area

❖ targets set

❖ break into sub-tasks (**WHAT?**)

❖ responsibility (**WHO?**)

❖ process (**HOW?**)

❖ timescale (**WHEN?**)

❖ resource implications

❖ success criteria

❖ review and evaluation

Let us look at a simple specific example from audit to action plan. A new housemaster in his first term in post becomes aware of the absence of a proper induction process for the new intake of boarders. A quick audit confirms the extent of the problem he has inherited. The 'data' collected may well have been gathered by:

❖ observations made by housemaster and tutors;

❖ discussions between matron and new pupils;

- reports from concerned parents;

- group discussion with new pupils;

- increased incidence of new pupils not doing what is expected of them.

Were he in any doubt as to the shortfall from desired standards, the criteria for NBS 21 (see Appendix 2) specify that:

- *"new boarders should be given suitable information about boarding routines and rules, including key information in writing";*

- *"there are arrangements for new boarders to have guidance from more experienced boarders".*

So there is clearly a welfare issue to be resolved, namely that new pupils feel lost and confused on arrival.

This suggests two clear priority targets; a short-term one of immediate action to resolve the problem for the current new pupils, and a slightly longer one to create an effective induction procedure for the arrival of the next new intake.

The housemaster and his team (because he has developed a strong corporate commitment to raising welfare standards) agree on four tasks needed to meet the targets set:

- send out welcome letter to new pupils before arrival;

- prepare new boarders' handbook or information leaflet;

- create system of shadows/sponsors;

- institute briefing sessions after new pupils arrive in the house.

They then use their combined talents and strengths to allocate specific action points to different members of the team, not forgetting matron and a particularly responsible group of house prefects. These are to:

- consult with house staff team about what is needed;

- consult this year's new pupils;

❖ use prefects' meetings to identify the briefing and induction sessions needed;

❖ ascertain practice in other houses;

❖ draft the welcome letter;

❖ draft the boarders' handbook;

❖ appoint and brief shadows/sponsors.

Each of these will have a clear indication of the person with overall responsibility for ensuring successful completion, with a specific time frame stated (including, perhaps, some interim dates set for further planning meetings).

The team considered resources and recognised that a limited but acceptable financial cost is needed, involving printing / photocopying / postage / coffee and biscuits. The most 'expensive' resource is obviously time. They spent a while developing their success criteria, and decided that a successful outcome of their initiatives could be signalled by:

❖ parents and pupils reporting satisfaction with induction procedures;

❖ prefects and staff reporting that new pupils appear settled and happy;

❖ staff reporting that few incidents occur where pupils are unclear about expectations and action.

Finally, they would review and evaluate the improvements they hoped to make by:

❖ carrying out a survey/questionnaire among new pupils at half term;

❖ evaluating and reviewing procedures and documentation before the next intake.

Needless to say, the new induction arrangements and improvements in the welfare of the new pupils were highly effective!

Now it could be argued that improvements such as these could have been quickly resolved and effected by the housemaster responding on his own to his initial recognition that things were not right, without going through this whole procedure in the manner just outlined. However, if he were to analyse such spontaneous actions, it is likely that he would have covered precisely the same process, albeit informally. A slightly more complex welfare issue identified, such as the improvement of the leadership and responsibility shown by senior pupils, would need a more precise identification of the action needed and, in a busy school routine, with perhaps a limited and inexperienced house staff team to draw upon, careful planning of new initiatives and improvements would be vital.

References and Notes

71. Hargreaves, David H. and Hopkins, David (1998), *The Empowered School: the management and practice of development planning*, Cassell, Chapter 5.

72. Ibid., p. 38.

73. Ibid., Chapter 7.

74. Department of Education and Science (1989), *Planning for School Development*, HMSO.

75. Hargreaves, David H. and Hopkins, David (1998), *The Empowered School: the management and practice of development planning*, Cassell, p. 140.

POSTSCRIPT

Twenty tips for a new housemaster or housemistress

- ❖ Staff are often said to be acting *in loco parentis*; therefore, the house could be regarded as an extended family. Thus, the care and concern of the good parent for each individual should be the guiding light. In a disciplinary situation, one should show one's disapproval of the offence, rather than the person. "Hate the sin; love the sinner."

- ❖ Good communication, up and down, is vital. Staff need to be approachable to the pupils, which involves an important element of trust that the staff will be discreet when necessary. Staff should be seen around the house regularly; there should not be any 'no go' areas round the house.

- ❖ A disciplined framework is, of course, necessary, and respect and courtesy must be the guidelines. Formal rules should be kept to a minimum, only being valid if they contribute to the good running of the community and the welfare of pupils.

- ❖ Consistency is important, and pupils respond to fairness. However, there are times when one needs the confidence to be flexible, and treat cases on their own merits. One often needs to be *inconsistent* in order to be fair. A pupil guilty of a serious misdemeanour as a reaction to a bereavement, for example, may not necessarily warrant the standard sanction. The ability to turn a blind eye on occasions is necessary, providing that one knows the pupils well.

- ❖ Wherever possible in a disciplinary situation, delay some while before acting. Never act in haste or anger. It frequently does no harm for a rule-breaker to reflect on his sins overnight. Keep things in proportion.

- ❖ Always be able to forgive. Young people change rapidly throughout the traumas of adolescence, and they must feel that they can be given a fresh start. Guard against the temptation to write off a pupil.

- ❖ Build effective relationships with the senior pupils, who are crucial in helping to promote the welfare of the house. Work hard to help them to share your vision for the house.

- Good and frequent communication with parents is a priority. Alerting them to possible minor problems, before major troubles arise, can often work well, as will passing on positive information to them. Parents can make useful allies when kept fully informed.

- Give time to the 'middle-of-the-road' pupils, as much as the outstanding or difficult ones. We often fail to give the unobtrusive pupils their fair share of our attention. It is worth regularly going down the house list, identifying those with whom you have not recently talked.

- Set your heart and soul against bullying or harassment of any sort, mental or physical. Declare yourself clearly and strongly on this issue, and rally the support of senior pupils.

- Don't forget the importance of the house's non-teaching and domestic staff, particularly your matron and any Gap students. They are constantly in situations where they may pick up problems and identify troubled pupils. Make sure that they know how to respond in cases of bullying or potential child protection situations.

- Boarding houses and schools are nowadays expected to have complaints procedures. Consider adapting yours and give it a more positive tone by calling it 'Discussing Problems' or something similar.

- Roll calls can occasionally be something of a chore. One way of doing this is to require pupils to report in to you over a ten-minute period. This provides a good opportunity to see each pupil, and hand out messages, etc.

- Recognise that you will probably not communicate easily with every one of your pupils. Other members of the house staff team should be used, and you will need to accept that they may relate better to some of these difficult pupils.

- It is also important to recognise that many teenagers will go through agonies trying to reconcile their desperate wish for individuality with a desire to conform with the peer group 'norms' and not stand out as being different.

- You will need to spot those who are under pressure and trying to cope with conflicting priorities. The pupil who is over-stretched in many directions, for example, from the simultaneous demands of sport, music and academic work, may need help to cope.

❖ In a single-sex house, with both male and female tutors, it will be important to establish clear protocols and expectations in terms of duty routines in the house at bedtimes.

❖ Ensure that the house staff team have as much information about pupils' circumstances and family background as possible. Their response to pupils' needs may depend on it.

❖ Try to remain neutral to start with, when intervening in a dispute between one of your boarders and another member of staff. Misunderstanding and over-reaction can be initiated by either party!

❖ Parents can sometimes have over-inflated expectations of their offspring's academic ability. You may find yourself having to resolve a situation where a child simply cannot cope with this, and reacts to the pressure inappropriately.

When things are at their lowest, and you are under pressure yourself (as you undoubtedly will be from time to time), try if at all possible to keep things in perspective. Being a housemistress or housemaster is certainly an awesome responsibility, and it is often incredibly demanding. But it should ultimately be richly satisfying and enjoyable.

CASE STUDIES

A selection of case studies and boarding scenarios is provided to enable staff to discuss issues and strategies to deal with a variety of welfare situations.

Case Study 1

Charlie (16) is at odds with his family, and with school. His parents are hardly able to communicate with him, and his father often takes out his frustrations at not being able to get through to his son on the school and the house staff in particular. "The school ought to be able to motivate my son." Charlie checked in at the start of prep but at 10.30 p.m. roll call he was not around. No one seems to know where he is. By 11.30 p.m., you are frantic. Midnight – you hover over the phone not sure whether to ring the head, the police or parents. Your resident house tutor still hasn't got back from the staff dinner night elsewhere in school. At 12.01 a.m. the phone rings. It is the police saying that they have found Charlie covered in blood, sitting in a bus shelter, three miles out of town. The cuts and bruises are only superficial – a police surgeon has cleaned him up and there is nothing broken. However, he doesn't seem to be very communicative. Will someone come and collect him from the police station? They will want to talk to him again in the morning. You put the phone down, and the fire alarm goes off. . . .

❖ What are your immediate thoughts and actions?

❖ How will you deal with Charlie – now, and in future?

Case Study 2

Marti is 16, and on exchange for a year from a German school. She has been an excellent member of the house, and is well liked. Earlier this evening (Saturday), she and a group of other lower sixth pupils went into town with permission to collect a take-away meal. There was an altercation involving local youths, during which the group scattered. Tragically, Marti ran across the High Street in panic, and was hit by a vehicle. She is in a critical condition in the local hospital. It is nearly midnight (1 a.m. German time). You are not sure how well her parents speak English. The phone rings. It is a journalist from the regional newspaper, not known for its strong support of the school. He has just got wind of the accident.

❖ What actions will you now take?

❖ How will you respond tomorrow (Sunday)?

Case Study 3

It is the first morning back after the holidays. You go into the dormitory as the pupils are getting up. One has bruises on his/her back and legs. You noticed exactly the same thing last time s/he returned to school after a holiday. When you asked him/her about it then, s/he looked uncomfortable and said s/he had fallen off his/her bike.

❖ What would you do this time?

Case Study 4

One of the 14-year-old boarders confides in you that s/he is in trouble, and needs advice. S/he has been in with bad company during the recent holidays. A couple of weekends ago, there was a party and, while the host's parents slipped out for a few hours, people got very drunk and noisy, and some cannabis was used. The police were called. The student is afraid of what action they might take. The student is a weekly boarder and clearly needs help. The student is not prepared to give any more details but s/he is clearly worried, and performance in the classroom and on the games field is very badly affected. All the staff are complaining. You mull over these matters overnight, and have a further talk with the student the next day. S/he seems very depressed, and the conversation gets around to home and family. It doesn't take much to read between the lines and recognise an acrimonious and disintegrating marriage. The student is now weeping openly as s/he describes his/her fear of what split parents will mean to him/her and the 8-year-old twins. By tea-time, you hear that the student has been caught smoking and that the deputy head is breathing fire at yet another misdemeanour.

❖ What are your thoughts?

- ❖ Who will you discuss the matter with? Are there any confidentiality issues here?

- ❖ Draw up an action plan to involve other support staff in school.

- ❖ As the constant resident presence in the house, you clearly have a major on-going role. How will you hope to resolve the situation over the next days and weeks?

Case Study 5

Jim is an upper sixth boarder, Sue is a lower sixth day girl. They have been going out with one another for about two years. The relationship is somewhat of a joke among 'the lads'. Jim's claims concerning his exploits with Sue defy even their adolescent imaginations. The girls are worried on two counts: they are becoming fed up at seeing Jim in their common room every break-time and they are embarrassed at seeing Sue and Jim draped over one another in public. Sue has cut herself off completely from the girls.

Both housemaster and housemistress have had informal chats with them, together and individually. Both sets of parents have been consulted over a longish period of time. The parents say that they would like the relationship to end but encourage the pair to spend holidays away together and, in holiday time, allow them to spend evenings alone together.

- ❖ How should house staff and the school now respond to:
  - Jim and Sue?
  - their parents?/other parents?
  - other pupils?

- ❖ How can staff ensure acceptable and appropriate behaviour (in public and private) without being unduly restrictive?

Case Study 6

Sarah is 15 years old. Last school year she was noted to be academically bright, and a happy, sociable girl, with many extra-curricular interests, especially art and debating.

This term, she has been absent from these, appears much thinner and paler in her appearance, and is noticeably less social with her peers and school staff, often showing wild fluctuations in mood and character.

One of her closest friends lets slip to you that she suspects Sarah is "losing it" – always on about how she looks and staying by herself to finish assignments. "She's no fun anymore", and refuses to eat with her friends at McDonald's – "she just sips black coffee".

You ask Sarah, during a quiet moment, if there is anything wrong but her response is curt and negative.

❖ How might you and your colleagues in school respond to Sarah?

Case Study 7

In order to be able to care for the boarders effectively, staff need to have the right level of information about new pupils on their arrival in the school. In the new intake, there are girls and boys in the following categories:

(*a*) asthmatics;

(*b*) a girl raped at the age of 12 – now 16 and seems to have recovered from it;

(*c*) a parent who is an alcoholic but who is denied access to the child *via* the courts;

(*d*) a bed-wetter;

(*e*) a boy whose twin died at birth;

(*f*) a child whose stepfather has been accused of child abuse but who was cleared by the courts;

(*g*) a Down's Syndrome sibling;

(*h*) a family with financial problems;

(*i*) a girl who has self-harmed;

(*j*) a boy who was on the verge of being suspended from his previous day school for consistently poor behaviour;

(*k*) a pupil who is HIV-positive;

(*l*) a pupil who is joining the school after being expelled from a previous boarding school for a minor cannabis offence.

- ❖ Who should have access to the full background circumstances of each of the above pupils?

- ❖ Is there any other information that should be made available about these pupils to those staff who will come into contact with them?

Case Study 8

Chris, a pupil in your house, comes to get something one evening for a 'headache'. He eventually tells you that he and a friend, who is a day pupil in the school, have tried cannabis during the Easter holidays.

They were at home alone, and had found the substance belonging to his father, who has a very liberal view about this sort of thing. Chris is worried because his friend is feeling increasingly uncomfortable about it and may tell his parents. Chris does not want his father to get into trouble and does not know what to do. He has talked it over with a few other close friends in the house but he does not think that they have told anyone else yet.

- ❖ How may Chris be helped on the evening of the disclosure?

- ❖ What would you do next? Who would you tell and what would be your course of action?

- ❖ Possible outcomes to the situation?

Case Study 9

Jo is new this year, and to start with seemed very outgoing and quite gregarious and lively, perhaps even a bit of a show-off at times. Two weeks into term, s/he was suddenly and painfully homesick. S/he now feels no one likes her/him. Parents live abroad, and the guardians, a quite elderly uncle and aunt, live over 100 miles away. Jo has been coming in to you regularly complaining of a bad cold, throat, head and anything else s/he can think of.

* ❖ What can you do to help, and who else might you involve?

Case Study 10

John is a bright and intelligent sixth former. He has become increasingly concerned with his own sexuality. He thinks he is gay. Although he says he gets on well with girls, he says he does not remotely fancy them physically. He is afraid to talk with parents, and reads too much about what might (or might not) be his 'condition'. He has kept his worries bottled up from his friends for a long time, for fear of what they might say. He chooses a quiet time in the late evening and just pops in for a chat.

* ❖ What is your response?

* ❖ How do you help him, and who else might you involve?

* ❖ Are there any confidentiality issues here?

Case Study 11

Michael (13) is a prep school boarder and is physically quite mature. Recently, he has 'discovered' girls, and has been showing off to some of the older girls. On Sunday, the Gap student found him having a hug behind the cricket pavilion with Rosie, with whom he has become infatuated, and in the boarders' common room he is repeatedly found in a close cuddle on the sofa, much to the embarrassment of some of the younger boarders. Last night, you overheard some of the 10-year-olds telling each other what they thought Michael and Rosie had been up to – using explicit language that you found distasteful and disturbing. They suddenly realise you have overheard them; some look embarrassed, others clearly wonder how you will react.

* ❖ How would you respond in the short term – to them – and to Rosie and Michael?

* How might you and the boarding house staff ensure that things are dealt with appropriately over the next few weeks, before the pupils go home.

Case Study 12

One of the 12-year-olds in your boarding house is complaining of sleeping poorly, has a lack of appetite and is alienating his peers because he is starting to become careless with his personal hygiene. You do know that the child has low self-esteem and can be emotionally fragile.

* How would you respond to this child? Who else might you involve?

* What other information about the child would you like to know?

* Would your 'diagnosis' and 'solution' be different, depending on whether the child is a boy or a girl? Would it be different if the child was aged eight . . . or aged 16?

The editor is grateful to Alison Scott, Roger Morgan, Clive Thorpe, Emma McKendrick and Ian Small for contributing additional case studies and ideas included in the above.

BOOK LIST AND REFERENCE MATERIAL

The following titles appear in the order in which they appear in the chapters, or are relevant to the topics covered.

Department of Health, *The Children Act 1989: Guidance and Regulations (Volume 5 – Independent Schools),* The Stationery Office.

Bee, Helen (1997), 8th ed., *The Developing Child,* Longmans.

Department of Health (1995), *The Children Act 1989: The Welfare of Children in Boarding Schools (Practice Guide),* The Stationery Office.

Birch, Ann (1997), *Developmental Psychology,* Macmillan.

Simmons, R. G., Blyth D. A. and McKinney R. L. (1983), in *Girls at Puberty,* Penguin.

Best, R. *et al.* (1995), *Pastoral Care and Personal–Social Education – Entitlement and Practice,* Cassell.

Hamblin, D. H. (1978), *The Teacher and Pastoral Care,* Blackwell.

Department for Education and Employment (1996), *Boarding Accommodation – A Design Guide* (Building Bulletin 84), The Stationery Office.

Morgan, Roger (1993), *School Life – Pupils' Views on Boarding,* London, HMSO.

Kahan, B. (ed.) (1994), *Growing up in Groups,* London, HMSO.

Lewis, C. (1996), *Aspects of Human Development,* Leicester, British Psychological Society.

Lloyd, P. (1995), *Cognitive and Language Development,* Leicester, British Psychological Society.

Schaffer, R. (1995), *Early Socialisation,* Leicester, British Psychological Society.

Smith, P., Cowie, H. and Blades, M., 3rd ed. (1999), *Understanding Children's Development,* Oxford, Blackwell.

Turner, P. J. (1995), *Sex, Gender and Identity,* Leicester, British Psychological Society.

Brierley, J. (1994), *Give Me a Child Until he is Seven,* London, Falmer Press.

National Children's Bureau (1991), *Residential Care and the Children Act 1989: A Resource Pack for Residential Care Staff,* London, NCB.

Coleman, J. and Hendry, L. (1999), *The Nature of Adolescence,* London, Routledge.

Waddell, M. (1994), *Understanding 12- to 14-year-olds,* London, Rosendale Press.

Bradley, J. and Dubinsky, H. (1994), *Understanding 15- to 17-year-olds,* London, Rosendale Press.

Goleman, D. (1996), *Emotional Intelligence,* London, Bloomsbury.

Kindlon, Dan and Thompson, Michael (1999), *Raising Cain: Protecting the Emotional Life of Boys,* London, Michael Joseph.

Rogers, Carl (1990), *The Carl Rogers Reader,* Constable.

Egan, Gerard (1990), *The Skilled Helper,* Pacific Grove, Brooks/Cole.

Bovair, K. and McClaughlin, C. (eds.) (1993), *Counselling in Schools,* London, Fulton.

Nelson-Jones, R. (1993), *Practical Counselling and Helping Skills,* London, Cassell.

Olweus, Dan (1993), *Bullying at School,* Oxford, Blackwell.

Department for Education (1994), *Bullying: don't suffer in silence,* HMSO.

Smith, Peter and Thompson, David (eds.) (1990), *Practical Approaches to Bullying,* David Fulton.

Department of Education and Science (1991), *Boarding School Line,* London.

Besag, Valerie (1989), *Bullies and Victims in Schools,* Open University Press.

Sharp, S. and Smith, P. K. (1995), *Tackling Bullying in your School,* London, Routledge.

Judson, Stephanie (ed.) (1983), *A Manual on Non-violence and Children,* Philadelphia, New Society Publishers.

Fine, Nic and Macbeth, Fiona, *Playing With Fire: Training for the Creative Use of Conflict,* Youth Work Press.

Adair, J. (1987), *Effective Team Building,* Pan Books.

Bennett, N. (1995), *Managing Professional Teachers,* London, Paul Chapman.

Covey, S. (1989), *The Seven Habits of Highly Effective People,* Simon & Schuster.

Covey, S. *et al.* (1994), *First Things First,* Simon & Schuster.

Handy, C. B. (1990), *Understanding Schools as Organisations,* Penguin Books.

Department for Education and Employment (1998), *Health and Safety of Pupils on Educational Visits,* DfEE Publication HSPV2.

Department of Health (1999), ***Working Together to Safeguard Children,*** The Stationery Office.

Association of Teachers and Lecturers (2000), ***Taking Students Off-site.***

Yule, William and Gold, Anne (1993), ***Wise Before the Event,*** London, Calouste Gulbenkian Foundation.

Hay, Ian (1914), ***The Lighter Side of School Life,*** T. N. Foulis.

Rae, John (1998), ***Letters to Parents,*** Harper Collins.

Scottish Office (1998), ***Improving the Care and Welfare of Residential Pupils.***

Smith, Jonathan (2000), ***The Learning Game,*** Little, Brown & Co.

Anthony, Vivian and Bush, Charles (2000), ***Head to House,*** John Catt.

Gania and Powell (1999), ***Seeding Intercultural Sensitivity in the Classroom,*** The British Council.

The British Council, ***Feeling at Home: A guide to cultural issues for those working with international students.***

The British Council, ***Next Steps: An orientation booklet for international students.***

Department of Education and Science (1989), ***Report of HMI on Pastoral Care in Secondary Education: An Inspection of Some Aspects of Pastoral Care in 1987-8,*** DES.

Crisp, A. H. (1980), ***Anorexia Nervosa: 'Let me be',*** London, Academic Press.

Brownell, K. D. and Foreyt, J. P. (1986), ***Handbook of Eating Disorders – Physiology, Psychology and Treatment of Obesity, Anorexia and Bulimia,*** New York, Basic Books.

Hargreaves, David H. and Hopkins, David (1998), ***The Empowered School: the management and practice of development planning,*** Cassell.

Department of Education and Science (1989), ***Planning for School Development,*** HMSO.

Everard, K. B. and Morris, G. (1996), ***Effective School Management,*** London, Paul Chapman.

Macgilchrist, B. *et al.* (1995), ***Planning Matters,*** London, Paul Chapman.

Appendix 1

A SUMMARY OF BOARDING WELFARE LEGISLATION

Note: these notes should not be taken as an absolute or definitive statement of either the law or of government guidance.

Primary legislation is the law of the land passed by Parliament in Acts of Parliament and must be obeyed. *Secondary legislation* is also law, but issued by the Secretary of State under delegated powers from Parliament – usually in the form of Regulations. *Statutory guidance* is not law, but is issued by the Secretary of State, and statutory authorities such as social services departments and the National Care Standards Commission must usually follow such guidance. *Practice guidance* has no statutory force, but is issued by a government department to be used where useful.

Welfare Legislation and Guidance

Section 87 of the Children Act 1989

This is the primary legislation that imposes a welfare duty upon schools towards their boarders, and upon (at present) local social services authorities (and, in the future, the National Care Standards Commission) to inspect the performance of that welfare duty. The key wording at present is:

"It shall be the duty of the proprietor of any independent school which provides accommodation for any child, and any person who is not the proprietor of such a school but who is responsible for conducting it, to safeguard and promote the child's welfare." (Subsection 1).

"Where accommodation is provided for a child by an independent school within the area of a local authority, the authority shall take such steps as are reasonably practicable to enable them to determine whether the child's welfare is adequately safeguarded and promoted while he is accommodated by the school." (Subsection 3).

"Where a local authority are of the opinion that there has been a failure to comply with subsection (1) in relation to a child provided with accommodation by a school within their area, they shall notify the Secretary of State." (Subsection 4).

From (provisionally) 2002, the wording of these sections will change to read:

"Where a school or college provides accommodation for any child, it shall be the duty of the relevant person to safeguard and promote the child's welfare." (Subsection 1).

"Subsection (1) does not apply in relation to a school or college which is a children's home or care home." (Subsection 2).

"Where accommodation is provided for a child by any school or college the appropriate authority shall take such steps as are reasonably practicable to enable them to determine whether the child's welfare is adequately safeguarded and promoted while he is accommodated by the school or college." (Subsection 3).

"Where the Commission are of the opinion that there has been a failure to comply with subsection (1) in relation to a child provided with accommodation by a school or college, they shall:

(*a*) in the case of a school other than an independent school or a special school, notify the local education authority for the area in which the school is situated;

(*b*) in the case of a special school which is maintained by a local education authority, notify that authority;

(*c*) in any other case, notify the Secretary of State." (Subsection 4).

"Where accommodation is, or is to be, provided for a child by any school or college, a person authorised by the appropriate authority may, for the purpose of enabling that authority to discharge its duty under this section, enter at any time premises which are, or are to be, premises of the school or college." (Subsection 5).

Note:

❖ the welfare duty applies to ALL children *accommodated*, not just boarders – including overnight accommodation of non-boarders, and of children not educated at the school;

❖ the duty applies to accommodation the school arranges, as well as that on site – *e.g.* lodgings, guardian or hostel arrangements;

❖ the welfare duty relates to individual children, not the group;

❖ the duty includes *promoting* welfare, as well as protecting from harm;

❖ Section 87 currently applies only to independent schools – but the amended wording from 2002 extends this to cover all types of school with boarding and also further education colleges with residential provision;

❖ the inspecting authority may take steps other than inspection to monitor welfare;

❖ failures in welfare *must* be reported by welfare inspecting authorities to DfEE (the Registrar of Independent Schools) or to the LEA in the case of a maintained school – the authority has no discretion;

❖ the amended legislation from 2002 will transfer the responsibility for inspecting boarding welfare from social services authorities to a new National Commission for Care Standards (in England) and (in Wales) the National Assembly.

Other subsections give inspectors (provided they carry both ID and authorisation) right of access to premises, pupils and records relevant to boarding. (There is also provision for Government to appoint bodies other than social services or the National Care Standards Commission to carry out welfare inspections – this power has, however, never been used.)

The National Care Standards Commission will inspect schools to a single set of National Boarding Standards, using a single national methodology.

Inspection of Premises, Children and Records (Independent Schools) Regulations 1991*

Secondary legislation, currently detailing social services rights of access to premises, pupils and relevant records.

"Volume 5" (full title "The Children Act 1989 Guidance and Regulations, Volume 5, Independent Schools")*

The Government's current statutory guidance for welfare in independent boarding schools – the definitive document for both schools and inspection authorities. All welfare inspections and reports, and all local authority standards documents, should be based on this guidance – social services recommendations to DfEE for enforcement action on welfare grounds should specify where they believe this guidance has been breached. Also contains guidance on conduct of inspections. ***Beware*** – this guidance has been amended and expanded by Circular LAC(95)1 below.

Department of Health Circular LAC(95)1 – "Inspection of Boarding Schools (Section 87 Children Act 1989): Further Guidance"*

Current statutory guidance amending and extending the above definitive Volume 5 guidance – mainly in relation to inspection. Reduces the inspection frequency for most boarding schools to a full welfare inspection every four years with regular informal contacts between – the criteria for reduced frequency are set out in an appendix. Includes useful statutory guidance on a number of problematic issues – *e.g.* guardianship, use of pupil questionnaires in inspections, making complaints about inspection, inspection of staffing records and the difference between inspection and child protection investigation. Includes a very useful set of standard headings to be used in welfare inspection reports – these provide a framework for both self-assessment and statutory inspection, and effectively define what 'welfare' covers. Use Volume 5 and LAC(95)1 together as the definitive statutory guidance 'set' on welfare and welfare inspection.

The Children Act 1989: the welfare of children in boarding schools: Practice Guide*

A handbook of more general guidance from the Department of Health, to accompany the original Volume 5 guidance above. Intended for social services, but a useful elaboration for schools of the more formal Volume 5 statutory guidance.

Section 63 of the Children Act 1989

Primary legislation requiring all independent schools which accommodate (or intend to accommodate) four or more children (*i.e.* under 18) for 295 days or more a year, to register with the local social services authority as children's homes. Schools providing *or arranging* accommodation of children outside normal term times (including arranging accommodation with guardians or in lodgings during school holidays) should check whether they are subject to this requirement. Social services authorities can take enforcement action in extremis to cancel registration as a children's home (subject to representations and appeals procedures), which has the effect of making it illegal for the school to accommodate or arrange accommodation for any child for 295 days or more. ***Beware:*** (1) the law was amended to introduce the 295 day criterion – the original criterion based on having 50 or fewer boarders has been repealed; (2) in 2002, there will be a further amendment to the detail of the 295-day definition.

Children's Homes Regulations 1991

Detailed secondary legislation with which schools registered as children's homes must comply – and against which social services authorities must inspect them. ***Beware:*** (1) these Regulations have been amended, mainly to apply an adapted (lighter) version to schools as opposed to 'ordinary' children's homes; (2) there will be a completely new set of Children's Homes Regulations from 2002.

---

*These documents are likely to be superseded in 2002. They represent current guidance until then, and continue to reflect good practice.

The Children (Homes, Arrangements for Placements, Review and Representations) (Miscellaneous Amendments) Regulations 1993

The secondary legislation amending the Children's Homes Regulations when applied to boarding schools registered as children's homes (plus some other amendments).

Department of Health Circular LAC(93)24

The statutory guidance which explains the amendments to the current Children's Homes Regulations for schools registered as children's homes. Also includes some useful other miscellaneous guidance relevant to all schools (*e.g.* on guardianship arrangements).

Volume 4 (full title "The Children Act 1989 Guidance and Regulations, Volume 4, Residential Care")

The current statutory guidance for schools that have to register as children's homes, together with comprehensive guidance on operating a children's home. ***Beware*** that the Regulations behind this guidance have been amended to lighten their load slightly for schools registered as children's homes.

School Life – pupils' views on boarding (Stationery Office)

A compendium of the (remarkably sensible and consistent) views of boarders themselves about a wide variety of welfare issues in boarding. Based on research in Oxfordshire, and published by the Government as a source document on welfare in boarding schools – intended to be readable and applicable on most boarding issues on any 'wet Monday' in the boarding house. Contains a useful summary of the 'Boarders' Best Buy' in welfare issues.

Permissible Forms of Control (Department of Health)

Practice guidance from the Department of Health on the tricky issue of using physical intervention and restraint with children likely to injure themselves or others or severely damage property. Intended for children's homes accommodating children with serious behaviour problems – but useful reference if a school finds itself having to contemplate use of restraint.

Choosing with Care (Stationery Office)

The Warner Report into selection of staff to work in children's homes. Has become the definitive practice guidance on safer staff selection methods, and recent Government announcements clearly indicate that its recommendations are likely to become required practice for boarding schools in the future. Merits purchase in preparation for future Government welfare requirements.

DfEE Circular 9/93

The definitive DfEE statutory guidance on conduct of staff recruitment checks, operation of List 99 and the criminal record checking system, and referral of cases of staff leaving under circumstances making them unsuitable to work with children in the future.

Developing the Protective Culture (NSPCC)

Useful Training Pack on child protection, produced by NSPCC with schools in Oxfordshire. Contains 'photocopiable' pages and sections of use in staff handbooks.

Working Together under the Children Act 1989 (Department of Health)

The definitive statutory guidance on child protection, investigation of child abuse allegations, and co-operation between different authorities in child protection. An updated version was published in December 1999.

The Education (School Premises) Regulations 1999

Detailed regulations on school premises design issued by DfEE, and including definitive requirements for boarding accommodation (*e.g.* ratios of toilets, size of rooms). Constitutes statutory regulations for maintained boarding schools – but does not have statutory force for independent schools, for whom it should therefore be regarded as guidance. However, the regulations are the single national Government source for boarding house design requirements, and should be followed by independent schools unless there is very good reason not to do so – they could become statutorily binding in the future. As the only national regulations, most other premises guidance (*e.g.* social services authority standards used in welfare inspections) is based on these.

Boarding Accommodation – a Design Guide – DfEE Building Bulletin 84 (Stationery Office)

A useful handbook on design of premises, to accompany the School Premises Regulations. Readable practice guidance, based on practical and operational considerations, with plenty of useful examples of different layouts and alternatives. Essential reading for any school (and architect) planning new or adapted boarding accommodation.

The Government's Response to the Children's Safeguards Review (and accompanying Department of Health Circular LAC(98)27)

Published November 1998 – the Government's action plan in response to the Utting Report on safeguarding children living away from home. Includes significant proposed Government actions relevant to boarding schools, including increased emphasis on complaints procedures for pupils, increased emphasis on staff recruitment procedures and checks (in line with the 'Warner Principles' of the Choosing with Care document above), clarification of the position of schools requiring registration as children's homes, promotion of welfare training for boarding school staff (already started through BSA), a revised accreditation system for services funding, stronger enforcement (with a revised DfEE registration system) where schools are found to be failing to safeguard and promote welfare, establishment of a single Criminal Records Agency to improve the recruitment checking of staff, and consultation on possible requirements for schools to have governing bodies.

School Standards and Framework Act 1988

The Act that from 1st September 1999 completed the legal prohibition of corporal punishment in schools by banning use of corporal punishment of privately funded pupils in independent schools.

The editor is most grateful to Dr Roger Morgan, Chief Inspector, Oxfordshire Social Services, for compiling this summary of boarding welfare legislation.

Appendix 2

NATIONAL BOARDING STANDARDS

National Minimum Standards for Sound Boarding Practice in Boarding Schools

These National Boarding Standards have been agreed and adopted by those bodies represented on the National Boarding Standards Committee (see below). After extensive trialling and consultation with the 594 ISC accredited boarding schools and 36 accredited state boarding schools, the final version was adopted unanimously by the national committee and was submitted in June 2000 to the Department of Health and the Department for Education and Employment for consideration and approval. They were compiled and written by Dr Roger Morgan, Chief Inspector for Oxfordshire Social Services.

CONTENTS

Staffing

Premises

List of Policies and Documents
List of Records

NATIONAL STANDARDS FOR BOARDING SCHOOLS

The National Boarding Standards are intended to provide nationally required minimum standards for the provision of welfare in boarding schools, together with accompanying criteria for use in assessing schools against each standard during inspection. They are intended to form the basis for all statutory and accreditation inspections and reports on boarding welfare, carried out under the Children Act 1989 by the National Care Standards Commission, and by ISI and OFSTED, in order to ensure that all inspection and accreditation processes assess boarding to the same agreed minimum standards and by the same criteria.

The standards and criteria have been constructed from the standards developed by:

- The Office for Standards in Education;
- The Independent Schools Council (ISC);
- HQ Services Children's Education (UK);
- Local Social Services Authorities.

They are also drawn from the following Government documents:

- Department of Health Children Act Guidance and Regulations;
- Department of Health Practice Guidance;
- Department of Health Local Authority Circular LAC(95)1;
- The Education (School Premises) Regulations 1999 (DfEE);
- DfEE boarding accommodation design guidance (Building Bulletin 84);
- School Life – boarders' views on boarding (Department of Health);
- DfEE Circular 9/93 (Protection of Children);
- Department of Health Guidance "Working Together to Safeguard Children" 1999.

The standards are consistent with guidance and requirements relating to boarding welfare issued under both the Children Act 1989 and by OFSTED, and reflect DfEE guidance on boarding premises for maintained schools. The standards and criteria are structured in accordance with the Department of Health's statutory guidance for reporting on welfare in boarding schools.

The standards cover the three main areas of good boarding welfare practice:

- Policies and Practices;
- People;
- Premises.

The standards have been drawn up by the National Boarding Standards Committee, comprising representatives of the following organisations. An essential feature of the National Boarding Standards is that they have been accepted as national standards for sound and satisfactory welfare in boarding schools by these organisations:

- ❖ Boarding Schools' Association (BSA);
- ❖ Department for Education and Employment (DfEE);
- ❖ Department of Health (DH);
- ❖ Girls' Schools Association (GSA);
- ❖ Governing Bodies' Association (GBA);
- ❖ Governing Bodies of Girls' Schools Association (GBGSA);
- ❖ Headmasters' and Headmistresses' Conference (HMC);
- ❖ Incorporated Association of Preparatory Schools (IAPS);
- ❖ Independent Schools' Association (ISA);
- ❖ Independent Schools' Bursars' Association (ISBA);
- ❖ Independent Schools' Council (ISC);
- ❖ Independent Schools' Inspectorate (ISI);
- ❖ Maintained boarding schools (STABIS);
- ❖ Medical Officers of Schools Association (MOSA);
- ❖ Office for Standards in Education (OFSTED);
- ❖ Oxfordshire County Council (OCC);
- ❖ Services Children's Education (SCE);
- ❖ Society of Heads of Independent Schools (SHMIS);
- ❖ Scottish Council for Independent Schools (SCIS).

While the National Boarding Standards are concerned with the welfare of boarding pupils, many of the standards and criteria will have wider application to the welfare of all pupils in a school. Similarly, the welfare of boarding pupils extends to their whole life at school and not solely their boarding experience; thus the standards inevitably relate to whole school activities and policies which affect boarders, and not exclusively to matters which do not affect day pupils.

Some standards are designated as *Core Standards*; these are identified in the following schedule of standards. Schools will be expected substantially to meet all the criteria for assessment of each Core Standard, while for each of the other standards an overall assessment of whether the school meets the standard will be made on the basis of evidence on the criteria listed. To be reported as meeting the National Boarding Standards, a school should substantially have met all the Core Standards, and the number and extent of any failures to meet other standards should not be such that inspectors conclude that there is a failure to safeguard and promote the welfare of its boarding pupils.

Where terms such as "reasonable", "satisfactory" and "appropriate" are used, this allows flexibility in the precise provision made, but requires the welfare objective of the standard to be met fully by the provision made.

Accommodation space standards and ratios of physical provision to boarder numbers are derived from the School Premises Regulations 1999, published by DfEE.

The National Boarding Standards are designed to be assessed through an accompanying inspection methodology, inspections using the National Boarding Standards being reported in a standard report format.

Principles of the National Boarding Standards

The National Boarding Standards are based on the following overarching Principles:

1. **Assessment of a school using the Standards should focus upon the extent of positive pastoral and welfare outcomes for boarders, and any risks to boarders, rather than upon structures and systems for their own sake.**

2. **The welfare objective of all boarding provision should be to safeguard and promote the welfare of each individual child accommodated.**

3. **Inspections of boarding schools should be carried out with consideration for the school's legitimate purpose and admissions policy, and its constant answerability to parents who have chosen that school for their child.**

These are supplemented by the following further Principles:

4. The same minimum standards should apply to all boarders in all boarding schools.

5. Where there is sound and satisfactory welfare, the standards should not inhibit the proper individual characteristics of different schools.

6. Assessment criteria should be equally valid for different types and organisation of school, and for different types and organisation of boarding.

7. Standards and criteria should be sufficiently specific to maximise the consistency, reliability and validity of assessments, regardless of who conducts them.

8. Criteria for the assessment of standards should enable corroboration of evidence from different sources.

9. Criteria for assessing standards should include both objectively observable facts and evidence from the views of boarders, staff and parents.

10. Assessment criteria should encourage positive appraisal as well as enabling shortcomings to be identified.

11. Criteria should where appropriate include comparisons with normative data for comparable schools.

12. Sound welfare provision should comprise both sound policies and procedures, and the delivery of satisfactory outcomes for boarders.

13. Standards should be derived from relevant Government guidance.

14. Inspections should give a valid appraisal of a school against published standards, but cannot ensure compliance with those standards at other times – it remains the responsibility of schools themselves to ensure continued compliance with the National Standards.

15. Standards should provide a basis for schools to use in self-appraisal of boarding welfare.

16. Standards should relate specifically to the welfare of boarding pupils, but should be consistent with good practice in the wider school.

The order of the standards and criteria in this document does not reflect any order of priority in importance to the welfare of boarders.

POLICIES, PROCEDURES AND PRACTICE

Welfare Policies and Procedures

STANDARD

> **1. A suitable statement of the school's boarding principles and practice should be available to parents, boarders and staff.**

CRITERIA

(*a*) The statement (which may be included in the Prospectus or similar document) covers the aims and organisation of boarding at the school, admission criteria, outline of facilities and welfare support services for boarders, any special religious or cultural aspects of the school, and relates as appropriate to relevant school policies and practice.

(*b*) This statement is up to date and is made available to parents, prospective parents, staff and boarders.

(*c*) The statement reasonably reflects the actual current boarding practice at the school, as identified through the inspection.

CORE STANDARD

> **2. The school should have, and follow, an appropriate policy on countering bullying, which is known to boarders and staff and is effective in practice.**

CRITERIA

(*a*) The school has a satisfactory policy on countering bullying, covering both measures to prevent bullying and to respond to observed or reported bullying.

(*b*) This policy is available and known to both staff and boarders, including junior and recently appointed staff.

(*c*) Discussion with boarders and staff confirms that suitable measures both to prevent and to respond to observed or reported bullying are being implemented in practice.

(*d*) No 'initiation ceremonies' intended to cause pain, anxiety or humiliation are reported by boarders or staff.

(*e*) Reported rates of bullying at the school (*e.g.* through boarder survey), as defined by boarders, do not significantly exceed the norms for comparable schools.[76]

CORE STANDARD

> 3. **The school should have, and follow, an appropriate policy on child protection and response to allegations or suspicions of abuse, which is consistent with local Area Child Protection Committee procedures, and is known to staff and as appropriate to older boarders in positions of responsibility.**

CRITERIA

(*a*) The school has a written child protection policy which is consistent with the requirements of the local Area Child Protection Committee procedures and which includes the requirement for timely referral (in writing or with written confirmation of telephoned referral) of allegations or suspicions of abuse[77] to the local social services department to carry out child protection investigations, rather than internal investigation by the school.

(*b*) The school's child protection policy includes procedures for all staff (including school medical and nursing staff) and others employed by the school, who receive allegations of abuse or suspect that abuse may be occurring at school or at home or elsewhere, from adults or peers, to consider measures that may be necessary to protect individual boarders, to avoid asking leading questions or giving inappropriate guarantees of confidentiality, to make and keep written records, and to report the matter to the school's designated person for further action[78].

(*c*) The school's child protection policy should explicitly provide for staff to raise concerns about school practices or the behaviour of colleagues which puts boarders at risk of abuse or other serious harm.

(*d*) The school's child protection policy is available to all staff and adults working at the school.

(*e*) All staff, at all levels, (including newly appointed and ancillary staff) have been given briefing or training on responding to suspicions or allegations of abuse.

(*f*) Staff with different roles and at different levels of seniority are able to describe what action they would take in response to an allegation or suspicion of abuse, consistent with the school's child protection policy.

(*g*) A senior member of staff is designated to take responsibility for the child protection policy, to liaise with the social services authority, and to co-ordinate action with social services and (where applicable) the police following any child protection allegation or suspicion affecting a boarder. This staff member has received training in child protection, and holds copies of relevant Government child protection guidance and local Area Child Protection Procedures.

(*h*) The local social services authority confirms that it has no current concern on child protection grounds regarding the way in which the school is safeguarding and promoting the welfare of its boarders, and that the school has responded appropriately to any recent suspicions or allegations of abuse and co-operated with any statutory child protection enquiry that has taken place involving the school since the previous inspection, contributing appropriately to the formulation and implementation of any child protection plan made.

(*i*) Where appropriate, senior pupils given positions of responsibility over other pupils are briefed on appropriate action to take should they receive any allegations of abuse.

(*j*) The school has satisfactorily dealt with any recent child protection issue that has arisen at school or involving a pupil while accommodated by the school away from the school site.

CORE STANDARD

> **4. The school should have, and follow, a fair and appropriate policy on discipline and use of punishments, known to boarders, staff and parents.**

CRITERIA

(*a*) The school has a written and appropriate policy on discipline, punishments and any rewards for good behaviour, which includes a statement of policy on use of restraint, which is available to all staff and parents and known to boarders.

(*b*) Any individual boarding house disciplinary policy or practice is both consistent with overall school policy, and formally sanctioned by the school.

(*c*) Discussion with boarders and staff demonstrates that discipline practice is in accordance with the school's policy.

(*d*) Observed standards of pupil behaviour are generally satisfactory.

(*e*) Corporal punishment is not used, and there are no reports that children have been hit as a disciplinary measure or in anger.

(*f*) No unacceptable or excessive punishments are used, or reported to be used by boarders or staff, including deprivation of access to food or drink, enforced eating or drinking, prevention of contact by telephone or letter with parents or any appropriate independent listener or helpline, requirement to wear distinctive clothing as a punishment (or night-clothes by day as a punishment), use or withholding of medical or dental treatment, deprivation of sleep, fines exceeding two thirds of the boarder's available pocket money provision, locking in a room or area of a building as a punishment.

(*g*) Any disciplinary powers of prefects or equivalent are clearly defined.

(*h*) Discussion with boarders and staff does not identify use of idiosyncratic punishments by individual staff or prefects which are not sanctioned by the school.

(*i*) Discussion with boarders identifies the school's use of punishments as generally fair.

(*j*) Administration of major punishments[79] is recorded in writing in a suitable book or log, with the name of the boarder concerned, the reason for the punishment, and the person administering the punishment.

(*k*) Any use of physical restraint is by reasonable and non-injurious means, only for the minimum time necessary to prevent injury to self or others or very serious damage to property, and always recorded in writing.

CORE STANDARD

> **5. The school should have, and follow, an appropriate policy on responding to complaints from boarders and parents, known to boarders, parents and staff.**

CRITERIA

(*a*) The school has a written and appropriate complaints procedure for complaints by boarders or parents, available and known to all staff and boarders.

(*b*) Documentation to parents identifies the means for parents to raise complaints or concerns about the care of their children at school.

(*c*) Discussion with boarders demonstrates that boarders know how to make a significant and reasonable complaint, and confidence that such complaints are/would be properly dealt with if made.

(*d*) A written record is kept of serious complaints and their outcome, for regular review[80] by the head or a senior member of staff.

(*e*) There is evidence that any recent complaints have been resolved either to the complainant's satisfaction, or with an otherwise appropriate outcome which balances the rights and duties of pupils.

STANDARD

> **6. The school should have, and follow, an appropriate policy on countering major risks to health, including substance abuse, which is known to staff and is effective in practice.**

CRITERIA

(*a*) The school's provision for personal, social and health education provides age appropriate content on alcohol and illegal substance abuse, smoking, sex education, HIV infection, hepatitis and sexually transmitted diseases, and protecting oneself from abuse.

(*b*) Staff demonstrate knowledge of the school's policy on response to alcohol, smoking and illegal substance abuse by boarders, and where such problems have been discovered, have followed that policy in practice.

STANDARD

> **7. Adequate records should be kept in relation to individual boarders' health and welfare needs and issues.**[81]

CRITERIA

(*a*) There are individual records for boarders, containing relevant health and welfare information provided by parents and recording significant health and welfare needs and issues during the pupil's time as a boarder.

(*b*) Boarders' records include identification of the persons with parental responsibility for the boarder, contact details for parents and any other emergency contact arrangements, and any court orders affecting parental responsibility or the care of the boarder.

(*c*) Boarders' records (*e.g.* school, rather than NHS, records kept by school nursing or matron staff) show any significant known drug reactions, major allergies and notable medical conditions, and this information is available to staff likely to administer medication or treatment to those boarders.

(*d*) Welfare needs and any special provision to be made for individual boarders are effectively made available to those staff with a need to know that information.

(*e*) There are no significant concerns from boarders or staff concerning confidentiality of personal information about boarders.

Organisation and Management

CORE STANDARD

> **8. There should be clear management and leadership of the practice and development of boarding in the school.**

CRITERIA

(*a*) Discussions with staff confirm that there is clear management and leadership of boarding at the school[82].

(*b*) Where applicable, members of the school's governing body are involved in consideration and monitoring of boarding provision.

(*c*) There is a training and development programme for staff with boarding duties, commensurate with their roles, experience, rate of turnover of staff, and any changes or planned changes in boarding in the school.

(*d*) Senior boarding staff have a satisfactory level of experience or training in the management and practice of boarding.

(*e*) There is a satisfactory staff disciplinary procedure, which includes provision for precautionary suspension of staff where necessary pending investigation or final decision following allegations or concerns having a potential significant effect on boarding welfare.

CORE STANDARD

> **9. The school should be capable of satisfactorily managing crises affecting boarders' welfare.**

CRITERIA

(*a*) Any major incidents or crises, such as outbreaks of illness, fires, serious allegations or complaints, significant accidents, have been satisfactorily managed.

(*b*) School documentation and discussion with staff demonstrate that reasonable plans are in place for the management of a range of foreseeable crises involving boarders' welfare.

STANDARD

> **10. The organisation of boarding houses or units should operate satisfactorily and provide appropriate protection and separation of boarders by age and gender.**

CRITERIA

(*a*) Discussion with boarders and staff demonstrates no major concerns regarding the school's house structure (*e.g.* vertical, horizontal).

(*b*) Discussion with boarders and staff does not identify any individual house or houses with significantly poorer physical provision, facilities or standards of welfare than other houses.

(*c*) There is no major or problematic discrepancy in standard between boarding provision for different genders.

(*d*) There are no major inappropriate or problematic discrepancies in principles or practice of boarding between different boarding houses.

(*e*) Sleeping areas, recreational areas, toilet and bathroom provision are reasonably separated for boarders of significantly different ages in vertically organised houses.

STANDARD

> **11. There should be an appropriate range and choice of activities for boarders outside teaching time, with adequate free time.**

CRITERIA

(*a*) School timetables, observation and discussion with boarders and staff demonstrate that boarders have suitable, and suitably timed, free time each day.

(*b*) School documents, and evidence from boarders and staff, demonstrate that the school provides a satisfactory range and choice of activities for boarders out of class time, throughout the year and both indoors and outdoors as appropriate.

(*c*) Boarders have appropriate access to school sports, recreational and hobby facilities outside class time.

(*d*) Boarders and staff do not report a significant lack of activities for boarders at weekends.

(*e*) There are sufficient appropriate supervised activities for any boarders remaining at school when most boarders have returned home (*e.g.* at 'exeat' weekends, half terms or holidays).

(*f*) Where boarders have access to the Internet, suitable supervision or safeguards exist to counter risks of access to inappropriate material.

STANDARD

> **12. Boarders should have opportunity to contribute views to the operation of boarding provision.**

CRITERIA

(*a*) There are formal opportunities (*e.g.* school councils, meetings, surveys) for boarders to express views on relevant aspects of boarding provision, either directly or through representatives.

(*b*) Discussion with staff and boarders demonstrates that boarders' views and concerns, properly expressed, are taken into account in the development and practice of boarding.

CORE STANDARD

> **13. Any prefect system (or equivalent) should give prefects (or equivalent) appropriate specific duties and responsibilities, with adequate staff supervision and measures to counter possible abuses of the role.**

CRITERIA

(*a*) Prefects are selected as suitable for the duties and responsibilities of the role (rather than on age or non-relevant factors).

(*b*) The duties, responsibilities and any powers of prefects or their equivalent are clearly stated to those appointed in writing.

(*c*) Prefects are not given undefined general duties or powers, nor used as direct general substitutes for staff.

(*d*) Prefects or their equivalent are given an induction into their role on appointment, which includes how to contribute to the school's anti-bullying practice and how to respond to allegations of serious bullying or abuse.

(*e*) Prefects (or their equivalent) and staff confirm that prefects are regularly supervised and directed in their duties by responsible staff.

(*f*) Discussion with boarders and staff demonstrates that prefects are generally fulfilling their roles appropriately, without abuse of the role (*e.g.* to bully others).

(*g*) The school also provides opportunities for boarders to learn and take on roles of leadership and responsibility, through other means than the prefect or equivalent system.

CORE STANDARD

> **14. Each boarder should have one or more members of staff to whom he or she can confidently turn for personal guidance or with a personal problem.**

CRITERIA

(*a*) The school has a clear policy that boarders may take a personal or welfare concern to any member of staff (not solely their own designated house or tutor staff), including the head.

(*b*) Boarders confirm that they are able to contact any member of staff with personal or welfare concerns.

(*c*) Boarders confirm that staff of both genders are available for them to approach with personal or welfare concerns.

(*d*) Boarders and staff confirm that any personal tutor system functions satisfactorily and that boarders use tutor contact as appropriate for discussion of personal and welfare issues as well as academic or administrative matters.

(*e*) Survey data confirm that boarders generally report being able to take personal problems or worries to a satisfactory range of different staff, without a significant proportion of boarders reporting that they could not take such issues to any member of staff.

(*f*) The school identifies to boarders at least one person outside the staff of the school (who may be a school counsellor) whom they may contact directly about personal problems or concerns at school.

(*g*) All persons identified to boarders for such contact have been subject to the same police and DfEE checks as school staff having substantial unsupervised access to boarders, with a satisfactory outcome.

(*h*) Boarders demonstrate to the inspector an awareness of the person(s) the school has designated for them to contact outside the school staff, and how they may be contacted.

Welfare Support to Boarders

CORE STANDARD

> **15. Appropriate first-aid and minor illness treatment should be available to boarders at school, with access to medical and dental services as required.**

CRITERIA

(*a*) The school has satisfactory arrangements to secure medical and dental attention for boarders as necessary, without undue delay (*e.g.* through registration with a local GP, or through a visiting school medical officer)[83].

(*b*) Any designated school nursing staff hold an RGN qualification, and the school has confirmed on appointment that they are registered with the United Kingdom Central Council. The title of 'nurse' is not used for staff not so qualified.

(*c*) If the school has a designated school nurse, that nurse should have access to a named doctor for professional guidance and consultation.

(*d*) Boarders report that they can freely choose whether or not they are accompanied by staff when being seen by the doctor or dentist.

(*e*) Boarders specifically wishing to see either a male, or a female, doctor are able to do so where this is feasible.

(*f*) Boarders competent to do so are able to make appropriate choices concerning medical or dental treatment.

(*g*) First-aid and minor illness treatment is given at school by competent designated staff (*e.g.* by or under the supervision of a qualified nurse or first-aider).

(*h*) Prescribed medication is only given to the boarder for whom it was prescribed, in accordance with the prescription or instructions from the pharmacy, and is not kept for general use for other boarders or added to 'stock' for such use.

(*i*) The school has secured, and follows, qualified medical or nursing advice in a written protocol on the provision of non-prescription 'household' medicines to boarders.

(*j*) Prescribed and 'household' medication, other than that kept by individual boarders able to administer and control their own medication, is kept securely (*e.g.* in a locked cabinet).

(*k*) Boarders keeping and administering their own medication are assessed by staff as sufficiently responsible to do so, and are able to store their medication safely and appropriately.

(*l*) A written school[84] record is kept of all medication, treatment and first-aid administered to boarders, giving name, date, medication/treatment, reason for administration (if not prescribed), which is signed by the responsible member of staff and is regularly monitored by an appropriate designated senior member of staff.

(*m*) A written school record is kept of all significant illnesses, accidents or injuries to boarders (either as part of the above school medication and treatment records or separately).

(*n*) The school has obtained prior written parental permission for the administration of first-aid and appropriate non-prescription medication to boarders, and to seek medical or dental treatment when required.

CORE STANDARD

> **16. Boarders who are ill should be regularly checked by a member of staff, and be able to summon staff assistance readily and rapidly when necessary.**

CRITERIA

(*a*) Boarders and staff confirm that boarders who are separated from others, in bed or otherwise, through illness, are regularly checked by a member of staff.

(*b*) Boarders confirm that they are able to summon staff assistance readily and rapidly when being looked after separately from others because of illness, by both day and night.

CORE STANDARD

> **17. Significant health and personal problems of individual boarders should be identified and managed appropriately.**

CRITERIA

(*a*) The school prepares and works to a written and agreed individual 'care plan', agreed with a parent, for any boarder with major special welfare needs, significant emotional or behavioural difficulties, or who does not see his or her parent or legal guardian at least three times a year.

(*b*) Appropriate provision is made to meet the assessed needs of boarders with Statements of Special Educational Needs.

(*c*) Boarders with problems of enuresis are appropriately supported in managing the problem and avoiding undue embarrassment.

(*d*) Boarders with other medical difficulties (such as asthma), with disabilities, or requiring special treatment or management because of health or welfare problems, are given suitable support, and activities are adapted as appropriate.

(*e*) Boarders confirm that boarders who are homesick are suitably supported at school.

(*f*) Boarders confirm that pupils who are being bullied are suitably supported, and that pupils who may bully others are also given suitable help and guidance.

(*g*) Boarders confirm that boarders undergoing times of personal stress (*e.g.* because of problems at home, or bereavements) are suitably supported.

(*h*) There is evidence that outside professional services (*e.g.* social worker, psychologist) are used where needed by individual boarders.

CORE STANDARD

> **18. The school should avoid inappropriate discrimination on grounds of gender, disability, race, religion, cultural background, linguistic background, sexual orientation or academic or sporting ability, should appropriately take these factors into account in its care of boarders, and should appropriately support and integrate identifiable minority groups amongst boarders.**

CRITERIA

(*a*) School documents demonstrate an appropriate approach to equal opportunities and avoidance of inappropriate discrimination of all forms.

(*b*) Appropriate provision is made where feasible and requested for boarders with particular cultural or religious needs or customs[85].

(*c*) Discussion with boarders and staff demonstrate that no identifiable minority groups within the school population are excluded or suffer from discrimination.

(*d*) Discussion with boarders and staff demonstrates that the school supports those boarders who for any reason do not 'fit in' to the school, house or pupil body.

(*e*) Appropriate provision or exemption is made for boarders with special dietary, dress or religious observance requirements because of religious or cultural background.

(*f*) Appropriate support is provided for boarders for whom English is not their first language, in boarding as well as through the curriculum.

CORE STANDARD

> **19. The school should enable boarders to contact their parents and families in private.**

CRITERIA

(*a*) The school facilitates boarders' contact with parents, and visits by parents to their children at school, at reasonable times.

(*b*) Observation and discussion with boarders confirm that boarders have access to a telephone (and if numbers require, more than one) to contact parents in reasonable privacy at reasonable times without having to seek permission from, or inform, staff.

(*c*) Boarders and staff confirm that boarders are able to write letters home and to receive letters from home (and to send and receive e-mail or voice mail messages to and from home if the school provides these facilities to boarders), without letters or messages being censored or read by staff or others, and without having to seek permission from, or inform, staff.

(*d*) The school can demonstrate that staff contact parents concerning major welfare concerns relating to boarders.

(*e*) Boarders are provided, either in writing or on notices by pupil telephones, with one or more appropriate helpline or outside contact numbers to ring in case of problems or distress.

STANDARD

> **20. The school should provide reasonable protection for boarders' personal possessions and any boarder's money or valuables looked after by the school.**

CRITERIA

(*a*) If the school provides or distributes pocket money, or looks after personal possessions for boarders, this is done fairly and a proper written record is kept.

(*b*) Each boarder has a suitably secure place to keep personal possessions and valuables safe, with reasonable access by the boarder (*e.g.* a lockable drawer, cupboard, locker, box or trunk).

STANDARD

> **21. There should be an appropriate process of induction and guidance for new boarders.**

CRITERIA

(*a*) New boarders should be given suitable information about boarding routines and rules, including key information in writing.

(*b*) There are arrangements for new boarders to have guidance from more experienced boarders.

CORE STANDARD

> **22. Any guardians appointed by the school should be subject to the same recruitment checks as staff having substantial unsupervised access to boarders, and their care of pupils should be monitored.**[86]

CRITERIA

(*a*) The school makes clear in writing to parents whether any guardians used by pupils of the school are arranged by or on behalf of the school, or by parents, clarifying that, in the latter case, parents rather than the school are responsible for the welfare of their children while staying with the guardians concerned.

(*b*) Any guardians appointed by the school to look after pupils are subject to police and DfEE checks, and the staff recruitment procedures set out in Standard 37, with a satisfactory outcome before any pupil is placed.

(*c*) The school regularly monitors the suitability of any guardian arrangements it makes.

STANDARD

> 23. **The head, or a senior member of the school's staff, should regularly monitor the school's records of risk assessments, punishments, complaints and accidents, to identify any issues requiring action.**

CRITERIA

(*a*) Records of risk assessments, major punishments, complaints and accidents are regularly (at least once a term) monitored by the head or a designated senior member of staff (see Standards 28 and 47 relating to risk assessments).

(*b*) Staff confirm that reasonable action is taken to reduce risks identified by risk assessments.

(*c*) Staff confirm that action has been taken in relation to any concentration or trend in recorded punishments, offences, complaints or accidents (*e.g.* relating to particular places, groups or times).

Other Provision for Boarders

CORE STANDARD

> 24. **Meals should be provided to boarders, which are adequate in quantity, quality, choice and provision for special dietary, medical or religious needs, with clean and suitable cutlery, crockery and dining facilities.**

CRITERIA

(*a*) Observation, inspection of recent or planned menus, meals taken by the inspector with boarders, and discussion with boarders and staff demonstrate that meals provided for boarders are nutritious, reasonably balanced, and adequate in quantity, quality, hygiene and temperature.

(*b*) Boarders have a choice of main dish at main meals, including a vegetarian choice.

(c) Boarders with special dietary, medical or religious needs requiring special catering provision are adequately catered for.

(d) Crockery and cutlery is sufficient and properly clean.

(e) Dining-rooms and furnishings are suitable and of sufficient size for the numbers and ages of boarders dining.

(f) Observation demonstrates that there is sufficient time at meal-times, taking into account any necessary queuing time, for boarders to finish their meals properly.

(g) Staff and pupils involved in preparing food for others have received appropriate training in food handling and hygiene.

(h) There are no significant outstanding recommendations of the Environmental Health Service.

CORE STANDARD

> **25. Boarders and boarding staff should be aware of emergency evacuation procedures from boarding accommodation. The school should comply with recommendations of the Fire Service, and should regularly carry out and record fire drills and any routine tests recommended by the Fire Service.**

CRITERIA

(a) There are no significant recommendations of the Fire Service outstanding beyond any timescale set by that Service for their implementation.

(b) Boarding staff demonstrate awareness of emergency evacuation procedures from boarding accommodation in case of fire.

(c) Boarders confirm knowledge of emergency evacuation procedures from sleeping and living areas in each boarding house.

(d) Records demonstrate that fire drills have been regularly (at least once per term) carried out in 'boarding time'.

(e) Records demonstrate regular testing of emergency lighting, fire alarms and fire-fighting equipment.

(f) Fire doors in boarding accommodation are not observed or reported to be wedged open without the express approval of the local Fire Service.

STANDARD

> **26. Schools where there are unusual or especially onerous demands on boarders should ensure that these are appropriate to the boarders concerned and do not unacceptably affect boarders' welfare.**

CRITERIA

(*a*) Discussion with staff and boarders demonstrates that any special welfare concerns or issues arising from unusual or especially onerous demands on boarders (*e.g.* demanding performance or practice programmes in addition to the usual school day) have been identified and are satisfactorily managed.

(*b*) Boarders still have reasonable free time each day alongside any other major demands on their time.

CORE STANDARD

> 27. **The school should make satisfactory provision for the welfare of any children it accommodates other than its own boarders.**[87]

CRITERION

(*a*) The organisational arrangements and discussion with staff demonstrate that any residential activities in which the school accommodates and looks after children other than its own boarders (*e.g. residential holiday activities*), provide satisfactorily for the supervision, welfare and protection of those children while accommodated by the school.

CORE STANDARD

> 28. **Identifiably high risk activities provided for boarders should be competently supervised and accompanied by adequate and appropriate safety measures.**

CRITERIA

(*a*) The school carries out risk assessments, recorded in writing, in relation to identifiably high-risk activities for boarders (including cadet and other uniformed organisation activities, and activities or instruction the school arranges to be provided by outside bodies), and takes reasonable measures to minimise unnecessary risks.

(*b*) Identifiably high-risk activities are instructed or supervised by adults holding the relevant qualification from the appropriate national governing body or association for the sport or activity concerned, where such a body can be identified; and where no such body can be identified, the school can demonstrate that reasonable steps have been taken to confirm that those supervising or instructing such activities are competent to do so.

(*c*) Safety measures are taken, and safety equipment provided, for boarders participating in identifiably high risk activities, in accordance with the recommendations of the appropriate national governing body or association for the sport or activity concerned, where such a body can be identified[88].

(*d*) Written parental permission is obtained for boarders to participate in identifiable high risk activities run by the school or arranged by the school with other groups or organisations.

(*e*) Where the school takes boarders to a centre providing activities requiring licensing under the Adventure Activities Licensing Regulations, the school can demonstrate that it has checked that the centre is so licensed[89].

STANDARD

> **29. Boarders should have access to information about events in the world outside the school, and access to local facilities which is appropriate to their age.**

CRITERIA

(*a*) Supervision arrangements for boarders' use of any local facilities outside school are appropriate to the age of the boarders involved, and the facilities used are of a suitable type without unreasonable risks to boarders.

(*b*) Boarders and staff confirm that boarders leaving the school site without staff are in age-appropriate groupings, only older boarders in senior age schools being permitted to leave the school site alone.

(*c*) Any community service activities by boarders outside the school are suitable and suitably supervised with acceptable levels of safety.

(*d*) Boarders have access to newspapers, television or other suitable information media at school.

PEOPLE

Staffing

CORE STANDARD

> **30. The staff supervising boarders outside teaching time should be sufficient in number and deployment for the age, number and needs of boarders, and the locations and activities involved.**

CRITERIA

(*a*) Staff supervision levels outside school time (*i.e.* early mornings before school, recreational periods during the school day, evenings and weekends), as observed by the inspector and reported by both staff and boarders, are satisfactory in number and staff competence for the number, age and nature of the boarder population, the layout of the school and grounds, and the range and nature of the activities involved.

(*b*) There is at least one adult in charge of each identifiable group of boarders, with the means to call for immediate back up from at least one other member of staff if necessary.

(*c*) The number of staff accompanying and in charge of boarders on organised trips away from the school site, overnight stays and trips abroad should at least satisfy DfEE guidance on minimum ratios[90], with an increased ratio of staff to pupils where the nature of the trip necessitates this. Staff numbers and deployment should be sufficient to supervise the pupils and activities involved, ensure that people not on the school staff or subject to the school's recruitment checks for access to boarders (including activity instructors) do not have substantial unsupervised access to boarders, and to deal with foreseeable emergencies. Where only one member of staff is in charge of pupils on any trip, that staff member has the means to call for back up from at least one other member of staff if necessary.

(*d*) The school can show a duty rota which demonstrates satisfactory levels of staff supervision of boarders during the early mornings, during breaks in the school day, during any evening prep. time, during evenings outside prep. time, and at weekends both during the day and in the evenings.

(*e*) There are satisfactory arrangements for the supervision of any boarders remaining in school accommodation during 'exeat' weekends, half-terms and holiday periods.

(*f*) There are satisfactory cover arrangements for boarding staff sickness and absence.

(*g*) Staff supervision levels remain adequate at those times which are identified by staff or boarders as having the 'thinnest' staffing levels.

(*h*) Boarders and staff do not report an insufficient level of staff supervision of boarders in the evenings or at weekends.

(*i*) The school has, and follows, a satisfactory policy for the safety and supervision of boarders during journeys, covering school transport, use of private vehicles and school use of public transport.

(*j*) The boarding staff group in day-to-day contact with boarders includes staff of both genders where this is practicable within the school's staffing structure.

CORE STANDARD

> **31. Boarders should at all times be under the overall supervision of an identified member of staff, and should be able to contact a member of staff in emergency.**

CRITERIA

(*a*) Boarders are able to identify the member of staff in charge of them, and how they can urgently contact that person, during out of school, evening and weekend times.

(*b*) There are means whereby staff know the whereabouts of boarders in their charge at all times (including a signing out and back in system for boarders leaving the school where permitted).

(*c*) Gap students are not left alone in charge of boarders without a supervising member of staff contactable on site or accompanying them when away from the school.

(*d*) There is a policy, known to staff, for searching for and if necessary reporting, any boarder missing from school.

CORE STANDARD

> **32. Staff should be present, and accessible to boarders as necessary, in each boarding house at night.**

CRITERIA

(*a*) There is at least one adult member of staff sleeping in each boarding house at night, responsible for the boarders in the house[91].

(*b*) There are additional members of staff sleeping in each boarding house where necessary because of the age and number of younger children, or the particular needs of boarders.

(*c*) Boarders have a satisfactory means of contacting a member of staff in each house at night.

(*d*) There are means for staff to know which boarders are sleeping in the house each night (*e.g.* in case of fire or of an expected boarder being missing).

STANDARD

> **33. All staff with boarding duties[92] have job descriptions reflecting those duties, receive induction training in boarding when newly appointed, and receive regular review of their boarding practice, with opportunities for continuing training in boarding.**

CRITERIA

(*a*) The school can produce job descriptions for staff with boarding duties which reflect their boarding responsibilities and duties.

(*b*) Staff with boarding duties confirm that they have job descriptions which properly reflect their current boarding duties and responsibilities.

(*c*) The role of spouses and partners of staff within boarding houses is where relevant made clear.

(*d*) The school has clear arrangements for the supervision of ancillary and contract staff and any temporary or agency staff or volunteers working at the school.

(*e*) The school has an appropriate induction training programme in boarding responsibilities and duties for newly appointed boarding staff (including any assistant or 'gap year' staff).

(*f*) The school's staff induction and training programme includes guidance on child protection.

(*g*) Recently appointed staff confirm that they have received adequate induction training in their current boarding responsibilities and duties.

(*h*) The school has an appropriate process for the regular review of the performance of each member of staff with boarding duties by a more senior or experienced member of staff (*e.g.* through individual supervision meetings or a staff appraisal system).

(*i*) Staff with boarding duties confirm that they have regular supervision and guidance as necessary from more senior or experienced staff.

(*j*) Job descriptions clearly state, and staff are themselves clear about, the person to whom each member of staff with boarding duties is accountable.

(*k*) The school provides opportunities for training and updating in boarding practice for all its boarding staff, including experienced boarding staff.

STANDARD

> **34. All staff with boarding duties should be provided with up-to-date written guidance on the school's boarding policies and practice.**

CRITERIA

(*a*) There is a staff handbook or similar written guidance readily available to all staff with boarding duties, which is up to date.

(*b*) Such guidance adequately covers the school's approach to boarding and the safeguarding and promotion of boarders' welfare; child protection, anti-bullying and sanctions policies; the school's tutor or equivalent and prefect or equivalent systems; responding to boarders' personal problems; the handling of complaints by boarders and parents; any special features of boarding; and the organisation of the boarding day.

(*c*) Staff, including junior, recently appointed and 'gap year' staff, confirm that they have been given such guidance.

CORE STANDARD

> **35. There should be sound staff/boarder relationships, and the overall boarder view should be that their staff look after them well, without either favouritism or antipathy towards individual boarders or groups of boarders.**

CRITERIA

(*a*) The general view of boarders, as expressed to inspectors, is that staff look after them well and fairly.

(*b*) There are no consistent and corroborated reports from boarders or parents of significant concern about the treatment of boarders by staff.

(*c*) Observed communication between staff and boarders is generally positive.

(*d*) Discussion with boarders and staff indicates that disagreements between boarders and staff are dealt with reasonably.

(e) Discussion and any comments received from boarders do not suggest inappropriate favouritism or antipathy of staff towards individuals or groups.

CORE STANDARD

> **36. Staff supervision of boarders should avoid intruding unnecessarily on boarders' privacy.**

CRITERION

(a) Observation and discussion with staff and boarders shows that staff supervision of boarders is by appropriate patrolling and availability in boarding accommodation, but that staff do not intrude inappropriately or in a way that embarrasses boarders at sensitive times such as dressing/ undressing, changing, bathing or showering – staff at such times being seen as "supervising but not watching"[93].

CORE STANDARD

> **37. Recruitment of all staff and other adults to be given substantial unsupervised access to boarders, or to boarding accommodation, must include police and DfEE checks with a satisfactory outcome, together with a satisfactory recruitment process recorded in writing.[94]**

CRITERIA

(a) The school's system for recruiting staff and other adults who will have substantial unsupervised access to either boarders or to boarding accommodation includes all the following before appointment, which can be verified from recruitment records:

in the case of all staff and other adults who will have substantial unsupervised access to either boarders or to boarding accommodation (including adults not employed by the school but resident in boarding accommodation, such as partners, spouses or adult family members of boarding staff):

(i)   check of identity against an official document;

(ii) police, List 99 and Department of Health checks carried out through DfEE, with a written record demonstrating that checks have been done;

(iii) written references, including the most recent employer, with a reference request letter that specifically asks all referees to state any known reason why the person should not be employed to work with children and that there should be no material mis-statement or omission relevant to the suitability of the applicant;

(iv) direct contact by the school with each referee to verify the reference;

and additionally, in the case of all staff who are to have substantial unsupervised access to boarders or to boarding accommodation (including teaching staff, staff with boarding duties, ancillary, domestic, grounds and maintenance staff, student staff, volunteers and visiting instructors if they have such access):

(v)   interview, with a written record of the outcome;

(vi)   check on proof of relevant qualifications, with a written record of its completion;

(vii)   requirement that applicants supply a full employment history, stating that any previous employer may be approached by the school;

(viii) contact by the school with each previous employer involving work with children or vulnerable adults to check the reasons the employment ended;

(ix)   explanation of any gaps in cv, with a written record by the school that explanations for any gaps have been sought and are satisfactory.

(*b*) Staff members and others subject to the above checks do not commence duties (or residence) at the school until receipt of all references and satisfactory completion of police and DfEE checks, unless exceptionally this is inevitable – in which case the school can demonstrate that staff commencing duties pending receipt of a satisfactory outcome to checks and references are supervised at a level that avoids them having substantial unsupervised access to boarders or boarding accommodation.

(*c*) Appointment of 'gap' student staff includes every element of the above recruitment checking system that is possible (even if the student concerned is already known to the school or to a trusted school abroad or is recruited through an agency).

(*d*) Where police and DfEE checks are not available for 'gap' student staff, the school obtains a 'certificate of good conduct' or equivalent from the relevant authorities of the student's home country where such facilities are available[95].

(*e*) Offers of appointment to staff and others subject to the above recruitment checks are made subject to satisfactory completion of police and DfEE checks and satisfactory references if not all yet received.

(*f*) All appointments to work with boarders (including internal transfers and promotions) are subject to a probationary period.

(*g*) Police and DfEE checks and references are included in the recruitment process for any guardians arranged by the school, and all adults in lodgings arranged by the school, with a satisfactory outcome received and recorded in writing by the school before any boarder is placed.

(*h*) The school either has a satisfactory system for carrying out police and DfEE checks on contractors' staff to whom the school itself gives substantial unsupervised access to boarders or boarding accommodation (*e.g.* contract cleaning, maintenance or catering staff), or has satisfactory arrangements to ensure that the school does not give contract staff substantial unsupervised access to boarders or boarding accommodation. The school has taken reasonably practicable steps to carry out police and DfEE checks on taxi drivers booked by the school to drive boarders unaccompanied by staff.

(*i*) The school has not offered work with boarders or in boarding accommodation to any person listed on DfEE List 99 or the Department of Health Consultancy Service list, or legally barred from working with children under the Protection of Children Act 1999.

CORE STANDARD

> **38. The school should not allow any adult appointed since October 1991 to have substantial unsupervised access to boarders, or to boarding accommodation, unless that adult has been satisfactorily police and DfEE checked.**

CRITERIA

(*a*) Discussion with staff confirms that no adult (appointed since October 1991) is given substantial unsupervised access to either boarders or to boarding accommodation without having been subject to police and DfEE checks with a satisfactory outcome.

(*b*) The school is able to confirm that staff identified by the inspector as having substantial unsupervised access to boarders or boarding accommodation (*e.g.* visiting music staff, volunteers, instructors, adults other than teaching or house staff) have either been police and DfEE checked with a satisfactory outcome, or are sufficiently supervised to prevent them having substantial unsupervised access to boarders or boarding accommodation.

(*c*) The school is able to confirm that adults visiting boarding accommodation (*e.g.* visitors, outside delivery and maintenance personnel) are kept under sufficient staff supervision to prevent their substantial unsupervised access to boarders or their accommodation.

(*d*) The school takes all practicable steps not itself to entrust boarders to 'unchecked' adults for journeys (*e.g.* by taxi) which involve giving such adults substantial unsupervised access to boarders.

CORE STANDARD

> **39. The school should report to DfEE any member of staff or other adult employed to work with boarders, who is either dismissed, or who resigns, in circumstances which suggest that they are unsuitable to work with children.**

CRITERION

(*a*) If there has been any dismissal or resignation of a member of staff or adult working with boarders at the school, in circumstances which suggest their unsuitability to work with children, this has been notified promptly and in writing to DfEE. (The school also satisfies this standard if there have been no such dismissals or resignations.)

PREMISES

Boarding Accommodation

CORE STANDARD

> **40. Boarding houses (including dormitories and living areas) and other accommodation provided for boarders should be appropriately lit, heated and ventilated, suitably furnished, accessible to any boarders with disabilities, and adequately maintained.**

CRITERIA

(*a*) Boarding houses and other areas for boarders are adequately lit by natural and artificial light, adequately heated and adequately ventilated.

(*b*) Boarding houses and other areas for boarders are generally clean.

(*c*) The standard of decoration of boarding houses and other areas for boarders is adequate.

(*d*) Furnishing of boarding houses and other areas for boarders is suitable, comfortable and in satisfactory condition.

(*e*) Boarders' accommodation and its furniture, fittings and equipment are generally free from breakages and from numerous or significant items requiring maintenance.

(*f*) Boarding accommodation is not unnecessarily noisy.

(*g*) Where there are boarders with disabilities, their accommodation is suitable or suitably adapted for their access to all areas and facilities they need to use.

STANDARD

> **41. Boarding accommodation should be reserved for the use of those boarders designated to use it, and protected from access by the public.**

CRITERIA

(*a*) Boarders' sleeping areas are for the exclusive use of boarders and other pupils sharing study/bedroom provision with boarders, other than by the reasonable invitation of the pupils designated to use those areas.

(*b*) Boarders' living areas are for the exclusive use of boarders and other pupils designated to share that provision, other than by reasonable invitation of pupils designated to use those areas.

(*c*) There is a clear school policy on access to school premises and boarders by people from outside the school, which is implemented in practice.

(*d*) Suitable and adequate security measures are in place to prevent unauthorised access by the public to boarding houses and other school buildings used by boarders (*e.g.* where applicable, security locks, restrictors on vulnerable windows, use of intruder alarms).

(*e*) Where feasible, given the nature of the school site, reasonable measures are taken to prevent or deter unauthorised public access to the school grounds.

(*f*) Any public use of school facilities does not establish substantial and unsupervised access to boarders, or boarding accommodation while occupied by boarders, by members of the public (including members of organised groups using school facilities).

CORE STANDARD

> **42. Sleeping accommodation should be suitably furnished and of sufficient size for the number, needs and ages of boarders accommodated, with appropriate separation between genders, age groups and from accommodation for adults.**

CRITERIA

(*a*) Beds are of sufficient size for the age of boarders, stable and of sound construction and in good condition, with mattresses of reasonable depth, clean and in sound condition.

(*b*) Bedding is clean and suitable for the age of boarders, and is reported by boarders to be sufficiently warm in winter.

(*c*) There is not an excessive variation in the standard of beds or bedding within any one dormitory.

(*d*) Bunk beds[96] are only exceptionally used for boarders beyond Year 8, and use of bunk beds at any age does not lead to overcrowding of bedroom or studying space.

(*e*) Beds have adequate space around them for boarders to change comfortably, and sufficient headroom above them (particularly above bunk beds).

(*f*) The beds closest together in dormitories are at least 900 mm apart.

(*g*) Dormitories are not reported by boarders or staff as overcrowded, and the smallest and the most apparently crowded dormitories in the school provide at least 4.2 m^2 per boarder plus 1.6 m^2 per dormitory of usable floor area[97].

(*h*) The smallest individual sleeping cubicles in the school provide at least 5 m^2 of usable floor area.

(*i*) All dormitories, single bedrooms and individual sleeping cubicles have a window.

(*j*) The smallest single bedrooms in the school provide at least 6 m^2 of usable floor area.

(*k*) Sleeping areas are either carpeted or have other suitable floor covering.

(*l*) There is adequate storage space either in or adjacent to sleeping areas for boarders' clothing and property.

(*m*) There is evidence that boarders can if they wish personalise an area of their dormitory with posters and personal items.

(*n*) Boarders' sleeping accommodation is fully separated by gender and appropriately separated by age-group.

(*o*) Staff, staff family and visitors' sleeping accommodation is separate from boarders' sleeping accommodation.

(*p*) Requests from boarders to change bed or dormitory for good reasons are properly considered.

STANDARD

> **43. Suitable facilities for both organised and private study should be available to boarders.**

CRITERION

(*a*) There is suitable, suitably lit and reasonably quiet provision for both organised prep. and boarders' private study, either in or near to dormitories, elsewhere in boarding houses, or by use of nearby main school accommodation.

CORE STANDARD

> **44. Adequate toilet and washing facilities should be readily accessible to boarders, with appropriate privacy.**

CRITERIA

(*a*) Each boarding house has at least one WC for every five boarders (in boys' houses, urinals may be provided instead of no more than two-thirds of the required number of WCs).

(*b*) WCs are:

    (i) distributed within boarding accommodation to provide reasonable access from both sleeping and living areas;

    (ii) in individual rooms or separate cubicles, with partitions and doors which do not have sufficiently large gaps above or below to be susceptible to invasion of privacy;

    (iii) in working order, with paper (and for girls requiring them, suitable sanitary disposal facilities);

    (iv) fitted with room/cubicle locks that are observed to be in working order;

    (v) observed to be satisfactorily clean and adequately ventilated.

(*c*) There are washbasins, with soap, hot water and hand-drying facilities ('pull towel', hot-air blower, individual personal towels or disposable towels, not roller towels or single communal towels), adjacent to all WCs and urinals.

(*d*) Each boarding house has at least one wash-basin for every three boarders.

(*e*) Each boarding house has at least one shower or bath for every ten boarders, most of this provision comprising showers, and:

   (i)   showers or baths are distributed within boarding accommodation to provide reasonable access from both sleeping and living areas;

   (ii) all showers and baths used for personal washing in boarding houses are separated into individual rooms or cubicles, or where in the same area are capable of being individually separated by curtaining if boarders wish;

   (iii) shower and bath facilities are observed to be satisfactorily clean and adequately ventilated.

(*f*) Significant queues for toilet and washing facilities at peak times are not observed, or reported by staff or boarders.

(*g*) Boarders do not express significant concerns about lack of privacy of toilet and showering/bathing facilities for boarders.

(*h*) Toilet and individual bathroom doors in schools accommodating disabled boarders should where practicable open outwards, and have locks openable from the outside in emergency.

(*i*) Toilet facilities in boarding houses are not inappropriately shared by boarders of widely differing ages (*e.g.* the most senior and most junior boarders), showering and bathing facilities are not shared at the same time by boarders of widely differing ages, and toilet and washing facilities are not shared by boarders of both genders[98].

(*j*) Staff and other adults (including visitors) have separate toilet and showering or bathing facilities, and do not share boarders' facilities.

STANDARD

> **45. Suitable changing provision should be provided for use by day.**

CRITERIA

(*a*) Boarders not using their bedrooms for changing have access to changing facilities by day (*e.g.* to change for sports), of sufficient size and privacy, with separate facilities for each gender, which are not shared at the same time by pupils of widely different ages and are not shared by staff, adults or visitors other than visiting pupils of similar age to the boarders themselves.

(*b*) Changing facilities used by boarders have adjacent and suitably private toilet and washing provision.

STANDARD

> **46. Boarders should have access to a range and choice of safe recreational areas, both indoors and outdoors.**

CRITERIA

(*a*) There is a range and choice of common room or other recreational areas available to boarders outside school time, in the evenings and at weekends, enabling separation of genders, age-groups and activities as boarders wish.

(*b*) There is a range and choice of outdoor areas within the school grounds available to boarders for outdoor activities at suitable times.

(*c*) Boarders report that they are able to find safe areas at school to be alone if they wish.

(*d*) Boarders have reasonable access to boarding houses outside school time.

(*e*) Any boarder access to staff accommodation is properly supervised and does not involve inappropriate favouritism or inappropriate one-to-one contacts between staff and boarders.

CORE STANDARD

> **47. Indoor and outdoor areas used by, or accessible to, boarders should be free from reasonably avoidable safety hazards.**

CRITERIA

(*a*) Sleeping, living and recreational areas, indoors and in the school grounds, are free of significant hazards to boarder safety observed by the inspector (*e.g.* trailing flexes, overloaded sockets, unguarded heaters).

(*b*) Windows accessible to boarders above the ground floor and presenting a risk to safety are fitted with suitable opening restrictors or alternative safety measures.

(*c*) Windows where there is significant risk of impact are either made of safety glass (of a type satisfying the relevant British Standard), or are otherwise suitably protected.

(*d*) Boarders and staff do not report that there are significant hazards to boarder safety in indoor or outdoor recreational areas used by boarders.

(*e*) The school has a policy, implemented in practice, for controlling or supervising boarders' use of, and access to, high risk areas within the school buildings and grounds (*e.g.* for educational or recreational use outside class time, including areas such as gymnasiums, laboratories, workshops, swimming-pools).

(*f*) Boarders are able to define those areas and activities that are out of bounds.

(*g*) The school has a satisfactory health and safety policy, available to all staff.

(*h*) The school has an effective system of risk assessment, with written records (including consultation with boarders) to identify and reduce risk to boarders from inherent hazards in the school buildings, activities or grounds, including hazards that boarders may access without permission (*e.g.* roads, river frontage, flat roofs, hobby equipment, firearms, cleaning materials, plant and equipment rooms).

CORE STANDARD

> **48. Suitable accommodation should be available for the separate care of boarders who are ill.**

CRITERIA

(*a*) Boarders and staff report that boarders who are ill at school can be cared for satisfactorily and separately from other boarders where necessary, within boarding, sick-bay or sanatorium accommodation.

(*b*) Schools with over 40 boarders have a designated room or rooms for isolation of sick boarders when necessary, with its own toilet and washing facilities nearby and sufficient for the number of beds provided according to the ratios in Standard 44.

(*c*) Any sick-bay or room for isolation of sick boarders provides at least 7·4 m² of floor space per bed, with beds at least 1·8 m apart.

STANDARD

> **49. Adequate laundry provision should be made for boarders' clothing and bedding.**

CRITERIA

(*a*) Staff and boarders confirm that boarders' bedding and clothing (other than any clothing washed by boarders themselves) is regularly and frequently laundered by the school.

(*b*) Staff and boarders confirm that boarders' clothing is satisfactorily stored and issued to the right boarder following laundering.

STANDARD

> **50. Boarders should have access to drinking-water in both boarding and teaching areas, and to food or the means of preparing food at reasonable times in addition to main meals.**

CRITERIA

(*a*) Drinking-water is available in all boarding houses at all reasonable times.

(*b*) Drinking-water is available to boarders during the school day at reasonable times in addition to meal-times.

(*c*) Snacks are available to boarders at reasonable times other than main meal-times – either provided by the school, purchasable by boarders, or prepared by boarders themselves.

(*d*) Older boarders in senior age schools have facilities to store appropriate food and prepare their own hot and cold snacks and drinks hygienically.

STANDARD

> **51. Boarders should be able to obtain minor necessary personal and stationery items while accommodated at school.**

CRITERION

(*a*) Minor personal toiletries and stationery are purchasable from a school shop, where appropriate from a nearby shop, or are otherwise obtainable at school.

CORE STANDARD

> **52. Any lodgings arranged by the school to accommodate pupils should provide satisfactory accommodation and supervision, be checked by the school before use, and be monitored by the school during use.[99]**

CRITERIA

(*a*) It is clearly stated to parents whether any lodgings accommodating pupils are arranged by the school or by parents themselves.

(*b*) Any lodgings provided or arranged by the school provide:

    (i)   each pupil with either a single bedroom or a bedroom shared with one other pupil of similar age and the same gender;

    (ii)   bedroom accommodation not shared with any member of the 'host' family;

    (iii)   suitable bed, bedding and storage space;

    (iv)   adequate lighting and heating;

    (v)   access to usual and adequate toilet, wash-basin and bath or shower facilities, in private;

    (vi)   adequate, suitable and regular meals, provided under hygienic conditions, for meals not taken in school;

    (vii)   a telephone enabling pupils to make and receive calls at reasonable times, with only 'at cost' payment for calls made;

    (viii)   access for pupils to enter and leave the lodgings at all reasonable times, without being 'locked out' at any time they would be expected by the school to be at their lodgings;

    (ix)   adequate provision for laundering of pupils' bedding and clothing, either by the 'host family' or by the pupil, if not done at school;

    (x)   adequate private sitting and studying space for each pupil, either in a 'bed-sitting' room or in a room for pupils' use separate from the host family's own rooms;

(xi) accommodation free of obvious significant health and safety hazards (*e.g.* dangerous electrical fittings or equipment, fire risks);

(xii) a satisfactory level of general hygiene, decoration and cleanliness;

(xiii) a responsible adult present in the lodgings at night when the pupil(s) are sleeping there.

(*c*) For lodgings provided or arranged by the school, the school can demonstrate that adult members of the host family are checked through police and DfEE checks as for staff, with a satisfactory outcome known before any pupil is placed.

(*d*) The school has a satisfactory written agreement with each adult providing lodgings for pupil on its behalf.

(*e*) The school provides satisfactory written guidance to host families accommodating pupils on behalf of the school, covering the school's policy and practice for lodging pupils.

(*f*) The school visits all potential lodgings, and interviews the adult who will be responsible for the accommodation of the pupil(s) in each lodging, and has recorded a satisfactory assessment, before any pupil is placed there.

(*g*) The school provides documentary evidence that at least once per school term a member of staff discusses their lodgings separately with each pupil accommodated by or on behalf of the school in lodgings, recording the pupil's assessment in writing and taking action on any concerns or complaints.

(*h*) The school provides documentary evidence that at least once a school year a member of staff visits all lodgings in which it accommodates pupils to check the continued suitability of the accommodation and to review provision with the adult responsible for the pupil(s) in each lodging, recording assessments in writing and taking action on any concerns identified.

(*i*) Those adults providing lodgings for pupils who are interviewed during inspection are clear to the inspector about their responsibility to safeguard and promote pupils' welfare and on the school's requirements of them, use of any punishments or sanctions, and response to allegations or suspicions of abuse and to complaints.

(*j*) Staff and adults providing lodgings for pupils confirm satisfactory arrangements for host families to seek and receive advice over problems, including a satisfactory arrangement for contact in evenings and weekends.

(*k*) Pupils in lodgings report no major complaints or concerns to the inspector.

CORE STANDARD

> **53. Any off-site short-stay accommodation arranged by the school for any of its boarders should provide satisfactory accommodation and supervision, be checked by the school before use, and be monitored by the school during use.**

CRITERIA

(*a*) Staff and boarders confirm that boarders' accommodation is satisfactory at any field study centres, accommodation abroad, school owned accommodation for boarders away from the school site, and when boarders are staying away from school on exchange schemes.

(*b*) Staff and boarders confirm that when boarders are staying in accommodation away from the school (other than private households in exchange schemes), they are accompanied by school staff at all reasonable times.

(*c*) The arrangements described by staff and boarders for staff supervision and accompanying of boarders accommodated away from school satisfactorily minimise unsupervised access to boarders by 'unchecked' adults.

(*d*) Staff and boarders confirm that when boarders are staying away from school on exchange schemes, there are satisfactory arrangements for boarders to contact school staff in the locality at all times in case of difficulty or concern, that accompanying school staff have daily contact with the boarders, and that staff regularly ask boarders during their stay whether they have any concerns regarding their accommodation or care[100].

(*e*) The school provides documentary evidence that it has assessed the suitability of any accommodation to be used for boarders away from the school site prior to boarders being accommodated there (other than exchange accommodation in private houses, or accommodation already known to the school to be satisfactory), including a visit to the accommodation where this is practicable.

(*f*) Short-stay accommodation (including accommodation for field trips, activities and exercises and camping accommodation) provided for boarders away from school provides:

(i) sufficient and suitable bed and bedding for each boarder (or the camping equivalent);

(ii) separate sleeping provision for each gender wherever practicable;

(iii) sufficient access to toilet and washing facilities (separate for each gender if possible) appropriate to the nature of the activity;

(iv) regular provision of sufficient and appropriate food and drink, stored and prepared under sufficiently hygienic conditions to minimise risk of disease;

(v) ability to contact medical services, and provision for return to school or home, in case of accident or illness;

(vi) satisfactory and contactable adult supervision of boarders, competent to supervise activities involved and with back-up staffing to deal with emergencies;

(vii) for high-risk activities, instructors/supervisors with an appropriate qualification from the relevant national governing body or association;

(viii) appropriate equipment, safety equipment and facilities, and briefing/instruction for any high-risk activities to be undertaken;

(ix) sufficient clothing, suitable for the activities to be undertaken, and sufficient to ensure adequate warmth;

(x) adjustment of activities for any special needs of individual boarders (*e.g.* disability, asthma, enuresis, dietary needs, allergies);

(xi) safe storage and provision for administration of any boarder's medication, by staff or the boarder as appropriate.

LIST OF POLICIES AND DOCUMENTS

The following school policies and documents are required under the National Standards:

- ❖ Staff Handbook / guidance for boarding staff.
  [This document may include many of the following specific policy documents.]

    - Statement of the school's boarding principles and practice;

    - Countering bullying;

    - Child protection (including means for staff to raise concerns);

    - Discipline (including punishments, rewards and restraint);

    - Complaints procedure;

    - Responses to alcohol, smoking and substance abuse;

    - Plans for foreseeable crises;

    - Staff training and development programme;

    - Staff disciplinary procedure;

    - Prefect duties, powers and responsibilities;

    - Protocol for provision of non-prescription medication to boarders;

    - Key written information for new boarders;

    - Staff duty rotas outside teaching time;

    - Job descriptions for staff with boarding duties;

    - Safety and supervision on school journeys;

    - Access to school premises by people outside the school;

    - Pupil access to risk areas of school buildings and grounds;

    - Health and safety policy.

Where applicable:

- ❖ Clarification of whether any educational guardians or lodgings are arranged by the school or parents;
- ❖ Agreement with any adult providing lodgings to pupils;
- ❖ Guidance on welfare to host families accommodating pupils on behalf of the school.

RECORDS

The following school records are required under the National Standards:

- ❖ Child protection allegations or suspicions;
- ❖ Major punishments;
- ❖ Serious complaints;
- ❖ Individual boarders' records (containing personal, health and welfare information);
- ❖ Administration of medication, treatment and first-aid;
- ❖ Significant illnesses, accidents and injuries;
- ❖ Parental permission for medical and dental treatment, first-aid and non-prescription medication;
- ❖ Risk assessments (for risk activities and on premises/grounds);
- ❖ Staff recruitment records and checks (including checks on others given substantial unsupervised access to boarders or boarding accommodation);
- ❖ Fire precautions and drills.

(Where applicable) pocket money and any personal property looked after by staff.

(Where applicable) care plans for boarders with special needs.

References and Notes

76. Norms for this purpose are included in the Inspection Handbook.

77. The statutory guidance refers to situations in which a child may be suffering, or may be at risk of suffering, significant harm (including abuse from other boarders).

78. The policy should be clear on action should the school's usual designated recipient of such reports themselves be subject to allegation or suspicion.

79. Examples of "major punishments" to be recorded are those only used by the school for particularly serious offences, any serious punishment used which is not included in the school's written disciplinary policy, punishments for offences likely to be sufficiently serious to be quoted in future reports or references for the boarder concerned, and punishments for offences which would constitute criminal behaviour in the case of an adult.

80. Under Government guidance "Working Together to Safeguard Children", such review should check for patterns of complaints that might indicate welfare concerns, as well as checking action on major complaints.

81. This standard does not relate to any NHS records which may be held at the school or kept by a school nurse or school doctor, but includes any non-NHS school records kept by a school nurse, matron or other staff.

82. Self-evaluation systems for boarders' welfare would contribute to meeting this criterion.

83. Schools are encouraged to appoint a nominated school doctor.

84. *i.e.* separately from the boarder's NHS records.

85. Schools can, however, expect pupils to participate in the cultural and religious life of the school, subject to parental wishes.

86. Educational guardians appointed by schools do not have parental responsibility. This standard applies where an educational guardian is appointed for a child under 18 by the school, by a member of staff as part of their work for the school, or by an agency or organisation on behalf of the school. Where a school provides lists of possible guardians, written documents should be clear whether the school or parent is responsible for the arrangements made and thus the welfare of the child. Guidance for schools on educational guardians is available in the "Boarding Briefing" series published by the Boarding Schools' Association.

87. The school accommodates children other than its own boarders if the school, or any member of its staff as part of their work for the school, is responsible for looking after them during their stay at the school. Visiting pupils staying in school accommodation, even accompanied by their own staff, should be regarded as "temporary boarders". This standard does not apply where the school has let its accommodation to another organisation which is itself responsible for looking after the children.

88. A list of major National Governing Bodies is included in Annex B to the DfEE publication *Health and Safety of Boarders on Educational Visits.*

89. Licensing is likely to be required where a commercial company or local authority provides caving, climbing, abseiling, trekking, horse-trekking, mountain-biking, off-piste skiing, or watersports such as canoeing, rafting and sailing. Licensing concerns safety provision, and does not include checks on suitability of staff to work with children.

90. The DfEE publication *Health and Safety of Boarders on Educational Visits* advises staff:boarder ratios for organised trips away from the school site of one member of staff per 10–15 boarders aged 8 to 10, one member of staff per 15–20 boarders aged 11 and over, increased to one per 10 boarders for trips abroad or overnight stays.

91. Where a house comprises more than one building, sleeping in cover from one of its constituent buildings can only cover more than one building if the buildings are immediately adjacent, the responsible staff member is easily contactable by boarders at night, staff supervision is fully satisfactory in practice, and the boarders are at the upper age-level in a senior school (normally sixth formers).

92. Throughout these Standards, references to staff with boarding duties include matrons and any assistant or gap year staff working with boarders.

93. The appropriate level and nature of supervision will vary according to the boarders' age.

94. The Government has issued guidance on staff recruitment in "Working Together to Safeguard Children", 1999. Guidance for schools is also available in the "Boarding Briefing" series published by the Boarding Schools' Association.

95. Guidance on Certificates of Good Conduct and equivalents is given in DfEE Circular 9/93 *Protection of Children: Disclosure of Criminal Background of those with Access to Children.*

96. *i.e.* beds fully one above the other, as distinct from "cabin" style beds with desk areas or storage beneath.

97. "Usable floor area" includes bedroom floor area taken up by room furniture or behind doors when open, but not unfurnished areas below low or sloping ceilings where boarders cannot stand upright.

98. This standard does not prevent the full age-range involved in the same team games from sharing the same changing and showering provision for sports activities.

99. School-arranged lodgings are those provided or arranged for a pupil under 18 by the school, any member of its staff as part of their work for the school, or by an agent or organisation acting for the school, rather than by the pupil's parent or by an agent or organisation other than the school acting on the parent's behalf. They include term-time use of lodgings instead of on-site boarding accommodation, holiday lodgings arranged for pupils by the school, pupils lodging with staff members during holidays, and accommodation during either term or holiday time with school arranged educational guardians.

100. This criterion can be met by the school specifically appointing a suitable member of staff of the school with which it is exchanging to carry out these functions for its pupils during the exchange.

INDEX

abuse, and child protection legislation 48–50; and confidentiality 78, 79; see also named abuse, *e.g.* child abuse

academic work 27, 179

accommodation 26; as comfortable 164–5; legislation 38–9; off-site 276–9; physical aspects 131; sleeping arrangements 27; standards 28, 247, 270–9

activities/hobbies 28

adolescence 22, 23–4; at preparatory school 170–1; described 55; as grown-up or not 57–8; in practice 58–9; puberty 23–4; understanding 56–7

alcohol abuse 30, 56, 79, 87, 135, 170, 189–90

anorexia nervosa 196; see also eating disorders

anti-bullying, see bullying

attitudes/values 29

behaviour 23, 150; codes 115; patterns 191–2; poor/inappropriate 29, 62, 63–5

bereavement, see death

binge 196–7; see also eating disorders

boarding, aims and objectives 25, 26; case study scenarios 227–33; changes in 12, 163–4; cost 14; government/society expectations 15; growth in international dimension 14; investment in 17; marketing challenges for 17–18; modern 164–5; options 12–13; organisation/management 27–8; parental expectations 15; perceptions of 14; policies/procedures 90, 145–7; principles 21, 248; quality 14, 16, 17; as transparent 12, 13–14

Boarding Education Alliance (BEA) 17–18; Pupil Survey (1999) 13

Boarding Schools' Association (BSA) 16–17, 96, 246; Heads' Conference (2000) 17

bulimia nervosa 196, see also eating disorders

Bullies and Victims in Schools (V. Besag) 97, 101

bullying 29, 31, 106, 147, 213, 214, 225; assertiveness training 99; buddying/support groups 99–100; bullies and victims 92–3; bully boxes/complaints procedures 100; common concern/no blame approaches 100; counteracting 99–101, 248–9; dealing with 97–8; described 88–9; extent of 89–92; factors affecting 93–5; as gender linked 92–3; group 98; improving the environment 99; parental contact 101; peer counselling 99; preventive measures 95–7; training issues 101–2

Bullying at School (D. Olweus) 88, 93

Bullying: don't suffer in silence (DFE) 89

bursar 129, 141

care, see pastoral care and welfare

Care Standards Act (2000) 16, 35, 40–1; children's home registration 43–4; see also Children Act (1989)

Certificates of Professional Practice in Boarding Education 16–17

child abuse 50, 79, 139

ChildLine, Boarding School Line 92, 93; Bullying Line 92, 93

child protection 48–50, 87, 147, 249–50

Children Act (1989) 34–6, 77, 137, 139, 217, 237–9, 245; background 36–7; child protection 48–50; court orders 47–8; educational guardians 44–5; *in loco parentis* 45–7; safeguards 37; significant harm 37–8; welfare duty 37–41; welfare inspections 51–3; see also Care Standards Act (2000)

Children Act Guidance and Regulations 20, 42, 52, 217

Children's Homes Regulations (1991) 42, 43–4, 240

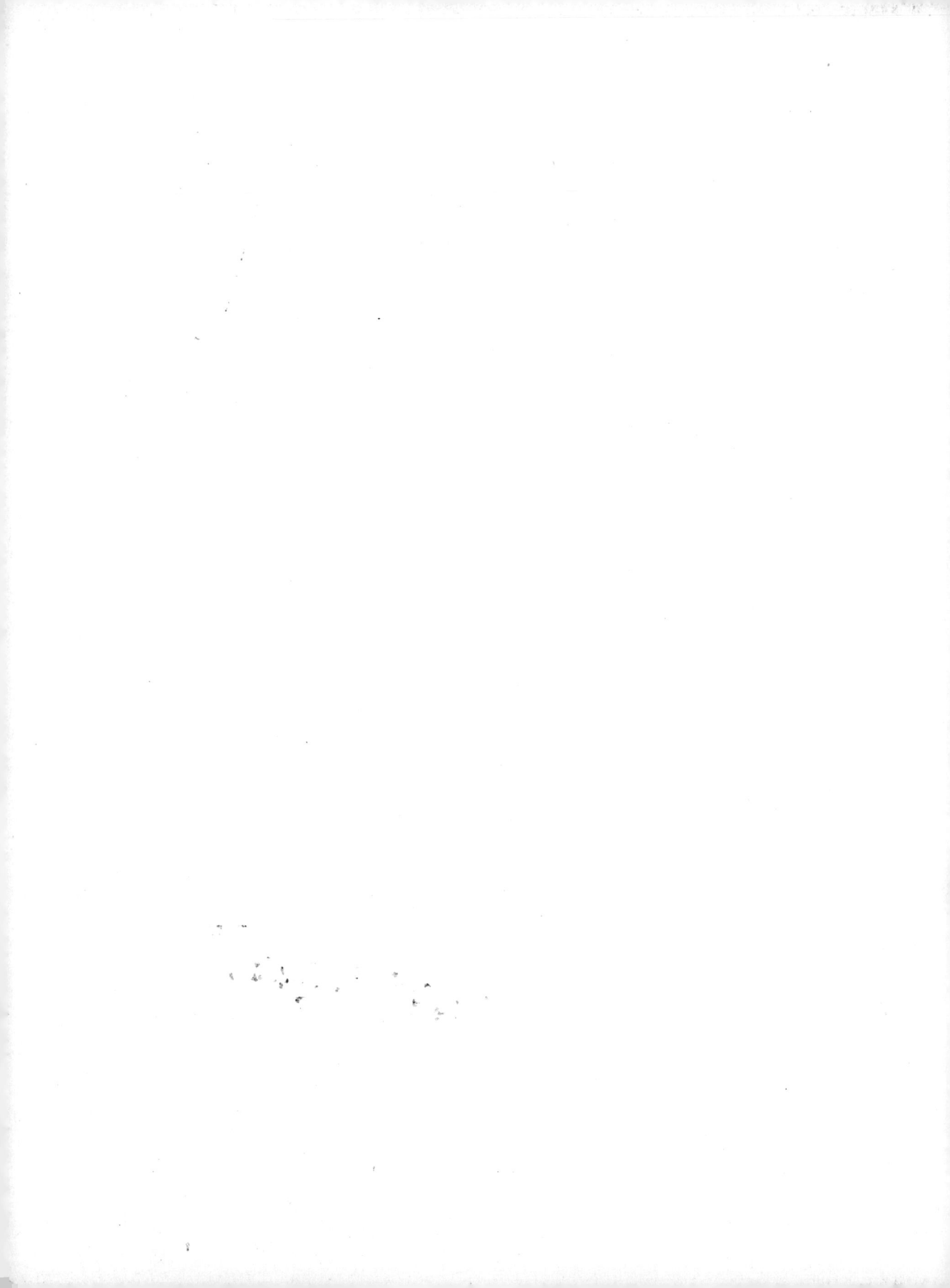